A Dramatic Pentecostal/ Charismatic Anti-Theodicy

A Dramatic Pentecostal/ Charismatic Anti-Theodicy

Improvising on a Divine Performance of Lament

Stephen C. Torr

Foreword by
David Cheetham

☙PICKWICK *Publications* · Eugene, Oregon

A DRAMATIC PENTECOSTAL/CHARISMATIC ANTI-THEODICY
Improvising on a Divine Performance of Lament

Copyright © 2013 Stephen C. Torr. All rights reserved. Except for brief quotations in critical publications or reviews, no part of this book may be reproduced in any manner without prior written permission from the publisher. Write: Permissions, Wipf and Stock Publishers, 199 W. 8th Ave., Suite 3, Eugene, OR 97401.

Unless otherwise indicated, Scripture quotations are from the New Revised Standard Version Bible: Anglicized Edition, copyright 1989, 1995, Division of Christian Education of the National Council of the Churches of Christ in the United States of America. Used by permission. All rights reserved.

Pickwick Publications
An Imprint of Wipf and Stock Publishers
199 W. 8th Ave., Suite 3
Eugene, OR 97401

www.wipfandstock.com

ISBN 13: 978-1-62032-854-5

Cataloguing-in-Publication data:

Torr, Stephen C.

    A dramatic pentecostal/charismatic anti-theodicy : improvising on a divine performance of lament / Stephen C. Torr, with a foreword by David Cheetham.

    xii + 237 pp. ; 23 cm. Includes bibliographical references.

    ISBN 13: 978-1-62032-854-5

    1. Theodicy. 2. Laments. 3. Suffering—Religious aspects—Christianity. 4. Pentecostal churches—Doctrines. 5. Pastoral theology. I. Cheetham, David (David A.). II. Title.

BT160 T677 2013

Manufactured in the U.S.A.

In memory of Muriel Torr.
Mum,
friend,
and teacher.

Contents

Foreword by David Cheetham | ix
Acknowledgments | xi
Abbreviations | xii

1. Introduction | 1
2. An Overview of Christian Approaches to Evil and Suffering | 22
3. Pentecostal/Charismatic Approaches to Evil and Suffering | 58
4. A "Dramatic" Pentecostal/Charismatic Hermeneutic | 98
5. Humans, Evil, and Suffering—A Theo-Dramatic Perspective | 131
6. Improvising on a Divine Performance of Lament | 170
7. Conclusion | 220

Bibliography | 227

Foreword

AMONGST THE MANY WORKS written on the problem of evil and suffering, Stephen Torr's work stands out as a strikingly original addition to the debate. His book uniquely fulfils a need to articulate the problem not as yet another finely-tuned adjustment of its "classic" form—as a formal and existential challenge for the existence of God—but as a question about how the problem of suffering is understood and, above all, responded to within the Charismatic and Pentecostal traditions in Christianity. As such, Torr's work constitutes a bold venture that walks the tightrope between giving a proper *voice* to the laments of the sufferer and the acknowledgment of faith in, and testimony to, the healing work of the Spirit within Charismatic and Pentecostal practice.

Often, a book's value is not solely to be found in its conclusions. Or rather, a good book should repay close attention to all of its chapters! This is certainly the case here. As we read through Torr's work, we see that rather than just supply a survey of the problem of suffering and the various common responses to it, he offers us a very insightful engagement with Pentecostal and Charismatic responses. So, even if readers do not wish to listen to his provocative recommendations towards the end, they can profit from the earlier chapters that have systematically gathered together and critiqued the work of Pentecostal and Charismatic scholars.

Engaging with Pentecostal and Charismatic traditions sympathetically—as well as giving voice to the sufferer—is not an easy task. It might have been easier had Torr decided to take sides and refute either the significance of suffering, on the one hand, or the forceful and often idealistic "supernaturalism" operative in his home tradition, on the other. Instead, his argument is constructive and creative, seeking ways in which the voice of suffering can be heard in a key that resonates deep within the practices of that tradition. This is not an uncritical process and within these pages Torr wrestles with the use of Scripture and how the right interpretation of it might actually find its way into the practices within the tradition. Furthermore, the problem

A Dramatic Pentecostal/Charismatic Anti-Theodicy

of suffering is a notoriously difficult problem for philosophers and theologians, and the danger is that a response to the problem may become rigidly formulaic or defensively apologetic. Or else, such is the unfathomable nature of individual or particular experiences of suffering that we are unable to deal with them and often neatly dispose of them within broad systematic generalisations—which are too often exercises in sheer avoidance. Torr opts for a different path. He wants to confront the fact of suffering—the fact of, say, the unhealed person who sits for years in a Pentecostal/Charismatic congregation that proclaims the healing power of the Spirit. He also wants to be a Pentecostal/Charismatic Christian. Given this, he seeks a method and approach that deeply affirms the tradition but which also wants to make suffering visible and a legitimate part of the Spirit-led practices within a community of faith.

Vanhoozer's *The Drama of Doctrine* (2005) has become an important text for many who are attempting to construct a new approach to the practice of theology. Vanhoozer's theory describes Scripture as a script and the theologian or the believer as a performer of this script. This kind of idea (similar perhaps to the Balthasarian theo-dramatics of Ben Quash) is becoming increasingly influential in theology with a new emphasis on aesthetics and, above all, performance. Torr seeks to utilise such approaches for the development of a "fitting Pentecostal/Charismatic performance" in the context of suffering. Influenced by another writer, Walter Brueggemann, he seeks out a Biblical voice that will deeply connect with the tradition of "testimony" and the emphasis on experience in Pentecostal/Charismatic circles. Torr's chosen focus on Biblical traditions of "lament" seems wholly appropriate and fits very well into such circles. Moreover, the way in which he wrestles with how his "theoretical" reflections might operate in the "ordinary" believing community means that this book ought to be read by the leaders and pastors of Pentecostal/Charismatic churches and not just academic theologians. In the end, this book seeks to draw together both the logical and existential dimensions of the problem of suffering into a dramatic work of theatre that involves all players. The fitting performance of Scripture in the context of suffering is about finding the Spirit of God in the lament of His people and testifying to His presence in the perplexity of life.

David Cheetham
University of Birmingham

Acknowledgments

UNDERTAKING AND COMPLETING a project such as this one is extremely difficult, if not impossible, to do without help along the way. On the journey I have taken to reach this point there are a number of people who I owe a debt of gratitude for the support, encouragement, insight and guidance they have provided.

Dr. David Cheetham and Revd. Dr. Mark Cartledge, have continually given of their time and energy in enabling me to complete this work. Their reading and re-reading of what I have produced, as well as the constructive criticism and on-going encouragement that has poured forth in our many conversations, has provided invaluable aid for the journey. It is primarily these contributions that have enabled the movement from some rough ideas, to the focused argument found in this work. For their help and friendship I am extremely thankful.

I also wish to thank Dr. Scott Ellington and Prof. J. Richard Middleton for their contributions. The various conversations I have had with them in the course of this project have helped me to clarify my own thoughts as well as find fresh direction and inspiration.

About the last quarter of this project was undertaken whilst training for ordination at Ridley Hall, Cambridge. With that in mind I wish to acknowledge and thank the various staff at Ridley who found ways for that training and this project to continue alongside each other.

There are too many friends and family, who have provided in various ways to enable me to undertake and complete this project, to name individually here. I hope you know who you are and that I am deeply grateful and thankful for your love and support.

Lastly, but most importantly of all, is my wife, Holly. Undertaking a project such as this one is no easy task, but it is much easier than having to live with and love the one who is doing it! Holly, thank you for your patience, sacrifice, support and love in walking this somewhat bumpy journey with me.

Abbreviations

CBQ	*Catholic Biblical Quarterly.*
DPCM	*Dictionary of Pentecostal and Charismatic Movements.* Edited by S. M. Burgess and G. B. McGee. Grand Rapids, Michigan: Zondervan, 1988.
EPCC	*Encyclopedia of Pentecostal and Charismatic Christianity.* Edited by Stanley M. Burgess. Abingdon, Oxon: Routledge, 2006.
HTR	*Harvard Theological Review.*
IJST	*International Journal of Systematic Theology.*
JAAR	*Journal of the American Academy of Religion.*
JBL	*Journal of Biblical Literature.*
JCTR	*Journal for Christian Theological Research.*
JPT	*Journal of Pentecostal Theology.*
JSOT	*Journal for the Study of the Old Testament.*
NDBT	*New Dictionary of Biblical Theology.* Edited by T. D. Alexander et. al. Leicester, UK: InterVarsity, 2000.
NDPCM	*New Dictionary of Pentecostal and Charismatic Movements.* Edited by Stanley M. Burgess and Eduard M. Van Der Maas. Grand Rapids: Zondervan, 2002.
NIB	*The New Interpreters Bible.* 12 vols. Edited by Leander E. Keck et. al. Nashville: Abingdon, 1996.
PQ	*Philosophical Quarterly.*
SJT	*Scottish Journal of Theology.*
ZAW	*Zeitschrift für die Alttestamentliche Wissenschaft.*

1

Introduction

My Story

IN OCTOBER OF 2002, after a fairly long illness, my mother died suddenly and unexpectedly whilst undergoing investigative surgery. I was aged twenty-one at the time and already suffering from a mild bout of depression that had kept me from returning to university for my second year of a Theology degree. Upon being told that my mother had died, I felt as if my heart had been torn in two and the bottom had dropped out of my life. I remain unconvinced that anyone, even when knowing what is coming and when, can ever be fully prepared for this kind of experience, but I was far from prepared or equipped.

    I had been taken to church by my mother since I was very young. Until the age of twelve my mother, my sister and I had attended a small Assemblies of God church and from the age of twelve onwards I had attended Charismatic free churches of one sort or another. I had grown up hearing various triumphalistic rhetoric and had found myself, at least partially, convinced by it. Believing that God still heals I had also believed the "prophecies" and "words of knowledge" concerning my mother's healing and was waiting to see those promises fulfilled. Some may say that those promises were fulfilled and that she now has total healing, but that would seem to sidestep the point that when initially delivered, those promises, and those stating them, seemed to suggest it would be a here and now healing. So, what does one do in the wreckage of the aftermath? How does one think about, talk about and, most importantly, talk *to* a God who it was believed could do something but actually seemed absent at the most crucial moments? Is one

A Dramatic Pentecostal/Charismatic Anti-Theodicy

simply to "have faith" that all will be well, not question the Almighty, and repeat after Job "the Lord gave, and the Lord has taken away; blessed be the name of the Lord" (Job 1:21)? Is one supposed to feel a deep sense of guilt for not praying enough, not praying the right prayer, or not having enough faith at the right time?

There were many good people around me at the time that gave out love and support and created safe space for me to begin to explore these questions. To these people I am immensely grateful. And, let the reader not misunderstand, I feel no ill will towards those who delivered the promises of triumph, it is more than likely that they were doing what they believed right and were probably left as bewildered as I was. However, for all the love and safe space, no-one from within the traditions I had been a part of could provide tools or answers that seemed helpful or satisfying in my quest to face the above questions.

I tell this part of my own journey because it provides the context from which the current project emerged. I maintain belief in a God that can and does produce signs and wonders, a God who can and does heal. I maintain belief in a God who is active in the world in tangible ways through his Holy Spirit. I retain much of my Pentecostal/Charismatic heritage. However, what I wish to suggest is that for a tradition that maintains a high view of Scripture, there is an imbalance regarding how Pentecostals and Charismatics respond to suffering, particularly suffering which appears innocent and meaningless and in which God seems somehow absent. Kathleen Billman and Daniel Migliore make the point that, "The true believer, especially in the practice of prayer, is expected to exhibit compliance rather than resistance. As a result, instead of providing space for protest and grief, what churches often offer are worship services that are 'unrelentingly positive in tone.'"[1] Billman and Migliore are here referencing Christianity in general but I suggest their point is even more apparent in Pentecostal/Charismatic churches. I suggest that an imbalance exists because this response does not seem to fully reflect what is evidenced in Scripture regarding correct responses to suffering. In Job 42:7–9, in the aftermath of the horrors Job had experienced, God states twice to Job's three friends that they had "not spoken of me what is right, as my servant Job has." What does it mean to speak rightly of and to God in the face of suffering? To broaden that a little, what does it mean to *communicate* rightly of and to God in the face of suffering (as to communicate includes speech but involves other forms of communication such as body language, facial expression etc.)? More specifically, what does it mean to communicate rightly of and to God in the face of seemingly

---

1. Billman and Migliore, *Rachel's Cry*, 14.

Introduction

innocent, meaningless suffering when God appears to be absent? How does one communicate rightly about and to God when faced with this situation? And how does one do that from within a theological perspective that is conducive to Pentecostal/Charismatic theology?

These questions are here drawn together into the single research question that will stand at the heart of this study: *What does it mean to communicate rightly of and to God in the face of seemingly innocent, meaningless suffering when God appears to be absent, in a way that is conducive to Pentecostal/Charismatic theology?* The primary aim of this study will be to provide an answer to this question.

However, although on the surface the question and the aim may appear clear, a closer look, or perhaps a moment of reflection, reveals that this is not the case. Instead, we are drawn into asking the further questions of, "What kind of answer is to be given?" and "How is this answer to be reached?" The first of these questions is a disciplinary context question, the answer to which can only be determined by way of clarifying which disciplinary context this project is anchored in. In short, the kind of answer produced in response to the research question will be governed by the discipline in which this study is operating.

In a similar way, *how* this answer will be achieved—the method—will also, to a great extent, be determined by the disciplinary context, as this will narrow the field of methodological options available. Further determination regarding method will occur by way of appropriate selection by the author.

Before we can proceed any further, both of these secondary questions need addressing. This will be the subject of the following two sections of this chapter. Having provided answers to these questions I will then move on to provide an outline of the study (section 4).

The final three sections of this chapter will examine the relationship between this and other Pentecostal/Charismatic work on lament (section 5), the limitations of the study (section 6), and terminology (section 7). We begin by answering the first of the secondary questions by way of examination of the disciplinary context in which this study will be anchored.

Disciplinary Context

In order to clearly illuminate what kind of answer will be produced in this study, the primary place to start is by stating that this project is located within the field of Systematic Theology. However, given the on-going discussions and multiple perspectives regarding how one defines this particular realm of theology, simply placing oneself within it still does not tell us much. It is important, therefore, to clarify my understanding of this field and how that specifically relates to this project.

Thomas Weinandy states,

> Systematic theologians, their reason guided by faith . . . and the light of the Holy Spirit, clarify and advance what has been revealed by God, written in the scriptures, and believed by their fellow Christians. In so doing they wish to make what has been revealed more intelligible, lucid, and relevant to the Christian community.[2]

Weinandy's statement offers helpful direction regarding the view of Systematic Theology ascribed to in this study. Daniel Migliore, in response to his own question of "What is theology?" states, "It is neither mere repetition of church doctrines nor grandiose system-building. It is faith asking questions, seeking understanding."[3] As both note, the starting point is faith, and as Migliore in particular notes, it is a faith that creates conversations. The initial conversation is one that exists between what one experiences and what one believes and the apparent incongruence between those two. The second conversation, in the light of the first, is one with the divine, seeking illumination and understanding. Weinandy draws us back to the point that the role of the systematic theologian is to act as the go-between in the tension created by the incongruence or mystery. The faith that seeks understanding is one that believes that God has revealed enough to aid in providing guidance for the voices that ask the questions. The systematic theologian is charged with returning to the divine source so that clarity and relevance regarding this revelation can be achieved. As Weinandy notes, "divine revelation, as the acts of God to which scripture bears witness, is a mystery to be grasped in faith and intellectually discerned and clarified."[4] However, Migliore is right in warning against system-building and repetition as neither of these have as their goal the aim of making intelligible and relevant that which has been revealed. Instead, following Colin Gunton, Systematic Theology "is, when rightly understood, dedicated to thinking in as orderly a way as possible *from* the Christian gospel and to the situation in which it is set, rather than in the construction of systems."[5] This is not to say that systems should, therefore, be dismissed. The point is that the system constructed should be done with the aim of conveying

2. Weinandy, "Systematic Theology," 131.
3. Migliore, *Faith*, 19.
4. Weinandy, "Systematic Theology," 126.
5. Gunton, "Rose?," 22.

Introduction

information and guidance that originates in the divine, to humans, in a way that illuminates truth and enables communion. The system, then, is not the end but the means.

There must also be a level of consistency within the system as well as "comprehensiveness and coherence."[6] Although, due to the finite nature of humans, there are of course limits to this, as Gunton notes, "if Christianity is to claim to be a true and rational faith, there must be consistency *of some kind* among its various doctrines."[7] We can say then that the aim of the system is both to convey something whilst at the same time displaying a level of consistency, comprehensiveness and coherence within itself.

Readers may be forgiven for thinking that I am heading towards a Tillichian style correlation approach to the Systematic Theology to be employed in this study (or perhaps even a praxis driven one) given my starting point with my own story and the question that emerges.[8] However, this is not the case. Gunton's point, noted above, is that the movement occurs from the "Christian gospel" to the current situation, and this is a response to the faith that seeks understanding that I will be heartily endorsing. Although it is important to listen to questions both from the culture in which we find ourselves and those "on the ground" in concrete situations, these voices are not the pinnacle of authority—that rests with God alone. Therefore, as my doctrinal starting point for doing theology, I begin with Scripture as authoritative, as I am suggesting this is the primary way in which God has revealed and communicated Himself. However, as Kevin Vanhoozer has highlighted, in reality it is difficult to opt for starting with the authority of Scripture without also beginning with God, as it is by holding certain beliefs about God that one can understand Scripture to be authoritative. In the same way, Vanhoozer also notes that it is impossible to begin with a belief in the Trinitarian Christian God without also starting with a belief about the authority of Scripture as it is Scripture that is understood as being the authoritative revelation of the Christian God, particularly in the person of Jesus Christ as revealed in the Gospels. Therefore Vanhoozer's "First Theology" begins with a mutually referential circle that contains both a belief about God and the authority of Scripture.[9] Likewise, I will be following a similar pattern.

6. Webster, "Introduction," 2.

7. Gunton, "Historical and Systematic Theology," 12.

8. See Tillich, *Systematic Theology*, particularly 1:3–68. Influenced by Tillich's work (amongst others) yet differing from it in certain aspects, Tracy's "Revisionist" approach also offers a significant example of a correlation method. See Tracy, *Blessed Rage*. For a good example of a praxis driven approach see Gutiérrez, *Theology of Liberation*, particularly pp. 3–12.

9. Vanhoozer, *First Theology*, 38.

A Dramatic Pentecostal/Charismatic Anti-Theodicy

Pentecostal/Charismatic theology has traditionally held to a high view of Scripture. Frank Macchia notes, "For all of its advantages and limitations, theology for pentecostals from the beginning has been a biblical theology."[10] It has also held to a strong view of God's sovereignty and interaction with creation, therefore the starting point suggested here would seem to fit comfortably within a broadly Pentecostal/Charismatic theological viewpoint. However, although a more detailed examination of the nature of the hermeneutical method to be employed in this study will be discussed in chapter 4, it is important to briefly note two significant points of possible contention regarding how conducive the type of theology to be done in this study is to Pentecostal/Charismatic theology.

Pentecostal/Charismatic theology has traditionally placed much emphasis on the work of the Spirit in the life of believers and with that, although not necessarily worked out in a rigorously academic way, the importance of pneumatology. It has also placed significant emphasis on belief in a "Full Gospel" in which Jesus is understood as Savior, Sanctifier, Baptizer with the Spirit, Healer and Soon-Coming King. In what I have described so far in this section, and in particular my appropriation of Vanhoozer's "First Theology" as starting point, it may appear that the theology I am undertaking here is not pneumatological enough and not Christ-focused enough in emphasis to be considered Pentecostal/Charismatic. However, in response to this I wish to make two points.

Firstly, I join with Veli-Matti Kärkkäinen in asking, "is it really the case that the Spirit is the 'first theology' for Pentecostals? Or should it even be?"[11] As noted above, this author does not believe so, however, that does not mean that the Spirit is therefore dismissed or relegated to a lesser role. As will become apparent as the study unfolds, the role of the Spirit is central to the work of the community, the interpretation of Scripture, and the revelation of God. However, this can only be brought to the fore once one has engaged with the first theology proposed here and begun travelling the mutually referential circle that Scripture and its author create.

Secondly, Kärkkäinen further notes that "An emerging scholarly consensus holds that at the heart of Pentecostal spirituality lies the 'Full Gospel,' the idea of Jesus Christ in his fivefold role as Savior, Sanctifier, Baptizer with the Spirit, Healer and Soon-Coming King."[12] As with the previous point, this author would affirm (although implicitly in this study) a "Full Gospel," but, would not make it the "first theology." In addition, the focus of

---

10. Macchia, "Theology," 1121.

11. Kärkkäinen, "Pneumatologies," 223–24.

12. Ibid., 224.

Introduction

this study is more a question of right Pentecostal/Charismatic belief and practice in the midst of awaiting the Soon-Coming King—a period in salvation history when salvation, sanctification and healing have not yet been brought to completion.

In a discussion regarding the nature and role of Systematic Theology Amos Yong states of the enterprise in question, "It is Pentecostal to the extent that it listens to and incorporates the narratives and 'babblings' of the marginalized. It is Christian to the extent that it listens prayerfully to the Word of God and to those in the Christian tradition who have faithfully preceded us."[13] Drawing together the above points, the current work is Pentecostal/Charismatic in that it listens to those who are marginalized—namely the minority who question the sufficiency of Pentecostal/Charismatic theology and practice in response to the situations of suffering in question here. And it is Pentecostal in that it is attentive to, and places emphasis upon, the work of the Holy Spirit in the life of the community and the reception and interpretation of the Biblical text in that community. It also implicitly affirms a "Full Gospel" and particularly the continuation of the work of Jesus as healer in the current context. Although implicit, this latter point is of great importance as it is this particular belief that makes the issue at the center of this study such a fundamental one for Pentecostal/Charismatic theology to face. The current work is also Christian in that the revelation of God in Christ is at its epicenter and it is an enterprise undertaken in the light of that revelation and its reception in the community of the faithful.

This thus sets the disciplinary context as *Pentecostal/Charismatic* Systematic Theology. However, before we move on to offer a conclusive response to the question of "What kind of answer is to be given?" in this study, a note on levels of discourse is in order.

In *Testimony in the Spirit*, Mark Cartledge describes three levels of discourse with which he interacts in his study of a Pentecostal community: "ordinary," "official," and "academic."[14] Cartledge describes the "ordinary" level as coming from those "participants in the movement, who have the Pentecostal tradition mediated to them by means of corporate worship, small group meetings, their pastors and their own experiences and personal commitments."[15] In short, "It is the theology of the people on the ground."[16]

The second level, "official," is "Denominational or confessional theology . . . It is a second order reflection on the first order theology from

---

13. Yong, "Systematic Theology?," 93.
14. Cartledge, *Testimony in Spirit*, 18–20.
15. Ibid., 19.
16. Ibid.

the pew and is articulated in denominational material, official statements of faith and policy documents; it is ecclesial discourse."[17] This confessional level of discourse is also informed by academic theology, which provides information for the shaping of it.

The third level, "academic," "is theology that is not tied to confessional . . . theology but nevertheless shares similar sources and concerns."[18] It also "has a broader agenda" than the other two levels of discourse and tends to "abstract" information from them in order to "theorise more generally."[19]

Nicholas Healy notes that "Ordinary theologies have much of significance to offer academic systematic theology, for they reflect the vast experience of a multitude of experiments in living the Christian life concretely, as individuals and as communities."[20] In reference to the three levels outlined above, this study will primarily operate at the third level as it is not confined to "official" and goes beyond the "ordinary." However, Healy's point is a valid one and thus, as noted above, the starting point is with the "ordinary" voice of my experience that questioned the "official" voice of, initially, a particular community, but then in this wider discussion, the dominant "official" voice of Western Pentecostal/Charismatic confessional theology at large. However, also to re-iterate, although the central research question emerges "from the ground," the response is to be rooted in a theology that begins with God and his Holy Scripture. As the study operates at the "academic" level of discourse it will primarily be conceptional in nature. However, here, following Webster, "concepts" are understood as "'abstractions,' not in the sense that they discard the practical in favour of the purely speculative, but in the sense that they articulate general perceptions which might otherwise be achieved only by laborious repetition."[21] Having generated an answer to the central research question at the "academic" level of discourse, guidance can be offered to the other levels in the light of this answer.

Having clarified the placement of the study with respect to levels of discourse it is possible to address the issue of the kind of answer to be given to the central research question. This answer will be one that begins with and is rooted in Scripture as the authoritative source for right Christian belief and practice. It will be a conceptual answer that will draw on other doctrines and disciplines within the theological enterprise in its construction. It will therefore be an "academic" discourse that seeks to illuminate and

---

17. Ibid., 19–20.
18. Ibid., 20.
19. Ibid., 19–20.
20. Healy, "Systematic Theology," 32.
21. Webster, "Introduction," 9.

clarify divine revelation relevant to the research question with the intent of offering guidance in belief and practice to participants in all three levels of discourse. The answer will also pay special attention to relevant Pentecostal/Charismatic beliefs and practices as it is one that is to be conducive to Pentecostal/Charismatic theology. Of particular importance here is the view of and use of Scripture, the centrality of Jesus, the work of the Holy Spirit and the practice of testimony.

In the light of this we can restate the central research question—*What does it mean to communicate rightly of and to God in the face of seemingly innocent, meaningless suffering when God appears to be absent, in a way that is conducive to Pentecostal/Charismatic theology?*—and say that the aim of the study is: *to answer the central research question by developing Biblically rooted, systematic guidance for right communication of and to God in the face of seemingly innocent, meaningless suffering when God appears to be absent. And, to do this in a way that is conducive to Pentecostal/Charismatic theology.*

With this as the *kind* of answer to be generated, we can move on to examine *how* the answer will be reached.

Methodology

In drawing from my own experience to produce the questions to be examined in this study, there is always the danger that I am creating a straw man. Perhaps my experience of the Pentecostal/Charismatic tradition was simply an exception to the norm and perhaps the issue I have unearthed does not exist in Pentecostal/Charismatic churches at large. Or, if it does, perhaps it has been responded to in a way I would find convincing but am unaware of. How would I know? The answer is that I would not, as it is impossible to survey every Pentecostal/Charismatic church in the world to assess whether the issue in question is universal, particular or somewhere in between! As an alternative to this I have opted for what I consider to be the next best option—an examination of the relevant literature that has emerged from Pentecostal/Charismatic contexts. The first point of my method is thus that research into the reality of the issue to be examined and responded to—Pentecostal/Charismatic responses to suffering—is based purely on literary research. This option provides the broadest base from which to generate any meaningful conclusions regarding the theological view of, and response to, suffering offered by Pentecostal/Charismatic theology. Engagement at this stage is at discourse levels one and two. The literature that is surveyed is from "ordinary" sources but, these "ordinary" sources reflect at least some "official" teaching in certain churches and act as sources for "official" teaching in others. There is, however, nothing that one may consider "academic" discourse in any of this source material.

Linked to the first, the second point of my method is derived from the answer to the question: what does one do with the unearthed information? How this is answered will be partially decided by what the information is that is unearthed as this will set limits as to what one *can* do with it. A further limitation, or perhaps focus, as noted above, is provided by the discipline in which the study is set. What I am suggesting is that right practice that is affirmed and understood as right practice is rooted in right belief. Or, as Miroslav Volf states, "Christian practices are *by definition* normatively shaped by Christian beliefs."[22] Where there are suspected inconsistencies in either or both of these, investigation must ensue to attempt to find and correct them. Amy Plantinga Pauw makes the point that, "What seems like consistency may instead be a coerced or unreflective uniformity."[23] In such a situation, "Critical theological reflection is required in order to unmask perennial human tendencies to triumphalism and self deception."[24] With that in mind, the systematic method being employed here would, ideally, start with an interrogation of the practices of Pentecostal/Charismatic communities, as represented in the literature, and then move to examine the beliefs that underpin them. However, although this author believes that right belief generally precedes right practice, separating belief and practice out in the examination of the literature is unrealistic as the two can only best be understood in the light of the other. Therefore, the first step in the method will be to examine both practices *and* beliefs, within Pentecostal/Charismatic communities, with the aim of "unmasking" any inconsistencies. Practices here are understood as "*things Christian people do together over time to address the fundamental human needs in response to and in the light of God's active presence for the life of the world.*"[25]

Having done this, the second step involves making corrections regarding any inconsistencies found. At this point the level of discourse has moved to the "academic" as an answer to the research question needs to be as comprehensive, coherent, and consistent as possible and this will be achieved via engagement with various scholarly works.

The third step involves revising the beliefs accordingly in order to enable the fourth and final step of providing guidance for how practice may be revised in the light of this. This fourth step begins the transition from

22. Volf, "Theology," 250.
23. Pauw, "Attending Gaps," 42.
24. Ibid., 43.
25. Dykstra and Bass, "Theological Understanding," 18.

Introduction

the "academic" discourse back into "official" and "ordinary." However, due to the nature of the study, what is offered in this fourth step can only be the beginning of the transition as the primary focus is on revision at the "academic" level. The third step thus produces the answer to the central research question and the fourth step begins to show the implications of that answer in more concretized ways.

The third point to make regarding this method reinforces the systematic nature of this study in that the method used is intra-theological and inter-disciplinary. By this I mean that the study incorporates and draws on other disciplines within the boundaries of theology, in a systematic way, but does not step outside the bounds of theology. Primarily the disciplines to be engaged with are Hermeneutics, Biblical Theology, Biblical Studies, and Pentecostal/Charismatic Theology as these will be systematically drawn together to produce a Biblically rooted answer to the research question. There will also be some engagement with Philosophical Theology, however, due to the nature of the answer constructed, this will be only peripheral. The reason for this is that I will argue that the use of Philosophical Theology in responding to the problem of evil and suffering has generally caused more problems than it has solved. This issue will be addressed in chapter 2.

Having anchored the study in its disciplinary context and provided details of the method to be employed, it is now possible to unfold an outline of it.

Outline of the Study

Responses to the problem of evil and suffering from within Christian theology have a broad and extensive heritage and so it is important that the response developed in this study is contextualized within that. For this reason, chapter 2 aims to provide a broad sweep of the field in which the response to be developed will be located. This holds within it two specific intentions. Firstly, by doing this the approach to be developed here can be located relative to that which already exists in this field, thus showing points of overlap and connection. Secondly, knowledge of the field also acts as a way of clearing the ground in order to develop an approach that is different and unique in comparison to what has gone before. By examining perceived issues with approaches already in existence a way can be forged that seeks to draw on the strengths and overcome the weaknesses. Chapter 2 is thus an exercise in contextualization and ground-clearing.

Building on chapter 2, chapter 3 will examine Pentecostal/Charismatic responses to the problem of evil and suffering. Although in the light of chapter 2 it is possible to begin to generally place the approach to be developed

A Dramatic Pentecostal/Charismatic Anti-Theodicy

in this study within the field of Christian responses to evil and suffering, this is only partially and tentatively possible. To build from this alone would fail to fully address the issue of developing a response that is conducive to Pentecostal/Charismatic theology. In a similar way to chapter 2 then, the aim of chapter 3 is to map out the specifically Pentecostal/Charismatic field, again, in order to both contextualize and clear ground.

Placed together, these first two chapters have the combined effect of both describing and interrogating Christian responses to the problem of evil and suffering (chapter 2 generally, chapter 3 with specific reference to Pentecostal/Charismatic theology) and in doing so highlight both intra and inter inconsistencies that exist in the practices and beliefs. They also highlight positive aspects of approaches that have been generated so far that will act as threads to be re-engaged with at points in the study when the specific approach to be developed here begins to emerge. Having provided this context and highlighted the issues to be overcome in the production of the new approach, the next obvious port of call may appear to be the construction of that approach. However, before this is possible, tools are required to enable this construction. This brings us to chapter 4.

A significant issue for Christian responses to evil and suffering generally, and Pentecostal/Charismatic responses in particular, is the inconsistency regarding, on the one hand, *use* of Scripture and the practices that develop from this, and on the other, claims about belief in what Scripture is and the role it should take in guiding one's practice. In short, what is allegedly believed about Scripture does not appear consistent with how Scripture is used and the practices that come from this. The beliefs about Scripture may be correct but I suggest that a significant reason why the problem of poor communication about and with God in the face of seemingly innocent, meaningless suffering when God appears to be absent occurs, is because right belief is not translated into right practice. To begin to address this problem, before right belief and practice regarding communication to and about God can be developed, the issue of right practice regarding the reading of and use of Scripture must be examined. The issue of Pentecostal/Charismatic hermeneutics is therefore the subject of chapter 4.

More specifically, chapter 4 consists of a three-way engagement between two Pentecostal scholars and an Evangelical one. The aim of the conversation is to examine the methods employed by the two Pentecostal scholars—who are pioneers in their field—to discover whether there are any inconsistencies in belief and practice regarding approaches to and use of Scripture, and highlight what these are. The method employed by the third party in this conversation acts as a corrective to the inconsistencies, but, employs a method that, I suggest, will be acceptable to Pentecostal/Charismatic

Introduction

theology. The third party—Kevin Vanhoozer—uses a "dramatic" method that will be employed to frame the rest of the approach developed in the study. The basis of this method is that Scripture is the God-given script that we, as actors in the drama of salvation, are to follow as we seek to put on fitting performances in the parts for which we have been cast. It is important at this point to provide the rationale for the selection of Vanhoozer as dialogue partner.

In a paper presented at the British Evangelical Identities Conference in 2004, Mark Cartledge addressed the issue of "The Challenges posed by Pentecostal Theological Method to British Evangelical Theology."[26] Cartledge highlighted five areas of challenge as well as some Evangelical concerns regarding Pentecostal method. Point four in the discussion concerned the issue of a possible false dichotomy between theory and practice and how this relates to a community's view of and use of Scripture. Cartledge concluded the point by stating "The challenge is for Evangelical theology to become more holistic whilst still retaining its *a priori* commitment to the supreme authority of Scripture and being rigorously academic."[27] Within this discussion, two Evangelical scholars that Cartledge noted may be making ground on this issue were Vanhoozer and N. T. Wright. In the conclusion to the paper, Cartledge also noted the possible domestication of Scripture by Pentecostal communities in how they see and use it and suggested that Evangelical scholarship would highlight this as a concern.[28] In 2008 Richard Allan drew on N. T. Wright's appropriation of "critical realism" in order to propose it as a corrective epistemology for Pentecostal hermeneutics.[29] In the light of these discussions, I am in agreement with Cartledge and Allan in their highlighting of the Pentecostal hermeneutical issues and their highlighting of Wright as proposing a method that may be corrective and palatable to Pentecostal theology. However, I opt for Vanhoozer as dialogue partner in chapter 4 as I suggest Vanhoozer, in incorporating Wright's insights, supersedes him in the rigor and depth of his method and thus proposes a method that will better suit the situation in question.[30]

With Vanhoozer's hermeneutical method framing the approach to be developed in the rest of the study, the research question can be re-stated:

26. Cartledge, "'Text-Community-Spirit,'" This paper has been reproduced in a modified format in Spawn and Wright, eds., *Spirit and Scripture*.
27. Cartledge, "'Text-Community-Spirit,'" 8.
28. Ibid., 10.
29. Allan, "Contemporary Pentecostal Hermeneutics," particularly chapter 3.
30. Vondey's review of the *The Drama of Doctrine* also highlights several aspects of Vanhoozer's work that would find interest in Pentecostal/Charismatic theology as well as points of tension. See Vondey, Review of *The Drama of Doctrine*.

A Dramatic Pentecostal/Charismatic Anti-Theodicy

What does it mean to produce a fitting Pentecostal/Charismatic performance in the face of seemingly innocent, meaningless suffering when God appears to be absent? In conjunction, the aim of the study can also be re-stated: *to answer the research question by developing Biblically rooted, systematic guidance for the production of a fitting Pentecostal/Charismatic performance in the face of seemingly innocent, meaningless suffering when God appears to be absent.*

Having addressed the issues of belief *about* Scripture and use *of* Scripture, chapter 4 acts as the hinge point of the study as the turn is made from assessment of practices and beliefs and the inconsistencies that emerge, to the correction of practices and beliefs. Chapter 5 continues this theme of correction by examining how, based on the Script, the divine playwright sees, understands, and responds to evil and suffering, and how the human actors are to perform fittingly in response to it. This examination draws back in some of those scholars mentioned in chapter 2 as having potential for aiding in the construction of a fitting response to evil and suffering. Most notable among them is Walter Brueggemann and N. T. Wright as well as continued engagement with Vanhoozer.

Brueggemann is particularly important as it is engagement with his work that will aid in the highlighting and understanding of the lament genre. Currently Brueggemann stands as one of the leading scholars in psalms research and particularly with regard to the lament genre within that. In addition, he has engaged in Biblical Theology rather than simply Biblical Studies and so, his insights will complement the work in this study in a way that other Biblical scholar's work would not have so easily done. A further point that highlights Brueggemann as a suitable dialogue partner is that in developing his Old Testament Theology he has been a strong advocate of testimony as important in the life of a community—in his case Israel. As testimony has also commonly been understood as a central feature in the life of Pentecostal/Charismatic communities this latter point further commends Brueggemann as a relevant and significant dialogue partner in this study.

In a similar way, N. T. Wright is also a leading Biblical scholar who has engaged in Biblical Theology. Of particular importance for this study is that he is also a scholar who has sought to examine the problem of evil and suffering from a Biblically rooted perspective. As such an examination is a rare occurrence, Wright's work in this area is particularly relevant and significant to the current project.

Continued engagement with Vanhoozer as the study unfolds is an obvious move since it is his hermeneutical methodology that provides the tools for the construction of the answer to the central research question. In the light of this, as Vanhoozer has produced work regarding divine interaction

Introduction

with humans and divine perspectives on evil and suffering, continued dialogue with his work seems fitting. He is also one of the few scholars who have sought to approach the problem of evil and suffering from a Biblically rooted perspective.

In engaging with Brueggemann in particular, it will become apparent that the practice of lament appears to offer direction for what a fitting performance may look like. However, to simply extract lament texts—particularly from the Psalms—and perform them ignores a key problem that the use of Vanhoozer's dramatic method seeks to surmount. As the image of the divine playwright in human form, Jesus gives a divine, command performance. As actors seeking to follow in his footsteps, the questions should be: i.) how does Jesus perform when faced with experiences of suffering? ii.) does Jesus engage with the lament tradition and if so in what way? iii.) how does Jesus' performance offer direction for our own? These questions are the subject of chapter 6.

Having provided the background to enable understanding of the performance of Jesus in chapter 5, chapter 6 aims to amalgamate the perspective and action of the divine playwright and the performance of his actors by examining the performance of the one perfect, divine-human actor. By examining Jesus' performance, particularly in the midst of personal suffering, we can both get a closer look at the divine perspective on evil and suffering as well as taking direction as to how we, as actors in the drama, are to perform fittingly in the midst of seemingly innocent, meaningless suffering. At this point we can return to the question at the heart of the study: What does it mean to produce a fitting Pentecostal/Charismatic performance in the face of seemingly innocent, meaningless suffering when God appears to be absent? Having developed the necessary tools in chapter 4, foundations for the construction of the answer to this question are laid in chapter 5 and the first half of chapter 6. At this point the answer to the research question is constructed on these foundations with reference to the divine actor and most notably how the divine actor makes use of the lament tradition that has been handed on to Him. We must, however go beyond this, particularly from a Pentecostal/Charismatic perspective, and ask specifically what the role of the Holy Spirit is in the performance we are to give—a point also addressed in chapter 6. Having done this, the chapter returns briefly to the various responses to evil and suffering as outlined in chapter 2 in order to categorize the current approach in the light of them.

Chapter 6 closes with "stage directions" for the prepared actors. Although direction has been provided for how one is to perform generally and why this is so, there exists a final question mark over how space within the Pentecostal/Charismatic companies of actors can be created in order for a fitting performance to take place. The closing section of chapter 6 offers preliminary suggestions for how this question could begin to be answered as the transition from "academic" to "official" and "ordinary" discourse is initiated. The study finally concludes by summarizing where we have been, where we are, and by making suggestions for future research.

In producing this study the intent is to provide a previously underdeveloped challenge to Pentecostal/Charismatic communities and scholars regarding right belief and practice in the face of seemingly innocent, meaningless suffering when God appears to be absent. In doing so it also acts as a resource that can offer direction in the midst of the various questions that may emerge from such a challenge.

Before moving on to discuss the limitations of this study it is important to highlight and acknowledge a minority of scholars in Pentecostal/Charismatic theology that are supportive of the recovery of lament, and how this study differs from their work.

Relationship to Previous Pentecostal/Charismatic Work on Lament

Michael K. Adams, David Molzahn, Larry R. McQueen, Scott A. Ellington, and Leonard Maré have all, in the past twenty years, in various ways, highlighted the importance of the practice of lament and the need to attempt to bring it back into Pentecostal/Charismatic theology and practice.[31] Although this may be a hopeful sign of what lies ahead (and I hope it is!) there is a common problem, from a Pentecostal/Charismatic perspective, with the suggestions they make as to why and how lament is to be recovered. Although differing in their emphases due, in the main, to their own specialisms and interests, the common problem is the lack of importance and significance given to the Easter event in the recovery of lament. Adams notes that "Many Christians think that the lament is superseded by some christological claim" of which I would add that I believe this to be particularly true of Pentecostal/Charismatic Christians.[32] Although I disagree with the idea of lament being outdated and am in agreement—as will become apparent in what follows—with the championing of its practice, it seems naïve to ignore the fact that the Easter event did change how God and his people relate to one another. And further, this naivety becomes even more

---

31. Adams, "Music," and Adams, "'Hope'"; Molzahn, "Psalms"; McQueen, *Joel and the Spirit*; Ellington, "Reality, Remembrance and Response" and Ellington, "Loss of Testimony"; Maré, "Pentecostalism and Lament."

32. Adams, "Music," 9.

pronounced when this fact is ignored by those from a tradition whose central belief involves a "Fivefold" or "Four Square" gospel.[33]

Both McQueen and Maré note the importance of hermeneutics to Pentecostal theology and particularly to the appropriation of lament, however, neither seems to recognize that, particularly from a Pentecostal perspective, how one interprets the Old Testament must be affected by the Incarnation and in particular the Easter event. On the contrary, Maré, although in passing makes reference to Jesus' use of Ps 22 and states, "Jesus Himself verbalized his negative emotions, and we can surely follow His example," seems to suggest that use of lament is legitimate because the Old Testament is as valid as the New and our experiences of suffering are similar.[34] There is truth in the point about similarities in experience, however, my main point stands: how one interprets the Old Testament is significantly affected by the Easter event. One needs only to think of the abolition of the Levitical laws, or the role of the priest, to see that this is so. Once recognized, the problem that emerges is the question of how to read and re-appropriate the Old Testament in the light of the Easter event (in this case the lament texts in particular), particularly in a way that is conducive to Pentecostal/Charismatic theology. As noted above, this study supports the re-appropriation of lament suggested by the scholars mentioned here, however, where it differs considerably is in the consideration and justification given to appropriating lament in the light of the Easter event and the hermeneutical method required to justify that appropriation. This will become apparent as the argument builds.

A further difference between this study and the work of McQueen in particular is that the situation in which lament emerges as a fitting response in McQueen's work is different to that being discussed here. In seeking to recover lament in contemporary Pentecostalism, McQueen primarily links the book of Joel and the practice of lament in early Pentecostalism. However, neither the practice of lament found in Joel, nor the practice of lament

---

33. Both a "Fivefold" and a "Four Square" gospel are christological at root and dependent upon the Easter event. Jesus can only be Savior, Sanctifier, Baptizer in the Spirit, Healer, and Soon Coming King because of what was achieved through his death and resurrection. It therefore seems naïve that those who are championing the practice of lament whilst also maintaining such a christologically rooted belief fail to notice that the Easter event fundamentally alters the way God relates to his people. In the case of the present work, most notable is the emphasis on Jesus as Healer. This is so because if one believes healing is in the Atonement (a point to be addressed in chapter 3), it seems unavoidable to ask whether lament is legitimate and justified in the face of suffering, for one who maintains such a belief. All the proponents discussed above seem to have failed to ask this question.

34. Maré, "Pentecostalism and Lament," 17. See section 6—"Conclusion"—for a summary of his argument.

A Dramatic Pentecostal/Charismatic Anti-Theodicy

in early Pentecostalism occurs in response to the type of suffering in question in this study. Ellington rightly notes that the examples McQueen draws on from early Pentecostalism seem "to refer almost exclusively to seeking for salvation and the baptism of the Holy Spirit."[35] There is a question as to whether McQueen is justified in making the links that he does between Scripture and Pentecostal practice, however, of greater importance for this study is McQueen's various sources. Neither the Old Testament texts, nor much of the New Testament texts that he draws from, provide fitting direction for lament in response to the kind of situation being examined in this study. And in addition, both the situation that led to lament and the theology and practice of lament in early Pentecostalism is starkly different from that which will be discussed in what follows. Therefore, whereas McQueen may be trying to recover a certain kind of lament as a response to a certain situation in Pentecostal theology and practice, no such recovery is being attempted here. Instead, in fulfilling the aim of the study, new ground will be broken by justifying the practice of lament in situations that previously have not been understood as requiring lament as a fitting response. The uniqueness of the endeavors in this study will become apparent as it progresses.

Having described the methodology and layout to be used, as well as placing the current work in the context of previous, similar endeavors, it is important to briefly discuss the limitations and focus of the study.

Limitations

Having opted solely for literary research as the basis for this project, with such an approach comes specific limitations. Firstly, the theology to be engaged with is limited by the literary resources available. Secondly, it is limited by my selection of which proponents to engage with within those resources. It is impossible to have gleaned and engaged with every Pentecostal/Charismatic understanding of, and approach to, the problem of evil and suffering and so, in this sense, the term "Pentecostal/Charismatic" (which I will discuss in greater detail below) seems too general. However, I have chosen to use it because the proponents of the various approaches that are examined have beliefs and practices that, at their core, hold common elements that have been designated as central to Pentecostal/Charismatic worldviews. What I am not saying is that the approaches covered by my research are definitively the *only* ones. What I am saying is that they are the best representatives, in the literary data available, of the variety of responses from proponents within the ethnic and geographic focus of the research in

35. Ellington, "Reality, Remembrance and Response," 204.

Introduction

this study. I have therefore opted for the method employed because I believe that it yields the most reliable data from which to draw any meaningful conclusions regarding the truth of the situation.

A further limitation, or perhaps focus, is that engagement, regarding Pentecostal/Charismatic approaches to the problem of evil and suffering, is confined to white, North American proponents. The reasons for this are threefold.

Firstly, due to my own heritage from which the initial questions and subsequent key question central to this study emerged, this focus seemed an obvious one. The traditions I have been a part of have been significantly influenced by the various proponents discussed and so in having to limit one's scope, this seems a helpful factor with which to decide how.

Secondly, thinking along the same lines but broadening the perspective a little, the proponents discussed have also influenced the wider linguistic context of which I am predominantly linked—the primarily English speaking Pentecostal/Charismatic world. This acts as a further reason for focusing in on those discussed.

As noted in the "Methodology" section above, when doing literary based research, the literature will, to some degree, determine the limits and the focus. A third reason for this focus is therefore established by the literature. Within the spectrum of responses to the problem of evil and suffering from within Pentecostal/Charismatic theology, the proponents discussed here are some of the best examples of different points on that spectrum as well as being some of the most influential on the Pentecostal/Charismatic world. Again this is a major contributing factor regarding choice of focus.

As a response to these limitations, what I hope for is that, rather than this project simply being a stand-alone that is affirmed, or critiqued, or worse, ignored, it would instead be the opening move in a dialogue with those who are "on the ground" in situations in which the subject matter discussed here is relevant. Although the major proponents engaged with in examining Pentecostal/Charismatic responses to suffering and evil are from the primarily English speaking world, what I am arguing for in this study is not limited to that. A dialogue obviously requires multiple interlocutors and so, as well as being a directive for fitting performance, feedback is invited from the actors—on all parts of the stage—to enable further fine tuning and revision. The issue of communication—to make common—is at the heart of this study and so it is hoped that common ground can be found in the desire to perform fittingly in the parts in which we are cast in the scenes in which we find ourselves. We do, after all, stand on stage together. We may be on different parts of the cosmological stage with different scenery, props and unfolding plot lines, however, in what follows I suggest there is something to aid everyone in their respective performances.

Before we embark on the work of finding direction for a fitting performance in times of suffering, a final note on terminology.

Terminology

In a recent essay discussing Pentecostal taxonomies and definitions, Allan Anderson states, "It is probably more correct to speak of Pentecostalism*s* in the contemporary global context, though the singular form will continue to be used here to describe these movements as a whole."[36] He further states, "The terms *Pentecostal* and *Pentecostalism* refer to a wide variety of movements scattered throughout the world that can be described as having 'family resemblance'" of which it is "a family resemblance that emphasizes the working of the Holy Spirit."[37] Anderson continues his examination by suggesting that this family could be sub-categorized into four types: "Classical Pentecostals," "Older Independent and Spirit Churches," "Older Church Charismatics," and "Neo-Pentecostal and Neo-Charismatic Churches."[38]

In the light of the limitations of this study regarding its demographic and theological focus (as noted above), and Anderson's typology, I will retain the term "Pentecostal/Charismatic" as the label for communities I am engaging with. The reason for this is that although I agree with Anderson that the term "Pentecostal" covers a multitude of diverse communities that share a "family resemblance," the limitations and focus of this study mean primary engagement will be with communities that fall into sub-categories one, three and four of Anderson's typology. The use of the term "Pentecostal/Charismatic" enables an acknowledgement of the key resemblances and the differences, historically, sociologically and theologically between the groups in question whilst not being too cumbersome.

---

36. Anderson, "Varieties, Taxonomies, and Definitions," 15.

37. Ibid., 15.

38. Ibid., 16–20. The first of these, "Classical Pentecostals," Anderson defines as "those whose diachronous and synchronous links can be shown, originating in the early-twentieth-century revival and missionary movements" (17). The second type, "Older Independent and Spirit Churches," are those "especially in China, India, and sub-Saharan Africa, that sometimes have diachronous (but not usually synchronous) links with classical Pentecostalism" (18). The third type, "Older Church Charismatics," "remain in established older churches, are widespread and worldwide, and often approach the subject of Spirit baptism and spiritual gifts from a sacramental perspective" (19). The fourth type, "Neo-Pentecostal and neo-Charismatic Churches," are "often regarded as Charismatic independent churches, including megachurches, and influenced by both classical Pentecostalism and the Charismatic movement" (19).

That said, the term "Pentecostal" in the use of the term "Pentecostal/Charismatic" will cover that which is usually designated "Classical Pentecostalism." Although much doubt is now cast over the previously believed North American origin of this movement, this term is best associated with the example of Pentecostalism that originated at Azuza Street in 1906. Emerging from the influence of the Wesleyan-holiness tradition, a key characteristic of this movement is belief in the Baptism of the Holy Spirit as evidenced by speaking in tongues. This experience is subsequent to conversion and sanctification. In addition there is a strong belief in the on-going work of the Holy Spirit in the community, manifesting itself, in particular, in charismatic gifts.

The term "Charismatic" in the use of the term "Pentecostal/Charismatic" will cover what Anderson refers to as "Older Church Charismatics," and "Neo-Pentecostal and Neo-Charismatic Churches." Given the nature and subject of this study I am simply defining "Charismatic" as any church which, whether in existence before or since "Classical Pentecostalism" has been significantly influenced by it, particularly with regard to belief in the Baptism of the Holy Spirit and the operation of charismatic gifts.

As noted above, of particular importance in both cases is the belief in the gift of healing that is often central within all "Pentecostal" and "Charismatic" communities.

Although "Pentecostal/Charismatic" will be the most common term used, where a specific community or individual is being discussed, if relevant, more nuanced terminology and definitions will be used.

In connecting this term with the various resemblances there is always the danger that I am including or excluding those who should not be. This is the risk with the use of any defined term. However, although to exist without defined terms *per se* is impossible, to exist with defined terms that are potentially temporal and open to revision is not. This is the aim in my use of the term "Pentecostal/Charismatic" in what follows.

2

An Overview of Christian Approaches to Evil and Suffering

Introduction

IN THIS CHAPTER THE aim will be to provide a general overview of what is typically considered the most important responses to the problem of evil and suffering from the perspective of a Christian worldview. Doing this will enable us to map out a field of responses in which we will then be able to situate Pentecostal/Charismatic responses (chapter 3) and, more importantly, the response to be developed by the author (chapters 5 and 6). In order to create space for this development, this chapter will proceed by bracketing the various approaches into categories and critiquing each one in turn. By doing this it will become clear, as the study progresses, where the response to be developed exists in relation to other responses, but also where it differs from them. In short the aim is to map out a contextual field and at the same time clear the ground for the development of the author's response.

Before we can proceed, however, we must establish the categories in which the various responses will be bracketed.

Many Christian responses to the problem of evil and suffering have emerged by way of attempting to address the problem as formalized by Epicurus, who set it up as a logical incompatibility issue in need of resolution. David Hume stated the problem in Part X of his *Dialogues Concerning Natural Religion*: "Is he [God] willing to prevent evil, but not able? then is he impotent. Is he able, but not willing? then is he malevolent. Is he both

An Overview of Christian Approaches to Evil and Suffering

able and willing? whence then is evil."[1] As Christian responses to the problem of evil and suffering have, on the whole, centered on responding to this formulation of the problem, it seems fitting to categorize them according to the different responses that this conundrum has brought forth. With that in mind the three main categories that will be used in this chapter will be "Defense Against the Problem of Evil," "Theodicy," and "Anti-Theodicy."

The first category will cover those responses that are heavily theoretical and constructed in a negative apologetic fashion by the theist against the challenges of the problem of evil by the atheist. The second category will cover those responses that, although still heavily theoretical, are constructed in a more positive apologetic fashion. These responses are sweeping explanations as to how the God revealed in the Bible, and more specifically in the person of Jesus Christ, can be understood and believed alongside the realities of our world. The third category will cover those responses that have rejected the theoretical stances of defense and theodicy as practically unhelpful, and are instead more existential and practical in response. They are approaches that are driven by the need to provide the sufferer and those around them with a practical method of response that helps rather than hinders them in the midst of their suffering.

Within the categories I have chosen I will highlight the key approaches that fall under the various titles and key thinkers that have produced these approaches. With any categorization of this nature there is always the risk of oversimplification whereby the uniqueness of a position is lost in the desire to bracket it with other similar positions. However, for the sake of clarity I have chosen to take this risk believing firstly that the gain outweighs the risk and that secondly, in what follows, retention of all relevant nuanced differences has been achieved.

Defense Against the Problem of Evil

When faced with an attack on the existence of God by way of the problem of evil one approach that has been assumed in response is that of the defense.[2] Although this approach has primarily come from philosophers such as Alvin Plantinga—who would come under the banner of "Christian"—it is primarily theistic as opposed to Christian. The distinction I make between the two is that the theist generally understands the term "God" as describing a being that is omnipotent, omniscient, omnipresent, omnibenevolent,

---

1. Hume, *Dialogues*, 88.

2. For examples of the types of attack in question, see Mackie, "Evil and Omnipotence"; McCloskey, "God and Evil."

A Dramatic Pentecostal/Charismatic Anti-Theodicy

just, immutable, and simple but seemingly detached from any context or tradition. Under heavy influence from Enlightenment rationality, this God,

> is presented as an abstract entity with a number of characteristics, a God who can be described without reference to any particular narratives, without any discussion of Incarnation, Christology, Trinity . . . Christianity is generally seen as one of the things you can get by adding a few supplementary beliefs to the basic starter kit of theism.[3]

In turn, the way evil is dealt with within this approach is also very general and abstract.

The most popular approach coming from this camp is commonly known as the "Free Will Defense," with the most recent formulations of it being attributed to Alvin Plantinga. The aim for the theist is to disprove the atheist claim that an omnipotent, all-loving God cannot coexist with evil and in so doing prove that it is possible that such a world could indeed occur, and, that it is rational to believe in such a world and such a God. As Plantinga states, "the aim is not to say what God's reason *is*, but at most what God's reason *might possibly be*."[4] It is Plantinga's formulation of this approach that I will outline here.

Plantinga's Free Will Defense

The theist firstly makes the definitions of the characteristics of God clear. As the concept of "all-loving" is fairly self-explanatory, the emphasis is placed on the definition of omnipotence.[5] Plantinga states, "What the theist typically means when he says that God is omnipotent is not that there are *no* limits to God's power, but at most that there are no nonlogical limits to what He can do."[6]

This principle is then combined with the possibility that a world containing creatures that have free will is a better world than one in which all things and creatures are determined. If it is taken that, from God's perspective, this is true, then God is bound by his character and nature to make

---

3. Kilby, "Evil," 14.
4. Plantinga, *God, Freedom and Evil*, 28.
5. All-loving in this context means God loves all humans equally and does the best God can for them. However God also hates all evil.
6. Plantinga, "Free Will Defense," 108.

An Overview of Christian Approaches to Evil and Suffering

such a world.[7] The result of this could be that God creates a world whereby the creatures in it that have freedom are humans.

The focus then shifts to how the idea of free will is understood. Plantinga states, "If a person is free with respect to a given action, then he is free to perform that action and free to refrain from performing it; no antecedent conditions and/or causal laws determine that he will perform the action, or that he won't."[8] And further, the choice cannot be coerced or determined by any causal law. If the question of morality is brought into this, its presence means that if a person is free to choose, as long as they are aware of right and wrong, they are also, therefore, free to choose between right and wrong. "Moral evil" is thus defined as "evil that results from free human activity."[9]

Bringing all this together, the Free Will Defense claims that if a world that contains creatures—in this case humans—that have free will is better than one without, then God must bring it into being. If morality is also present, as the theist believes it is, this means that the free creatures can choose to do wrong as well as right. And, because God, although omnipotent, cannot do anything that is nonlogical, he therefore cannot override the freedom of the creatures, as this would contradict the freedom that they have. The result is that God can be all-loving and omnipotent and at the same time moral evil can exist. As Stephen Davis says, "the FWD must say that the amount of good and evil that exist in the world is partially up to us and not entirely up to God."[10]

Clear and concise though this defense may be, it does raise some important questions regarding possible flaws. These potential flaws include: could God not have created a world in which humans are free but never do wrong? Is this the best possible world, as surely God must create the best possible world? How does the Free Will Defense account for natural evil?

In response, Plantinga first dismisses the idea that it is possible to create a best possible world. This is based on the argument that regardless of how good the world is, there is always room for an infinite amount of more goodness so the idea of a best possible world becomes an incomprehensible idea.[11] Plantinga further suggests that "what is really characteristic and central to the Free Will Defense is the claim that God, though om-

---

7. He is bound to create it because God, by his very nature of being perfect, cannot make anything less than the best.

8. Plantinga, *God, Freedom and Evil*, 29.

9. Ibid., 30.

10. Davis, "Free Will and Evil," 75–76.

11. This is contra Leibniz who stated, "It seems to me that I have proved sufficiently that among all the possible plans of the universe there is one better than all the rest, and that God has not failed to choose it" (*Theodicy*, 268).

nipotent, could not have actualized just any possible world He pleased."[12] If God must create a world with humans in that have free will, then, by the very nature of their free will there will be certain worlds that God cannot actualize, as this would not be compatible with the nature of the free will that humans have. Plantinga goes on to suggest that "it is possible that every creaturely essence—every essence including the property of being created by God—suffers from transworld depravity."[13] By the term "transworld depravity" Plantinga means that given any world that is actualized a creature with transworld depravity will make at least one morally wrong decision, making it impossible for God to actualize a world in which humans have free will and never go wrong. Plantinga further states, "What is important about the idea of transworld depravity is that if a person suffers from it, then it wasn't within God's power to actualize any world in which that person is significantly free but does no wrong—that is, a world in which he produces moral good but no moral evil."[14]

With regard to the question of natural evil there are at least three responses.[15] It is possible that some natural evil is simply a result of the structure of nature and the eco-system necessary to maintain the planet and the life of creatures on it. It is also possible that due to wrong choices made by the free human beings regarding maintenance and nurture of the eco-system, it does not work the way it was made to. The second of these responses begins to blur the lines of natural and moral evil. The third response is that, as well as creating human beings with free will, it is also possible that God created nonhuman beings, such as angels, with a level of freedom. If this is true then we know from the brief discussion above that free will and the presence of a moral order create the possibility of choosing wrongly. This therefore means that the spiritual beings could choose to affect nature in such a way as to create what appears to humans as natural evil. Plantinga suggests that it is a "possibility that natural evil is due to the actions of significantly free but nonhuman persons."[16] Again, the fact that this idea is based on the choice of moral creatures with free will means that at least some apparent natural evil could in fact be placed in the bracket of moral evil.[17]

12. Plantinga, *God, Freedom and Evil*, 34.

13. Ibid., 53.

14. Ibid., 48.

15. Plantinga describes natural evil as "Evil that can't be ascribed to the free actions of human beings" (*God, Freedom and Evil*, 57).

16. Ibid., 58.

17. Plantinga combines this idea with moral evil and labels it "broadly moral evil," 59.

An Overview of Christian Approaches to Evil and Suffering

It must be noted again that these theories are not meant in a positive apologetic sense and therefore are not given as definitive about the way things are. They are simply meant to act as defensive apologetic possibilities that create a plausible response to the Epicurean trilemma employed in most atheistic attacks. In fact, Plantinga suggests that the Free Will Defense "solves the main philosophical problem of evil."[18] However, he also notes regarding actual suffering that humans face, that a Free Will Defense is not "designed to be of much help or comfort to one suffering from such a storm in the soul" and that it will probably not "enable someone to find peace with himself and with God in the face of the evil the world contains."[19]

A Critique

The great strength of an approach such as this is that, purely on an academic, logical basis, it is the strongest defense against attacks on the existence of God by way of the problem of evil. It also provides a foundation on which one may construct a theodicy. However, there are possible logical problems with this defense. One example is: why could God not have created humans (or angels) with free will but without "transworld depravity," therefore making them unable to go wrong at some point?

An interesting question though this may be, the key concerns for this study do not center on the internal inconsistencies of the philosophical argument that is proposed in the Free Will Defense. Instead the two points that are of concern here are firstly, how useful the Defense is in response to actual occurrences of suffering and evil, and secondly, as it is a "Christian" response, where the authority that justifies such a response is to be found.

The first of these concerns can be dealt with quickly and easily. As noted above, Plantinga does not see his defense as providing much pastoral aid and so is of little help to the one suffering. The second concern, however, is not so straight forward.

Richard Swinburne notes, "Neither the New Testament nor subsequent Christian doctrine contain more than parts of a full-blown theodicy and hints on how to construct one."[20] Marilyn McCord Adams also states,

---

18. Plantinga, *God, Freedom and Evil*, 64.

19. Ibid., 29.

20. Swinburne, *Providence*, 249. Swinburne defines theodicy as "not an account of God's actual reasons for allowing a bad state to occur, but an account of his possible reasons (i.e., reasons which God has for allowing the bad state to occur whether or not those are the ones which motivate him)" (ibid., 15). Swinburne's definition of theodicy is therefore not unlike Plantinga's Free Will Defense, hence my use of the quote here. There are differences, however, in that Swinburne seems more concerned with

A Dramatic Pentecostal/Charismatic Anti-Theodicy

"The Bible is short on explanations of why God permits evils and relatively long on how God makes good on them."[21] The points to draw out from both these observations are, firstly, that the Bible gives no real explanation for why evil exists, and secondly, that it seems God, as revealed in Scripture, is more concerned with responding to evil and suffering than to explaining its existence. With this in mind, one has to consider whether a response to suffering that is labeled "Christian," and yet does not seem to respond in a way that concurs with that which is revealed in Scripture, can still maintain such a label. The emphasis for Plantinga seems to be on whether something is logical and rational rather than whether it is a response that follows in the path of Jesus. And, although it is clinical and theoretical, it is not an approach that has simply emerged in a vacuum, nor is it purely objective. Instead the Free Will Defense has emerged within a western, post-Enlightenment narrative. John Swinton states, "Put simply, the Age of Enlightenment was that period in European cultural history that moved away from a theological worldview, which understood God, church and religion as central, and moved towards a worldview determined by science and reason."[22] He continues,

> Understood in terms of the Enlightenment, the problem of evil appears to be just one more of the problems that humans frequently encounter and strive to solve through reason and intellect. Once we answer the questions and solve the problem, the use of human reason verifies and legitimizes faith in God.[23]

All worldviews from the ground up must begin with a belief in something and in Plantinga's case it appears that his belief is in human reason. As Hauerwas points out, the result of this is that the response to the problem of evil that emerges is "more like a game than a serious activity."[24] As will become apparent, particularly in chapter 3, a Pentecostal/Charismatic worldview has a high view of Scripture. This said, a response to the problem of evil and suffering that is not anchored in a faith in the God revealed in Scripture, and, in particular, in his son, Jesus Christ, will have no place in Pentecostal/Charismatic worldviews or practice.

---

developing his view from inside a more Biblically grounded framework. Having said that, it is not as well anchored in this as those positions to be discussed in the "Theodicy" section of this chapter, meaning that Swinburne straddles both categories but is neither fully one nor the other.

21. Adams, *Horrendous Evils*, 137.
22. Swinton, *Raging*, 32.
23. Ibid., 33.
24. Hauerwas, *Naming Silences*, 2.

In addition, Pentecostal/Charismatic theology has traditionally approached rational, academic theology and philosophy with a high level of suspicion and has instead emphasized the experiential and practical. Bearing these various issues in mind it is hard to see how the Free Will Defense can retain the label "Christian" and even harder to see how it can provide any aid in the creation of a Pentecostal/Charismatic response to the problem of evil and suffering. On which note, we proceed to examine the area of "Theodicy."

Theodicy

Whereas the aim of the defense is merely to show that attacks by atheists on the existence of God by way of the problem of evil are flawed in some way, thus showing that the Epicurean trilemma *can* be "solved," the aim of the theodicist extends far beyond this into the realm of suggesting *how* it can be solved. Michael Peterson states, "a theodicy seeks to articulate *plausible or credible explanations* that rest on theistic truths and insights."[25] The point here is that the ground work done by the defense theist is built upon by the theodicist as they seek to construct explanations for the existence of evil and suffering from a Christian perspective. The aim of a theodicy is therefore to provide "*an intellectual defense of God in the face of evil and suffering.*"[26] As a general rule, one of the underlying principles of Christian theodicies is that there is a greater good at work that will be completed in the fullness of time.

As there is such a vast volume of literature on theodicy I will confine my discussion to four general areas for two reasons. Firstly, I would suggest that most theodicies are variations on the approaches I will outline here and secondly, a narrowing down such as this allows for greater clarity in understanding in such a constricted space. The four general approaches I will discuss here are: "The Free Will Theodicy," "The Irenaean Theodicy," "The Openness Theodicy," and "The Process Theodicy." There are areas of overlap between these categories and the various thinkers I will discuss, but, again I believe the gain of this approach outweighs the cost.

The Free Will Theodicy

This approach to the problem of evil and suffering is usually attributed in its common form to St. Augustine of Hippo. Most approaches after Augustine

---

25. Peterson, *God and Evil*, 85.
26. Swinton, *Raging*, 2.

A Dramatic Pentecostal/Charismatic Anti-Theodicy

are merely variations on his thought. I will therefore focus on Augustine and draw on other scholars where relevant.

Augustine held to the idea that God is omnipotent, omniscient, omnibenevolent, omnipresent, immutable, just, simple, and that he can do no evil. Augustine also believed God to be all-good, pure being, and the source of all things and suggested that all that God creates is good and that creation is ordered. All things have their place within the order both in a physical sense and a chronological sense and any misuse of anything in the order, or an attempt to move it to a different place, would result in corruption of the order.[27] This results in "plenitude" whereby the order contains everything that could be created and is lacking in nothing. Augustine affirmed this in a discussion with his friend Evodius stating, "Whatever might rightly occur to you as being better, you may be sure that God, as the Creator of all good things, has made that too."[28]

Included within the world that Augustine suggested God made, are mutable humans, with free will. They are given free will because they are made to be at their best when they are in a perfect, loving relationship with their creator. And, since a loving relationship involves them *choosing* to be in it, they must have free will in order to do this. However, the other side of this is that they can choose not to maintain their place in the order in the correct fashion. In the fall, we see wrong choice, resulting in the entry of sin and evil, leading to corruption of the order. "All the moral evil that exists in the world is due to the choices of free moral agents whom God created."[29]

At this point attention must be drawn to how Augustine defined evil. He stated, "There is no such entity in nature as 'evil'; 'evil' is merely a name for the privation of the good."[30] If all that God made was originally all-good, the entry of evil should really be understood as not the entrance of some substance but the absence of goodness. Evil is where goodness is lacking. Although it was Adam and Eve that committed sin, thus causing corruption, Augustine believed this was transmitted through all humans from then on, almost like a genetic disease. He therefore also believed that we can only be saved by what God does for us, not by what we can do for ourselves.[31]

This caused some problems for both Augustine and those who have followed his thought since, in his work, there appear to be two main,

---

27. See St. Augustine, *Free Choice* 3.9, for Augustine's view of order and corruption.
28. St. Augustine, *Free Choice* 3.5. This is a forerunner to Leibniz' "Best Possible World" view.
29. Davis, "Free Will and Evil," 76.
30. St. Augustine, *City of God* 11.22.
31. Ibid., 13.3.

conflicting, approaches in understanding the connections between God's attributes and character and the free will human's possess. The earlier Augustine seemed to suggest that we can still, as fallen creatures, turn to, or away, from God when God reaches out his hand to us. The later Augustine maintained that we have free will but that God chooses (or does not choose as the case may be) some to be saved and therefore some to be damned.[32]

When discussing the existence of evil in the post-fall state, Augustine also suggested that in an aesthetic way, some things that humans perceive as evil may actually be part of the overall beauty of the world. Like an observer staring at a dot on the canvas, we do not see how this dot contributes to the beauty of the painting because we do not have the right perspective. Augustine's point was that maybe some evil in the big picture is not really evil at all. And even when evil is rightly perceived as evil, God can bring good from it to the point that some suffering may even bring us closer to God. Augustine even went as far as saying that nothing falls outside of God's plans. The obvious problem with maintaining such a view whilst holding that God is all-loving and all-good is that a God who knowingly and willingly at the very least permits evil, if not causes it, seems to be incompatible with the labels "all-loving" and "all-good."

As with most theodicies, the Free Will Theodicy has a teleological aspect to it. There is also maintenance of belief in the existence of both Heaven and Hell and, therefore, no belief in universal salvation. With the belief in the existence of Heaven comes the idea that God will somehow outweigh the evil and the suffering that has been experienced by those who populate it, and, that he will restore and heal them.

A Critique

In building on the foundations of the Free Will Defense, the sister theodicy moves on to develop a solution to the Epicurean trilemma that gives a far more fleshed out response to the problem. The great strength of this is that the solution given is one that is far more specific and therefore understandable and useful for those who are grappling with the details of the problem of evil. Although it still remains heavily theoretical, it does provide for those who are inclined to face the problem at a theoretical level.

However, many of the internal problems raised against the details of the Free Will Defense can be raised against its sister theodicy and it retorts with much the same answers. Natural evil can be attributed to corruption of

---

32. The first of these is known as the "libertarian" approach and the second, the "compatibilist."

the natural order by humans or demonic activity, and the question of why humans fell can be pushed back to them being tempted by Satan, raising the seemingly unanswerable question of why angels fell.[33] Further problems created by this theodicy are actualized if one chooses the route of compatible freedom. Doing so results in God choosing some and not others, and, all experiences of suffering being understood as part of God's plan. Arguably this does not match up to our understanding of love and justice or concepts of love and justice revealed in Scripture. The proponent may answer by saying that this is because we do not understand God's ways. I do not find this a satisfying answer as this leaves God being actively responsible for evil and the damnation of some of his creatures. I therefore find the libertarian route more plausible. This, however, raises the question of why God only acts sometimes and not others, particularly if we consider atrocities such as the Holocaust, whilst maintaining the omnibenevolence and omnipotence of God. If a response is attempted that suggests there is some "greater good" to be drawn from it, or, that from a different perspective this is not really evil, then I am not sure the sufferers, or, any of us who take such horrors seriously, can accept this as anything less than blasphemy. As J. Richard Middleton suggests, "to claim that every evil in the world contributes to some equal or greater good which would be otherwise unattainable means quite simply that there is no *genuine* evil."[34] Arguably, not only is this of no help to those who are on the receiving end of some form of evil and suffering, but, the justification of the necessity of their experience for the greater good, at the very least, has the potential to increase their level of suffering, as it *encourages* apathy and *discourages* resistance. If the answer comes from the free will granted to humans, then we are back at the problem of why God created a world in which humans not only *could* sin, but, *would* sin.

As with the Free Will Defense, this critique shows the inconsistencies within the argument. However, as was also observed with regard to the Free Will Defense, a Free Will Theodicy seems to exist in order to produce a solution to the problem of evil—a sign of being heavily influenced by Enlightenment philosophy rather than the way of Jesus revealed in Scripture. More will be said about Jesus' response in chapter 6 but for now it will suffice to note that if one is seeking to follow in the way of Jesus it is paramount to begin with an examination of his response to evil and suffering.

---

33. For a discussion on the plausibility of an angelic fall, see Wright, *Theology of the Dark Side*, 62–65.

34. Middleton, "Why the 'Greater Good,'" 86.

The Irenaean Theodicy[35]

In an attempt to produce a theodicy that avoided or answered the problems faced by the Free Will Theodicy, John Hick drew on the thought of the church father Irenaeus.

In order to understand Hick's theodicy let us begin with his view of creation. The traditional view that Augustine and many before and after him have taken was one in which God created *ex nihilo*. He created in a certain order over a period of time, and this creation was completed with the first two humans—Adam and Eve—who then "fell," thus allowing sin to enter. This approach is in line with a fairly literal understanding of the Genesis narrative. However, Hick rejected a literal understanding as a myth, claiming that modern science had proven it as such. He then went on to replace it with a far looser, metaphorical understanding that heavily relies on scientific theories of evolution. According to this understanding, humans were not created perfect and neither was the world, instead both were created to evolve, which they continue to do. There was no literal Adam and Eve, they are merely representative of the humans that were made. Hick did however maintain the traditional understanding of God being all-loving, omniscient, and ultimately sovereign.

With this as his basis Hick then attempted to graft on to it what he interpreted as Irenaeus' view of how humans were originally created. The key to this in Hick's eyes was that there is a difference between being made in the image of God and being made in his likeness. Being made in his image is our original state whereby a human is an "intelligent creature capable of fellowship with his Maker" but at the same time immature and thus not perfect.[36] Our aim is to move from here to where we are in the likeness of God, where we are finally perfect, and the Holy Spirit aids us on our journey. Rather than seeing the fall as a literal fall from pure and perfect to sinful and corrupt, Hick saw the fall merely representing "the immense gap between what we actually are and what in the divine intention we are eventually to become."[37] He referred to this gap as "epistemic distance" between humans and God and saw the snake in the Genesis text as representative of the experimental side of humans, rather than as Satan. In connection to this, Hick maintained a similar view of freedom to that of the Free Will Theodicy. His view was that our progress in life has at its center the pursuit of a perfect loving relationship with God, and, we therefore must have free will to pursue

---

35. Or "Soul-Making Theodicy."
36. Hick, *Evil and God*, 217.
37. Hick, "Irenaean Theodicy," 41.

A Dramatic Pentecostal/Charismatic Anti-Theodicy

this as love cannot force. Hick also pointed out that progress is an individual thing so it may not necessarily be observed as overall progress in the whole of the human race throughout history.

If we now bring in Hick's view of evil, it is starkly different from the Free Will Defense or Theodicy. Hick believed we were not created in a perfect, pure state. In conjunction with that, he also believed much evil and suffering is the result of the various tests and temptations we must go through to get to the perfect state we are working towards. He suggested,

> one who has attained to goodness by meeting and eventually mastering temptations, and thus by rightly making responsible choices in concrete situations, is good in a richer and more valuable sense than would be one created *ab initio* in a state either of innocence or of virtue.[38]

And therefore, "In order to possess positive goodness men must be mutable creatures, subject to at least some forms of temptation."[39] The reason for the existence of moral evil from here becomes fairly clear. Bad choices in what Hick termed our "Soul-Making" result in moral evil occurring. Hick's explanation for natural evil was also similarly straight forward. Natural evil is either there as part of the eco-system of the world and as such acts as an education in the soul-making process, or, it is the result of bad choices by humans that have resulted in apparent natural evil. The former of these two educates because it provides an opportunity for soul-making in how one responds. The latter of the two would include such things as famine, and would therefore also challenge the choices that individuals make. Hick understood pain as a valuable tool in this education process as it protects us, deters us and warns us, all of which add to the educational process Hick believed we are involved in. When questioned over the horrendous and seemingly pointless nature of some evil, Hick's response was that it is a mystery, but, it does bring about some extremely positive responses such as compassion.[40] He also maintained that it is not possible for God to limit evil or remove some kinds of evil, since how would God decide which, or know where to stop? It is an all or nothing approach.

As with most theodicies, Hick's also has a teleological part to it. But, unlike the Free Will Theodicy Hick believed in universal salvation, "For if there are finally wasted lives and finally unredeemed sufferings, either God

---

38. Hick, *Evil and God*, 291.
39. Ibid., 307.
40. What Hick refers to as "excessive" or "dysteleological" suffering. See *Evil and God*, 363–67.

An Overview of Christian Approaches to Evil and Suffering

is not perfect in love or He is not sovereign in rule over His creation."[41] And for all those who are not ready for Heaven when they die because they have not gained sufficient purity for entry, he also proposed some sort of purgatory. The aim of this is that it causes the individual to progress to the state in which he should be in order to enter Heaven.

A Critique

Although this is only a brief summary of Hick's formulation of the Irenaean theodicy the main points, I believe, are clear. What Hick does well through this approach is to remove the problems related to "the fall" seen in the Free Will Defense/Theodicy (i.e., the problem of explaining why humans or supernatural beings chose to fall if there was no evil in the original creation) and alongside this provide an interesting variation on the reason for the existence of evil. Again, on a theoretical side, this approach also causes one to question the validity and plausibility of traditional doctrines applied in the Free Will Theodicy, thus potentially causing one to alter their worldview.

However, Hick's approach is also far from unproblematic. Firstly, his rather arrogant dismissal of the creation story seems a little premature. It is no secret that interpretation of the creation texts is difficult and scientific theories that support the various interpretations are varied with no solid conclusions emerging. In addition, post-modern scholarship with regard to science, such as Jean-Francois Lyotard's *The Postmodern Condition*, has exposed significant problems with claims of absolute proof for scientific theories.[42] The point being that the idea of science being more reliable than faith is a false dichotomy as both begin with faith based presuppositions. The concept that science is more reliable therefore seems short-sighted. This point is further supported by the history of changes in scientific theories due to the emergence of fresh insight. Hick's idea that science is more reliable completely misses the point that it is also based on beliefs, and that data still has to be interpreted and meaning generated by fallible human beings. Not only that but Hick seems happy to draw on "pre-scientific" beliefs in other areas of his theodicy thus creating somewhat of an inconsistency.

Secondly, Hick's account for horrendous evils seems unconvincing.[43] Are they just part of the test? And if so, what kind of God creates such a test

---

41. Hick, *Evil and God*, 376.
42. Lyotard, *Postmodern Condition*.
43. The term "horrendous evils" is borrowed from Marilyn McCord Adams. Adams describes horrendous evils as "evils the participation in which (that is, the doing or suffering of which) constitutes prima facie reason to doubt whether the participant's

and is it worth the cost? Hick seems happy to suggest that these, the worse evils—if indeed evils can be ranked—are a mystery, but that they also provide an opportunity for positive responses such as compassion. Considering Hick is attempting a theodicy, this response seems somewhat unacceptable as it fails to achieve what the essence of the theodicy is intended to do.

Thirdly, regarding Hick's teleology, if when we die we are not ready for heaven, and therefore have to go through purgatory, why could all not simply experience purgatory rather than having to experience horrendous "testing" in one's prior life? And, why is Hick happy to use the Christian God but not happy to use a Biblical understanding of Heaven and Hell, or creation? This last point raises a deeper problem that will be discussed further as the study unfolds. Where does Hick's authority lie in the creation of his theodicy? It cannot be with Scripture as he seems to take a "pick and mix" approach to it. The same could also be said of science as Hick takes a similar approach to this.

What is apparent is that although Hick may avoid some problems with his theodicy, this avoidance creates other serious problems that cannot be solved, thus reducing the plausibility of his theodicy quite significantly.

The Openness Theodicy[44]

In response to what it perceives to be the negative effects of the heavy Greek influence on Christianity, Open Theism has attempted to construct a less Hellenistic view of God, which has led to a different approach to the problem of evil. In order to understand this approach, we begin by briefly examining their view of God and his characteristics.

Open Theism, much like classic theism maintains that God is omnipotent, omniscient, omnipresent, and omnibenevolent as well as being all-good and just. The difference comes in how they define the first two of these, and, their rejection of God's supposed immutability and impassibility.

Richard Rice states, "We call this position the 'open view of God' because it regards God as receptive to new experiences and as flexible in the

---

life could (given their inclusion in it) be a great good to him/her on the whole" (Adams, *Horrendous Evils,* 26). She continues, "what makes horrendous evils so pernicious is their life-ruining potential, their power prima facie to degrade the individual by devouring the possibility of positive personal meaning in one swift gulp" (27–28). Hick uses the term "dysteleological suffering" rather than "horrendous evil," but I have opted for Adams's phraseology as her definition is clearer than Hick's but appears to mean the same thing. Hick's theodicy, if it is as strong as he suggests, must be able to respond to the problem of horrendous evil.

44. Open Theism is sometimes referred to as "Free Will Theism."

way he works toward his objective in the world."[45] In the light of this the open theist suggests that God is omnipotent in the broadest sense of the term, but, he has chosen to limit himself in order to work in partnership with the free creatures he has created. In this sense, God does not necessarily get his own way as he is not fully in control. Clark Pinnock states, "We must not define omnipotence as the power to determine everything but rather as the power that enables God to deal with any situation that arises."[46] In connection to this, Open Theism also places limits on God's omniscience. They believe that God is indeed omniscient but that "omniscience need not mean exhaustive foreknowledge of all future events. If that were its meaning, the future would be fixed and determined, much as is the past."[47] Instead, "God knows everything that can be known—but God's foreknowledge does not include the undecided."[48] This may not necessarily be the case if God were in a timeless eternity—suggested by Augustine—because God would be able to see things as they are happening all at once, thus making the idea of future, present and past collapse into one present. However, Open Theism does not believe that God is in such a state. Instead they believe that God is in time and constrained by it as, if the future is completely determined and fixed, it removes the libertarian free will they believe humans have.

The notions about God's relation to time stated above move us on to Open Theism's views on immutability and impassibility. Open Theism does not maintain that God is immutable or impassible for a number of reasons, all of which revolve around the belief that such characteristics are incompatible with his relationship with creation. Open Theism argues that "God . . . enters into dynamic, give-and-take relationships with us" meaning that as well as God being able to influence humans, they too can influence Him.[49] They believe, based on Biblical support, that God acts in time, and that he also changes his mind and experiences emotional changes caused by the actions of those he loves.[50] Such beliefs about God mean that he must be in time because, "After God acts, the universe is different and God's experience of the universe is different. The concept of divine action thus involves divine temporality. Time is real for God."[51] However, Open Theism also believes

---

45. Rice, "Biblical Support," 16.
46. Pinnock, "Systematic Theology," 114.
47. Ibid., 121.
48. Ibid., 123.
49. Pinnock et al., "Preface," 7.
50. For a good example of the texts used and the way in which they are used by Open Theists, see part two of Boyd, "Open-Theism".
51. Rice, "Biblical Support," 36.

A Dramatic Pentecostal/Charismatic Anti-Theodicy

that there are elements to God that are changeless. "They apply the 'changeless' statements to God's existence and character, to his love and reliability. They apply the 'changing' statements to God's actions and experience."[52] Thus, "God is immutable in essence and in his trustworthiness over time, but in other respects God changes."[53] Alongside this they maintain that God is both transcendent and immanent to his creatures.

The kind of theodicy that comes from this perspective shares many of the beliefs found in the classic Free Will Theodicy. Open Theism believes that God created *ex nihilo* out of choice rather than necessity as God is not dependent on creation. Pinnock also states, "Our understanding of the Scriptures leads us to depict God, the sovereign Creator, as voluntarily bringing into existence a world with significantly free personal agents in it, agents who can respond positively to God or reject his plans for them."[54] Therefore sin entered the world because of the wrong choice made by humans. However, the Open Theist's perspective on God causes the major similarities to halt there. Moral evil is simply the result of the decisions made by humans in conjunction with the somewhat limited power and knowledge of God. God cannot be held responsible as God could neither absolutely see it coming nor necessarily have the power to stop it. David Basinger notes, "we believe that God can never know with certainty what will happen in any context involving freedom of choice."[55] In addition William Hasker explains:

> According to free will theism . . . God knows that evils will occur, but he has not for the most part specifically decreed or incorporated into his plan the individual instances of evil. Rather, God governs the world according to *general strategies* which are, as a whole, ordered for the good of the creation but whose detailed consequences are not foreseen or intended by God prior to the decision to adopt them.[56]

Underpinning this approach is the belief that God, even though not responsible for moral evil, can still bring good from evil situations. Added to this is the idea that God, in his immanence, is emotionally affected by the evil that occurs. The sufferer may therefore be able to take some comfort in the belief that God is suffering alongside him, although, Basinger

---

52. Ibid., 48.
53. Pinnock, "Systematic Theology," 117.
54. Ibid., 104.
55. Basinger, "Practical Implications," 163.
56. Hasker, "Philosophical Perspective," 152.

An Overview of Christian Approaches to Evil and Suffering

further states, "we . . . believe that God does not as a general rule intervene in earthly affairs" so one wonders how this helps.[57]

Open Theism also maintains a typical teleology in which God will bring the world to an end in a final judgment. The result of this will be some going to Heaven and some to Hell. Due to the limits on God, this approach avoids the pitfalls associated with him determining everything and therefore leaves him free of guilt regarding the eternal destiny of all.

A Critique

There are a number of things that make this approach attractive and strong. Firstly, as stated above, the limits on God mean he is not responsible for the eternal destiny of humans. But, wider than this, it also removes divine responsibility for evil entering the world, as he may not have seen it coming and could probably not have stopped it if he had. Secondly, the God described by Open Theism is more immanent and interested in relationship than in other approaches. This becomes particularly important when he is understood as a faithful companion in our suffering. In a practical sense this is a God one can journey with.

However, it is also a theodicy that raises some serious questions regarding its plausibility. The biggest problems revolve around the consequences of attempting to redefine God's characteristics. If God is limited in knowledge and power in the ways suggested, how can we guarantee that God will bring any specific end about? If God cannot even say with certainty how things will turn out, and, he exhibits surprise that certain events occur, what kind of God is this, and does it even have the right to hale the title "God"? This approach might well remove the problem of God being held responsible for evil, but, the cost is that he is reduced to nothing more than a faithful companion that will suffer with, but ultimately cannot promise to be able to do anything to remove the suffering. Also, does the belief that God is affected by our responses mean that God can be manipulated? A fuller critique of this whole approach rests outside of this study, but, for the sake of what is to follow here, there are two important points to make.[58] Firstly, although the claim of Open Theism is that it is intended to be more rooted in the Biblical texts than its supposed overly Greek influenced counterparts, there is a distinct sense in which "proof-texting" is the order of the day.

---

57. Basinger, "Practical Implications," 173.

58. For examples of the debates that exist around Open Theism and conflicting views, see Beilby and Eddy, eds., *Divine Foreknowledge*; and Basinger and Basinger, eds., *Predestination and Freewill*.

A Dramatic Pentecostal/Charismatic Anti-Theodicy

Whereas the opponents of Open Theism are accused of watering down difficult texts under the heading of "anthropomorphisms," it seems that in the same way, proponents of Open Theism build a theology on certain texts and then attempt to force controverting texts into that mold. This seems an equally poor use of Scripture.

Secondly, my suggestion is that the reason why a "Procrustean Bed" style approach is used towards Scripture is because the driving force behind their approach to the problems of evil, predestination, free will and foreknowledge is actually based in a post-Enlightenment worldview rather than a Biblical one. As highlighted earlier in this chapter, the underlying aim in Enlightenment thought was to find a rational solution to a problem, something the Bible—and therefore God—does not seem interested in on these matters. Instead, God appears more concerned with responding to the problem of evil and suffering in a practical fashion. Thus, although an Openness Theodicy attempts to distance itself from the influences of Greek philosophy, it simply seems to substitute these for post-Enlightenment influences that then masquerade as Biblical ones.[59] This seems unsatisfactory from a Christian perspective.

The Process Theodicy

Process theodicy, as with all approaches considered so far, focuses on attempting to solve Epicurus' trilemma. And, as with Open Theism, the solution to the problem requires a re-examination and consequently a redefining of the term "omnipotence." However, before I discuss this aspect and the subsequent view of evil it produces, it is necessary to briefly outline parts of the philosophy and theology of Process thought on which the Process Theodicy is built.[60] In what follows David Ray Griffin's work will be our focus as the main proponent of Process thought in relation to evil.

---

59. Pinnock states, "Although it can be validated on other levels, open theism is primarily a biblical and practical theology for us. Unlike, say, process theism and even conventional theism, we do not weigh in with large assumptions about what God 'must be like,' dictated by philosophical ideas which cause us to ignore aspects of the biblical witness (the *dignus dei*)" (Pinnock, "Open Theism," 239). There is, clearly, something of a protest against "ontotheology" in the attempt to be biblically rooted in the construction of Open Theism, which this author wholly commends. However, although this may be the intention, in practice, particularly with regard to theodicy, the lens with which Open Theists come to the biblical text is one that is heavily influenced by the post-Enlightenment ideal of solving problems. The result is that in attempting to solve the problem of evil, *and* be biblically based, biblical texts are interpreted to suit a certain end and in doing so are distorted.

60. This foundation is attributed to Alfred North Whitehead and Charles Hartshorne

An Overview of Christian Approaches to Evil and Suffering

Process philosophy suggests that all "actual entities"—those things that are not inanimate objects—experience "events" in passing "occasions" and have the capacity to create.[61] During these occasions, the experiencing of events involves the transfer of energy. Each occasion is based on the content of the event and the previous experience of the entity, which come together to create feelings. This is called "concrescence."[62] The ability to create for an actual entity involves both the power to affect one's own creation/evolution as well as the power to affect the creation of other actual entities. The affecting of other actual entities by oneself involves the transfer of energy and is called "transition."[63]

The result of this foundation in thought is that no actual entity (of which God is included) has a monopoly on power. But instead, all actual entities are i.) evolving and ii.) determined to a greater or lesser extent by the influence of other actual entities. The most important consequences of this are that God must therefore be evolving and must also be necessarily dependent on the world and its creatures.

As opposed to classic theology, the Process God did not create *ex nihilo* as this would involve God being a separate entity free from influence. Instead the God of Process theology began to bring order out of the chaos that already surrounded him by the interactions he had with it.

At this point it is worth bringing back into the discussion the Process understanding of the term "omnipotence." Similar to Open Theism, the process view believes that the traditional view of omnipotence requires revision.[64] God is omnipotent as far as the Process theologian is concerned, but, this simply means that God only has all the power he can have in a world where all other actual entities also have some degree of power. For the Process theologian, "The problem is the assumption that the meaning

---

with David Griffin stating, it "is a theodicy based on Whiteheadian-Hartshornean process philosophy" (*God, Power, and Evil*, 275).

61. Whitehead defines "actual entities" as "the final real things of which the world is made up" (Whitehead, *Process and Reality*, 18). He later substitutes this term for the term "actual occasions" as the actual entity is only such momentarily—thus making it an "occasion" (73). "Events" are therefore defined as "a nexus of actual occasions, interrelated in some determinate fashion in one extensive quantum" (73).

62. Whitehead states, "The word Concrescence is a derivative from the familiar latin verb, meaning 'growing together'. It also has the advantage that the participle 'concrete' is familiarly used for the notion of complete physical reality. Thus Concrescence is useful to convey the notion of many things acquiring complete complex unity" (*Adventure of Ideas*, 236).

63. See Whitehead, *Process and Reality*, 210–15.

64. As can the term omniscience. Omniscience requires revision because clearly from the Process view, God is evolving and is therefore *not* all knowing.

of perfect power or omnipotence can be settled apart from a metaphysical discussion of the nature of the 'beings' upon whom this perfect power is to be exercised."[65] Of which they believe it cannot. Instead omnipotence must be understood in the context of the reciprocating relationship between God and creatures in which there cannot be a monopoly of power. In such a relationship the traditional view of omnipotence must be discarded. It therefore also entails that God experiences within time alongside his creatures.[66]

In the mind of God is the aim of what he is working towards in relation to the world and creatures. In his interactions with them he is attempting to persuade them in such a way as to eventually achieve these aims. The key word here is "persuade" as "God's power is persuasive, not controlling."[67] He does not have total control. In conjunction with this is the free will of the creatures. As stated above, all actual entities have a level of self-determination and the level of free will increases based on the evolution of the creature. As Griffin states, "The world must transcend God in the sense of having its own creativity."[68] The point being that although humans, as we understand them now, may not have been part of the original order that God brought out of the chaos, the evolution of creatures has led to our existence and the level of freedom that goes with it. The Process view may therefore suggest that creatures have not yet finished evolving and that there are creatures with higher levels of freedom yet to emerge.

With this as a brief outline of some of the main foundations of Process theology, we now turn our attention to the theodicy that is derived from these foundations.

It has already been stated that Process theology believes in an omnipotent God—with omnipotence being re-defined. It also believes that God is omnibenevolent and that evil exists. The solution to the theodicy problem for Process theology therefore lies in the revised understanding of omnipotence and the relationship that God has with the world and its creatures. Because all actual entities have a degree of freedom and power, creation "can refuse to conform to the divine input" and thus it is impossible for God to prevent evil from being done at some point.[69] And, since the Process view does not believe in God creating from nothing, but rather, out of chaos, he is not only constrained by the limits on his power but also by what he has

---

65. Griffin, *God, Power, and Evil*, 265.

66. Pinnock differentiates between Open Theism and Process Theism by stating, "Process theology denies ontological independence, maintaining that God needs the world as much as that world needs God" ("Systematic Theology," 112).

67. Griffin, *God, Power, and Evil*, 276.

68. Ibid., 280.

69. Ibid.

An Overview of Christian Approaches to Evil and Suffering

to work with. The result of this is that "Although an actual world without genuine evil is possible, it is impossible for an omnipotent being to guarantee such a world."[70] This removes responsibility for the existence of evil from God. And, although it is part of God's aim to persuade creatures to evolve in such a way that allows for the possibility of greater goods, the increase in the capacity for good is directly proportional to the increase in the capacity for evil, as well as being directly proportional to the increase in the level of freedom a creature has.

Griffin states that there are two types of evil—"disharmony" or "discord" and "triviality."[71] The former of these, as the name suggests, is a break down in the system due to misuse and wrong choices that ultimately lead to destruction. The latter of these involves "boredom, lack of zest and excitement".[72] This is classed as evil because the Process theologian believes that a greater level of goodness is achieved through a greater level of intensity of good feeling brought about through and contributing to further evolution. Triviality on the other hand leads to a regression or a slowing of the evolution process. It is worth noting at this point that such an understanding of evil leads to the possibility that what may be first perceived by a creature as evil may not necessarily be so, but, is instead, being masked by the perceiver's lack of knowledge and understanding of the situation.

Regarding God's relation to evil in the world, the Process theodicist believes that not only is God affected by it, but, that he somehow has the capacity to take it within himself and use it for good. This is not meant in some self-indulgent way but rather God experiences the suffering alongside the sufferer and allows it to affect him and alter his divine plan in such a way as to overcome it. It may be said in relation to this that the cost of the existence of evil is worth it when the good that will come out of it is considered. It is also important to note that the god of Process theodicy is therefore seen to have a degree of providence for his creatures, but, this is in "process," based on the changing circumstances.

When the area of teleology is considered it is held that, "belief in a life after death is not an essential element in a process theodicy because it is unnecessary and insufficient as well as too uncertain."[73] This is held because what is considered most important is the continual evolution of actual entities, which may continue into infinite epochs, amongst other possibilities.

---

70. Ibid., 270.
71. Ibid., 282–83. See also Whitehead, *Adventure of Ideas*, 259–64.
72. Griffin, *God, Power, and Evil*, 282.
73. Ibid., 312.

A Dramatic Pentecostal/Charismatic Anti-Theodicy

A Critique

Due to the characteristics of the Process Theodicy it carries with it many of the same strengths as the Open Theodicy. God is removed from having to shoulder responsibility for the existence of evil due to the limits in his character and nature. He is also the faithful companion to his creatures and is affected by them. Thus God suffers when his creatures suffer. Again this is a far more practically tangible approach than others, as it brings God close to his creatures.

However, the Process Theodicy is also open to many of the same criticisms as the Open view, particularly regarding the revision of the meaning of "omnipotence." As I discussed this above, I will not repeat the issues here. What I do think causes this to be made worse regarding the weakness of God is that unlike the Open view, God seems to have very little choice over such things as what substance he has to work with at the beginning and whether he necessarily has to have a relationship with creatures and the world. This seems to reduce God down to a being like humans that has just evolved a little more and is therefore a bit more advanced. But what kind of God is that? However, as with the previous positions outlined so far, this is not my main concern in this study. My main concern revolves around how well this approach is anchored in and takes authority from Scripture. This in turn leads to my secondary concern of how practical this response is in the face of evil and suffering—a point I believe to be intrinsically linked to the former point, as my argument will be that a Biblically rooted response is at core a practical one.

Rather than starting with and taking direction from Scripture the process approach seems to read scientific theory into the text. The result is twofold: firstly, authority rests with scientific theory, with sections of the Bible used almost as add-ons—a practice that is unpalatable to the Christian taste. Secondly, in gaining direction primarily from outside of Scripture, the Process Theodicy falls foul of the trap of the other theodicy representatives—namely trying to solve a post-Enlightenment problem. The issue this author takes with such an approach has been discussed above. The result of these problems is that, once again, one is left wondering if this approach to the problem of evil and suffering can realistically be labeled "Christian."

Having briefly surveyed the various approaches that are to be found under the title "Theodicy," a number of observations can be made.

A Critical Summary

Firstly, if rationalism and coherence is the plumb line by which we measure such approaches, then it has been highlighted that none of them are problem free. In all cases, it has been shown that there are issues with the internal coherence of the arguments being made. True though this is, in the case of this study, as has also been observed, this is not the most pressing of issues. Thus, secondly, and more importantly, is the very context from which theodicy emerges. In the same way as was noted of the "Free Will Defense," the whole project of theodicy, even if attempting to be rooted in a more Christian tradition, is still premised on the post-Enlightenment urge to solve problems—in this case the Epicurean trilemma. The unfortunate result of such a quest is that not only do all attempts fail to provide a solution that does not create further problems, but, in the very attempt at this provision, each proponent actually engages in seeking to *justify* the existence of evil by some form of the greater good argument, which is unacceptable.

This leads us on to the third point—that of foundations for approaches. As has already been noted in the discussion of each of the theodicy approaches, use of Scripture seems somewhat shallow. To a greater or lesser extent, in all cases considered, it seems that texts from Scripture are often extracted from their respective places and deployed as proofs for the argument of the proponent who is using them. What underpins such a method is that the foundation of the proponent is primarily built upon belief in the good of rationality rather than the goodness of God. Direction is thus taken from those who wish to solve a rational, logical problem rather than from the incarnate Christ who seeks to respond practically to the needs of creation. As this study develops it will be the latter of these that this author will seek to take direction from in the development of the answer to the central research question. For now we turn to explore "Anti-Theodicy."

Anti-Theodicy

As the title of this section suggests, the existence of the views of those who will be discussed below commonly originates as a response to the problems that the creation of a theodicy brings. We began to touch on what the key problems are above and this will be continued below as we begin by looking at the issues that proponents of an anti-theodicy response to evil and suffering highlight and respond to in the creation of their approaches. The opening sub-section will therefore be called, "The Problems of Theodicy: Re-stated." Categorization of anti-theodicists is far less straightforward than

A Dramatic Pentecostal/Charismatic Anti-Theodicy

in the case of theodicists, and this is reflected in the sections that follow. Once the problems have been re-stated, the way responses to these problems will be categorized is by looking at different ways anti-theodicists respond to them in their understanding of "The Nature and Role of God in Response to Evil and Suffering" and the "Role of Humans in Response to Evil and Suffering."[74] Having explored the various responses in this way I will then close this section by critically reflecting on how well the problem of evil and suffering has been responded to in the views being discussed.

The Problems of Theodicy: Re-stated

Karen Kilby states, "My proposal . . . is that these questions, these concrete and theological versions of the so called 'problem of evil' ought to be acknowledged as completely legitimate *and* as utterly unanswerable."[75] The point Kilby is making is not that there is no problem of evil but rather that it is not a problem that Christians can logically solve. In a similar way John Swinton suggests, "the problem of evil is a deeply meaningful and often spiritual human experience before it becomes an object for theological and philosophical reflection."[76] Swinton here highlights the fact that no problem of evil and suffering begins in discussion. It has already existed in an existential way long before there is any detached reflection undertaken. We have here then two key problems with theodicy from the view of anti-theodicy. Firstly, it attempts to solve the unsolvable—which we have earlier acknowl-

---

74. I am here modifying a classification that is made by Surin. In chapter 2 of *Theology and the Problem of Evil,* Surin separates out the theoretical questions involved in theodicy construction:
  1. Can *evil* in itself be rendered intelligible?
  2. Is the existence of *God* logically compatible with the *existence* of evil?
  3. Does the existence of evil constitute *evidence* that counts against (or reduces the possibility of the truth of) theism?

  And the practical questions:
  4. What does *God* do to overcome the evil and suffering that exist in his creation?
  5. What do we (qua creatures of God) do to overcome evil and suffering?

  I am using questions 4 and 5 as I think they provide an excellent mode of categorizing views. However, I am modifying them because the view proponents have of God's nature is as important as what they believe he does in response to evil and suffering in the construction of their anti-theodicies. Surin's phrasing does not allow for this. I have also used the term "role" as this incorporates more than just action, and the term "response," as not all response is to overcome. Overcoming is instead a subsection of response.

75. Kilby, "Evil," 24.

76. Swinton, *Raging*, 3–4.

edged as an Enlightenment driven project. Secondly, in spending time making theoretical arguments, theodicists ignore the sobering reality that the problem of evil and suffering is a felt experience to someone, somewhere that requires a practical response.

When a response does emerge from theodicy debates, because the underpinning belief is that explanation is required, explanation is what is produced. However, as David Bentley Hart points out, in the face of real life suffering, "Pious platitudes and words of comfort seem not only futile and banal but almost blasphemous; metaphysical disputes come perilously close to mocking the dead."[77] The third key problem then is that the response given by theodicists is not practically helpful to the sufferer. As discussed in the critique of Theodicy above, the greater good argument removes the possibility of genuinely defining something as evil and shuts down the cry of the sufferer. As Tilley notes, "to silence a suffering voice maybe to participate in one of the most despicable practices theodicists (or anyone else) can perform."[78] The fourth key problem that follows on from this is that God must be what Soelle refers to as "a sadistic God" of which "The ultimate conclusion of theological sadism is worshipping the executioner."[79] In chapter 4 of Book 5 of Dostoevsky's *The Brothers Karamazov*, the character of Ivan focuses on the suffering of children in particular and outlines why he cannot accept that such horrors are necessary. He further responds to the notion of heavenly reconciliation as a fixative measure by saying to Alyosha, "I hasten to return my entry ticket. And if I am at all an honest man, I am obliged to return it as soon as possible. That is what I am doing. It isn't God I don't accept, Alyosha, it's just his ticket that I most respectfully return to him."[80] If a sadistic God is what is suggested, then to worship it is masochism.

The fifth and final key problem for theodicy from an anti-theodicy perspective is summed up by Hauerwas, "there is no experience without mediation by a story. There is no primal experience of God, of suffering, or even of the death of a child."[81] He further states, "No two sufferings are the same; my suffering, for example, occurs in the context of my personal history and this is peculiarly mine."[82] Although wrapped in the narrative of post-Enlightenment philosophy, theists see "theodicy (in its ideal form) very much as an ahistorical and individualistic quest for logically stable no-

77. Hart, *Doors of the Sea*, 6–7.
78. Tilley, *Evils of Theodicy*, 110.
79. Soelle, *Suffering*, 28.
80. Dostoyevsky, *Brothers Karamazov*, 320.
81. Hauerwas, *Naming Silences*, 29–30.
82. Ibid., 3.

A Dramatic Pentecostal/Charismatic Anti-Theodicy

tions, exact axioms, and rigorous chains of deductive inference."[83] However, it is impossible to divorce how one understands and responds to evil and suffering from the narrative in which one is embedded. We are all embedded in communities with specific narratives, cultures, and practices and therefore specific worldviews, which have been shaped by, and will shape, the interpretation of our experiences.[84] This will affect how we understand and respond to evil and suffering, and theodicists seem to overlook this point.

With these issues as the backdrop, we move now to explore the contents of anti-theodicy approaches to the problem of evil and suffering by exploring the way different views answer the revised version of Surin's questions.

The Nature and Role of God in Response to Evil and Suffering

The understanding of the nature and role of God held by anti-theodicists with regard to evil and suffering is extremely varied. Perhaps the most commonly held view that impacts upon one's response to evil and suffering is that of im/passibility as an attribute of God. For some proponents, it is necessary for God to be passible as a central tenet of their belief and practice, of which Dorothee Soelle is a case in point. Soelle argues that in the midst of suffering, prayer is an important tool. However, she suggests that it is only useful in facing and dealing with suffering if it is done to a God who feels.[85] She states, "God suffers where people suffer. God must be delivered from pain."[86] She further suggests, "Redemption does not come to people from outside or from above. God wants to use people in order to work on the completion of his creation. Precisely for this reason God must also suffer with the creation."[87] She therefore concludes that "God, whatever people make of this word, is on the side of the sufferer. God is on the side of the victim."[88]

In a similar fashion Jürgen Moltmann sees a God who cannot suffer as a weak and poor God as well as suggesting that "the one who cannot suffer cannot love either. So he is also a loveless being."[89] In focusing on the activities of the Godhead at the cross Moltmann suggests that "The Son suffers

---

83. Surin, *Problem of Evil*, 13.
84. See Walsh and Middleton, *Transforming Vision*, in particular Part 1.
85. Soelle, *Suffering*, 75–78.
86. Ibid., 146.
87. Ibid.
88. Ibid., 148.
89. Moltmann, *Crucified God*, 222.

An Overview of Christian Approaches to Evil and Suffering

dying, the Father suffers the death of the Son" and thus "this event contains community between Jesus and his Father in separation, and separation in community."[90] He further suggests that in this moment God takes all suffering up inside himself in order to overcome it and from this the Holy Spirit is poured out into creation. The conclusion of such a view for the sufferer is that prior to the Eschaton, God suffers with the sufferer and "Where we suffer because we love, God suffers in us."[91]

At the other end of the spectrum, David Bentley Hart maintains a belief in divine impassibility as the very grounds on which the destruction of evil and suffering takes place. He states, "The cross is thus a triumph of divine *apatheia*, limitless and immutable love sweeping us up into itself, taking all suffering and death upon itself without being changed, modified, or defined by it, and so destroying its power and making us, by participation in Christ, 'more than conquerors' (Rom 8:37)."[92] He articulates this in another place by stating,

> And this is our salvation: for when the infinite outpouring of the Father in the Son, in the joy of the Spirit, enters our reality, the *apatheia* of God's eternally dynamic and replete life of love consumes every pathos in its ardour; even the ultimate extreme of the kenosis of the Son in time—crucifixion—is embraced within and overcome by the everlasting kenosis of the divine life.[93]

It is only because divine *apatheia* exists that God can overcome the evil and suffering in the world.

Somewhere in the midst of these approaches N. T. Wright offers an approach that focuses on the story of salvation history revealed in Scripture. He states, "Insofar as the Old Testament offers a theodicy . . . it isn't couched in the terms of later philosophy, but in the narrative of God and the world, particularly the story of God and Israel."[94] In this story, "The overarching picture is of the sovereign creator God who will continue to work within his world until blessing replaces curse, homecoming replaces exile, olive

---

90. Ibid., 243, 244.

91. Ibid., 253. Both Soelle and Moltmann draw on a story, recounted by Elie Wiesel of an experience Wiesel had whilst in a concentration camp during World War Two. In doing so, both use the story to further support their case for a God that suffers with the sufferer, (see Soelle, *Suffering*, 145–50; Moltmann, *Crucified God*, 270–74; and Wiesel, *Night*, 64–65).

92. Hart, *Doors of the Sea*, 81.

93. Hart, "No Shadow of Turning," 205.

94. Wright, *Evil*, 23.

branches appear after the flood, and a new family is created in which the scattered languages can be re-united."[95] He further argues that "the tortured young Jewish prophet hanging on the cross was the point where evil had become truly and fully and totally itself."[96] In the resurrection of Jesus, evil and suffering were defeated. "The long story of God and the world, of God and Israel, of God and the Messiah, has arrived at its goal. Death always was the ultimate denial of the good creation; now, with its abolition, the creator's new world can proceed."[97] For Wright then there appears an underlying belief in a sovereign, all-powerful, faithful, loving God, but, he is more concerned with what God does as a response rather than defining God's nature in detail. For Wright, God has overcome the power of evil and suffering and will banish it completely at the Eschaton.

In a similar story-centered—or rather, drama-centered—fashion, Kevin Vanhoozer's approach seems to attempt a union between that suggested by Wright and Hart but with some level of sympathy towards the passibilists. Vanhoozer, like Wright, believes that God's ultimate response to evil and suffering is to destroy it at the cross. He also explicitly argues for impassibility. However, he writes, "Divine impassibility means not that God is unfeeling—impervious to covenantally concerned theodramatic construals of what is happening—but that God is never overcome or overwhelmed by these feelings such that he 'forgets' his covenant or who he is as covenant Lord."[98] In arguing for this approach Vanhoozer then applies it to how God responds to us in our suffering:

> God consoles us by reminding us what he has done, is doing, and will do on our behalf in Christ through the Spirit. Communicating God's covenantal concern and theodramatic perspective may not remove our suffering, but it provides the power to resist what can be resisted and the power to consent to that which cannot, and the knowledge in both cases that nothing can separate us from the love of God (Rom 8:39).[99]

Although far less developed than Wright, Vanhoozer and the passibilists, in his "practical theodicy" John Swinton offers an approach that has

---

95. Ibid., 29.

96. Ibid., 49.

97. Wright, *Resurrection*, 476.

98. Vanhoozer, *Remythologizing Theology*, 433. We will unpack the concept of "covenantally concern based theodramatic construals" in chapter 6. For now it is sufficient to note that Vanhoozer's aim in its development and application is to give space to the concept that God "feels" whilst avoiding the pitfalls of a classic passibilist position.

99. Ibid., 447.

An Overview of Christian Approaches to Evil and Suffering

similarities with all of them.[100] Similar to Wright he suggests that "While suffering and evil are not immediately eradicated in the cross of Christ, they are ultimately defeated."[101] Similar to Soelle and Moltmann he suggests, "The solution to the problem of evil that God offers on the cross is not abstract condolence but costly solidarity."[102] But similar to Vanhoozer, he also seems to point towards endurance in the face of suffering as we await the Eschaton: "The goal and endpoint of practical theodicy is the enabling of the Christian community to live faithfully *despite* the presence of evil."[103]

A final way in which God is viewed by those who reject theodicies is that he is not all-good. Although not from a Christian perspective, Jewish theologian David Blumenthal believes that God is fair, passible, "powerful but not perfect."[104] He further states that "We recognize that God's action is sometimes evil."[105] He supports this argument by saying, "We must begin, under the seal of truth, by admitting that Scripture does indeed portray God as an abusing person; that God, as agent in our sacred texts, does indeed act abusively; that God, as described in the Bible acts like an abusing male: husband, father, and lord."[106] The result of such a view is that "Unity and reconciliation are no longer the goal; rather, we seek a dialogue that affirms our difference and our justness, together with our relatedness to God."[107]

---

100. Swinton defines "practical theodicy" as resistance to evil and states, "Practical theodicy takes seriously both the impact of what evil does and the embodied and practical ways in which God has responded to and continues to respond to the problem of evil and suffering" *(Raging*, 79–80).

101. Ibid., 71.

102. Ibid.

103. Ibid., 85. However, although there are similarities with Vanhoozer there are also differences. Swinton notes, "Practical theodicy assumes that God is in and for the world, not in abstract reasoning, but in compassionate actions of resistance and transformation. It does not view the problem of evil as a dislocated philosophical argument but rather as a grounded context for practical, faithful engagement with the reality of evil and human suffering. Such an approach calls not for *explanation,* but for the learning of faithful practices of *resistance* that open up the possibility of transformation and redemption" (86). There are then, moments in Swinton's work when he supports the idea that in the face of suffering one is not just seeking to endure but also resist and transform the situation—hence his examination of lament in his work. However, as was noted above, Swinton's approach is not as well developed, theologically, as others.

104. Blumenthal, *Facing the Abusing God*, 16.

105. Ibid., 223.

106. Ibid., 242.

107. Ibid., 267. From a Christian perspective, John Roth affirms a similar "protest theodicy" but Roth seems more aggressive in response to evil. He states, "Unjustifiable waste is everlasting, but it deserves no more victories" (Roth, "Theodicy of Protest," 12).

A Dramatic Pentecostal/Charismatic Anti-Theodicy

If this is a brief overview of the various understandings of the nature and role of God in response to evil and suffering proposed by those who reject theodicies, we move next to explore the role of humans in responding to evil and suffering from an anti-theodicy perspective.

The Role of Humans in Response to Evil and Suffering

Stanley Hauerwas, in the questioning of a universal response to suffering, states, "it is simply not the case that all people everywhere respond to the suffering of children with the same outrage or even perceive what the children endure as suffering."[108] At the center of Hauerwas' thought is the importance of giving space to recognize the context and narrative of the one suffering when providing a response, rather than imposing a narrative onto them. In this sense, Hauerwas aims to start with the sufferer and their story.

In conjunction with this Hauerwas seems to suggest the possibility of the story of the sufferer being taken up into the story of God in order give the sufferer fresh perspective. He states,

> The problem of evil is not about rectifying our suffering with some general notions of God's nature as all powerful and good; rather it is about what we mean by God's goodness itself, which for Christians must be construed in terms of God as the Creator who has called into existence a people called Israel so that the world might know that God has not abandoned us. There is no problem of suffering in general, rather, the question of suffering can be raised only in the context of a God who creates to redeem.[109]

In bringing the two stories together, a dialogue can emerge whereby the sufferer encounters companionship and hope and thus their suffering can be transformed. This is not to attempt to explain the suffering as, "the problem with all free-will defences of suffering is that they 'explain' too much."[110] Rather it is to give the sufferer hope in eternity and companionship on the journey, particularly from the community of the Church: "We have no theodicy that can soften the pain of our death and the death of our children, but we believe that we share a common story which makes it possible for us to be with one another especially as we die."[111] In this sense

---

108. Hauerwas, *Naming Silences*, 69.
109. Ibid., 78–79.
110. Ibid., 78.
111. Ibid., 148.

An Overview of Christian Approaches to Evil and Suffering

Hauerwas is arguing for community and companionship in suffering in order to aid the sufferer in banishing isolation and finding hope.

Soelle calls for a similar sense of solidarity with the sufferer, but without such a well-defined sense of narrative and meeting of stories. Instead she offers a three phase response by the sufferer, which the companion joins them in.[112] The first of these involves silence—"Respect for those who suffer *in extremis* imposes silence."[113] The second phase involves the sufferer finding expression through "specific elements" of "psalmic language" "such as lament, petition, expression of hope."[114] The third phase involves action, by which she means exploring the causes and effects and seeking to do something outward and positive with the findings. Soelle also builds on her view of the suffering God in order to suggest that we experience the suffering God in our suffering: "What matters is whether the suffering becomes our *passion*, in the deep double sense of that word."[115]

In phase two of Soelle's approach, she mentions the practice of lament, a practice Hauerwas also points towards.[116] This practice is anchored in the texts of the Old Testament and is a way God's people communicate their anguish to him in times of suffering, when he appears to be absent. In these times "the 'call of distress,' the 'cry out of the depths,' that is, the lament, is an inevitable part of what happens between God and man."[117] In his work on the Psalms Walter Brueggemann defines lament as "a painful, anguished articulation of a move into disarray and dislocation. The lament is a candid, even if unwilling, embrace of a new situation of chaos, now devoid of the coherence that marks God's good creation."[118] Brueggemann and other proponents of the lament tradition argue that it is in the midst of intense suffering that one uses lament to keep communication open with God. And, this is thought to only be helpful because "The passionate prayers of lament and protest assume that God can be affected, that God is vulnerable to the cries and questions of the afflicted."[119] However, these assumptions also, surprisingly, sit next to a belief in the omniscience and omnibenevolence of God.

---

112. Soelle, *Suffering*, 70–74.
113. Ibid., 69.
114. Ibid., 71–72.
115. Ibid., 125.
116. Hauerwas, *Naming Silences*, 79–84.
117. Westermann, *Praise and Lament*, 261.
118. Brueggemann, *Message of the Psalms*, 20.
119. Billman and Migliore, *Rachel's Cry*, 113.

A Dramatic Pentecostal/Charismatic Anti-Theodicy

As Middleton states, "The genre of lament is predicated on the expectation that God can and will rescue the supplicant."[120]

Swinton also picks up on the practice of lament as response but one way that he differs from most others is that in aiming at "a Christian response to the human experience of evil and suffering" he brings Jesus into the equation when most do not.[121] What is particularly interesting is that he appears to be aiming at giving guidance for how we respond to evil by looking at Jesus' response. However, this in itself, and in particular his exploration of Jesus' use of lament, remains largely under-developed.

Two final approaches we need only briefly touch on are suggested by Wright and Vanhoozer. In his work on the problem of evil Wright calls for an "Inaugurated Eschatology" which he defines as "beginning to live in the present by the rule of what will be the case in the ultimate future."[122] He further suggests "we are to *implement* the achievement of Jesus and so to *anticipate* God's eventual world."[123] He warns against false ideas of humans achieving this, but, also suggests that playing a part in it is an imperative of the Gospel.

Following on from his view of God outlined above, Vanhoozer seems to suggest that the aim is perseverance and endurance in the face of suffering. "Jesus provides a template for right theodramatic participation; patient yet joyful endurance is the way in which the church plays its part this side of the eschaton."[124] He further states "By revealing the end, the book [of Revelation] communicates grace—hope and strength—for the journey."[125] And on this journey "The church—the 'body of Christ'—most corresponds to God when its members pour out their lives for the sake of others in various kinds of communicative acts and, again like Christ, in the loss of the very capacity to communicate on earth (i.e., death)."[126]

With these various approaches both to God and humans in view a critical reflection can be offered.

---

120. Middleton, "Why the 'Greater Good,'" 100.

121. Swinton, *Raging*, 3. Ellington (*Risking Truth*, chapter 6) and Billman and Migliore (*Rachel's Cry*, 33–42) explore lament in the New Testament but none of them delve deeply into Jesus' use of it. However, in response to comments regarding his book, Ellington does seem to be aware that there is more to be said regarding Jesus' words and actions at the cross, and lament in contemporary theology. See Ellington, "So Much Still to Do," 191–92.

122. Wright, *Evil*, 77.

123. Ibid., 66.

124. Vanhoozer, *Remythologizing Theology*, 466.

125. Ibid., 467.

126. Ibid., 464.

An Overview of Christian Approaches to Evil and Suffering

Critical Reflection

On the Nature and Role of God

Although there is something appealing about the view of the passibilist in response to evil and suffering—as it depicts a God who feels and shares our suffering and is thus our companion on the journey—one wonders how practically useful this is. God may be able to share our suffering but surely the God we require and the God portrayed in Scripture is one that has the power to remove the suffering we experience? As much as a fellow suffering patient is some comfort in a time of illness, what we desire is the doctor to aid us in the removal of the suffering. The passible God fails to have the ability to do this, it would seem. This view also seems to hang on a rather selective reading of Scripture and instead seems more built on a human view of God than the one revealed in Scripture.

On the other hand, Hart's impassible God, although powerful and loving, seems somehow detached and difficult to relate to—characteristics not reflected in the accounts of Jesus' interaction with creation. It thus seems difficult to commune with a God who appears somehow unmoved by our suffering. This again seems to be selective in what parts of Scripture such a view is built upon.

Vanhoozer seems to offer a middle way through that maintains God's otherness yet suggests that God is not emotionless—as does Wright in a less developed way. Both of these also seem to rely more on Scripture for the development of their views. What is offered here then, is a view of God that understands his response as overcoming evil and suffering at the cross, as well as having emotions with which to "feel" with regard to how he relates to his creation.

The view put forward by the protest proponents, although practical and to some degree anchored in *parts* of Scripture, seems to fall foul of seeking to solve the Epicurean trilemma by compromising omnibenevolence. The twofold issue with this is that, firstly, although it gives space to start from the place of the sufferer, it selects certain texts on which to build a doctrine whilst ignoring contradictory ones. It therefore offers only a selective view of Scripture that bases authority of use in the hands of the sufferer. The God referred to thus becomes, to a fairly great extent, a human construct. Secondly, on the practical side, one is also left wondering why anyone would ever trust, worship, or want anything to do with a God that is sometimes evil and abusing. It seems that this view is, therefore, not all that practically helpful.

A Dramatic Pentecostal/Charismatic Anti-Theodicy

On the Role of Humans

Solidarity and companionship are key themes that emerge in most anti-theodicy responses, and with good reason. Community and the idea of suffering-with are themes that run throughout Scripture. In seeking to continue relating to God in the midst of suffering, lament is also a practice that is picked up by anti-theodicists and is particularly found in the Old Testament. However, what does one do, post death and resurrection of Jesus, with regard to lament? Wright calls for inaugurating eschatology and Vanhoozer and Swinton call for perseverance and endurance, of which all of these points are Biblically warranted. But neither Wright, nor Vanhoozer give space or direction for lament. This is particularly the case for Vanhoozer as he seems to see all suffering, post death and resurrection of Jesus, as persecution (hence the emphasis on perseverance and endurance)—something that seems a little narrow and naïve.[127] Although Swinton calls attention to lament and in particular picks up on the idea of looking to Jesus as an example of practice in a way most lament proponents do not, he fails to develop a Biblically rooted, rigorous method that shows how we may follow Jesus in this practice or why it is legitimate in the aftermath of the cross. Other lament proponents highlight the literature and the practice that this displays in the Bible, but fail to show what difference Jesus' incarnation has made to how this is understood and practiced.

Hauerwas, in picking up the theme of stories, highlights the need for relating to the sufferer in their suffering. However, in doing so he leaves the practice largely undeveloped regarding how it may outwork and how one uses Scripture to aid the sufferer in reframing how they see and experience their life. And, although he also points towards lament as an important practice, as with the criticism above, this practice is neither legitimized nor given any sense of direction as to how it is to be practiced.

Conclusion

There are a number of points to draw together as we look towards the next stage in this study. In order to highlight these points we must recall that the aim of the study is: to answer the central research question by developing Biblically rooted, systematic guidance for the production of a fitting Pentecostal/Charismatic performance in the face of seemingly innocent, meaningless suffering when God appears to be absent.

---

127. See *Remythologizing Theology*, 463–68.

An Overview of Christian Approaches to Evil and Suffering

As we reflect back on the responses to the problem of evil and suffering proposed by the Free Will Defense and the various Theodicies, the first point to make is that all views in these categories fall considerably short of achieving this aim. They also offer little in way of help to achieve this aim.

As we turn our attention to the responses produced in the Anti-Theodicy section, the outlook regarding usefulness in aiding the achievement of the aim is not as bleak. Although it appears that there is no complete response that fulfills this aim, the second point I wish to suggest and develop in what follows, is that there is the latent potential for significant aid in the resources of some anti-theodicy proponents. Vanhoozer and Wright appear to have the most Biblically rooted view of evil, suffering and how God sees and responds to it and so will act as worthy dialogue partners in the development process. However, the third point is that there is no serious mention of lament in their approaches—which seems a significant flaw as this practice appears central to Israel's continuing ability to relate to God amidst periods of suffering. Therefore, lament proponents—Brueggemann in particular—will also be sourced for aid in achieving the aim of the study.

There are, however, two problem areas that need to be faced before the development of an answer to the central research question can be achieved. Hauerwas, in his emphasis on the meeting of the sufferer in their particular context and narrative with the transforming narrative of Salvation History, points to the second of these problems. Put simply, how does one engage with Scripture as the revealed story of salvation, in order for God to direct the sufferer into a right response to him and the evil being experienced amidst the suffering? Or better, what is the hermeneutical method the sufferer is to engage in when seeking direction for right response. And further, what is the hermeneutical method a *Pentecostal/Charismatic sufferer* is to engage in? This will be the conundrum to be solved in chapter 4. The first problem, however, is to explore how Pentecostal/Charismatic theology has understood and responded to the problem of evil and suffering. In order to answer the central research question, it is important to situate ourselves within the field of responses that have preceded the guidance that will be developed here. We have looked at responses to the problem of evil and suffering from a general Christian perspective and can say that the answer developed in this study will resonate with the term "Anti-Theodicy." We must now turn to explore where it will situate itself amongst Pentecostal/Charismatic responses to the problem of evil and suffering.

3

Pentecostal/Charismatic Approaches to Evil and Suffering

Introduction

IN THE PREVIOUS CHAPTER an overview of the most common responses to the problem of evil and suffering from within the Christian tradition was laid out. This ranged from the deeply theoretical and philosophical approach of the negative apologetic "Free Will Defense," proposed most extensively by Alvin Plantinga, through to the more practical, existential approaches bracketed within the category of "Anti-Theodicy." We noted at the end of the previous chapter that the response to be developed in this study would resonate with those in this latter category. We also noted that before this response could be developed further, we must be aware of the Pentecostal/Charismatic field of responses in order to situate the current one within it. The aim of this chapter will therefore be to provide an overview of Pentecostal/Charismatic responses to the problem of evil and suffering in order to clear the ground and provide a context in which to situate the approach being developed in this study.

Pentecostals and Charismatics, like all other Christians, cannot avoid the real life existence of evil and suffering, and so, it is no surprise that during the evolution of these strains of Christianity, responses have been developed and deployed. However, the main approaches that are found in the literature available are very lop-sided. This is particularly apparent when one attempts to find any extensive literature specifically on Pentecostal or Charismatic approaches to evil and suffering, of which there is very little.

Pentecostal/Charismatic Approaches to Evil and Suffering

B. Scott Lewis writes, "Historically Pentecostals have not reflected upon the traditional problem of evil from a philosophical perspective."[1] He continues, "In other words, no formal theology of the problem of evil exists from a Pentecostal perspective."[2] Instead what is found is a vast array of literature regarding the removal of suffering by way of healing.

Those that are Charismatic and remain in a denomination outside of the specifically Pentecostal denominations, whilst maintaining key components of the Pentecostal worldview, will most likely borrow the approach to evil traditionally used in their denomination, and attempt to bolt on Pentecostal beliefs. However, one wonders how successful this has been, as again, there is little literature proposing such a collaboration.[3]

In attempting to provide an overview to Pentecostal/Charismatic approaches to evil and suffering there are, therefore, two main problems, of which one is more disturbing than the other. The first of these centers on the understanding that "Pentecostals . . . have not generally understood evil in a philosophical framework . . . rather, they have understood evil in terms of spiritual power."[4] The problem this creates is that describing their approach in a way similar to those outlined in chapter 2 is almost impossible as this is not how Pentecostal/Charismatics approach or understand the problem. They have therefore not written about it in such a formulaic way. However, since the approach by Pentecostal/Charismatics seems to be an existential one, a possibility may be to approach it in a similar way to the "Anti-Theodicy" section in the previous chapter and explore how evil and suffering are understood based on practical responses. A deeper look at this possibility, however, brings out the second and more disturbing problem, namely that, "Because Pentecostals have viewed existential evil as something to overcome by spiritual warfare, they have not adequately formulated a theology of suffering."[5] This is a problem, firstly, and least significantly, because it means there is no body of literature to draw on for research purposes. More concerning though is that, secondly, there are virtually no resources

---

1. Lewis, "Evil, Problem of," 186.

2. Ibid. Three exceptions to this are McLean, "Pentecostal Perspective on Theodicy"; McLean "Pentecostal Responses to Evil"; and Archer, *The Gospel Revisited*, chapter 5. However, each ultimately opts for the Open Theodicy which comes with all the problems outlined in chapter 2.

3. As noted in the previous footnote, the only literature proposing collaborations offers the reverse, where non-Pentecostal approaches to the problem of evil are attempted to be integrated into Pentecostal theology.

4. Lewis, "Evil, Problem of," 187.

5. Ibid., 188.

for those within these traditions to draw on when victory is not attained and suffering and evil persists. Jacques Theron states,

> it can be asked whether all Pentecostal pastors and churches know how to apply their theory of both salvation and healing based in the same way on the same verses when care is needed for those who suffer over a prolonged period of time and to those who are not being physically healed at all.[6]

The literature suggests that most do not. This in turn, as will be seen in the discussion below, leads to irresponsible and damaging pastoral responses that, as a general rule, I will argue do not accurately reflect God's intent for, and interaction with, his creation, and are not anchored in an adequate use of Scripture.

For now, however, the question remains, how do we access Pentecostal/Charismatic approaches to evil and suffering in order to assess and critique them and contextualize the approach being developed here? I propose that the answer can only come, with some exceptions, by returning back to the main resource for research within the Pentecostal/Charismatic tradition when looking at responses to evil and suffering—literature on healing. By examining this literature I aim to raise to the surface the implicit approaches to evil and suffering that they contain, in order to assess and critique them. My method for doing this will involve asking various questions of the text and examining how the approach would answer these questions. The questions will be: i.) How does this approach explain the entrance of evil and suffering into the world, ii.) What does this approach understand by the term "evil," and iii.) What can be done about it and who can do what?[7]

There is what seems sometimes like a limitless amount of literature on this subject in Pentecostal and Charismatic circles, so, discussing every proponent of an approach in the time and space available is impossible. However, in a similar way to a method employed by Henry H. Knight III, I suggest that the various approaches can be placed within a spectrum that spans between the two poles of God's responsibility and human responsibility.[8]

---

6. Theron, "Healing Ministry," 57.

7. This follows a similar pattern to that suggested by Walsh and Middleton in the construction of worldviews. Walsh and Middleton suggest that worldviews hang on the answers to four questions: (i.) "Who am I?" (ii.) "Where am I?" (iii.) "What's wrong?" and (iv.) "What is the remedy?" See *Transforming Vision*, chapter 2, esp. 35. I have focused my questions in a specific area in order to unearth specific parts of the worldviews being examined.

8. See Knight III, "God's Faithfulness." Although similar to Knight III, one important difference is the nature of the two poles used. Knight III opts for "God's faithfulness" and "God's freedom" whereas in the present work the two poles are "God's

By God's responsibility I mean an extreme view of determinism in which the presence and continuance of evil is controlled by God, as is its removal. This position understands God as the great puppet master that we are at the mercy of, who pulls the desired strings to cause his grand plan to be worked out.

In opposition to this, at the other end of the spectrum, is the view that the presence and continuance of evil in the world is purely due to humans, and thus its removal is their responsibility. As will be seen, this sets God up as the distant watchmaker God of Deism, who has set the world going with certain laws and rules regarding how it works. Humans have a choice as to whether they adhere to those rules and use the resources they have correctly, or not, the consequences of the latter choice being the invasion and continuance of evil.

These are the two extremes, of which few theologies actually take such positions—hence the use of a spectrum. Even when a tension is attempted to be held between the two, proponents generally favor one over the other. In what follows I will firstly, discuss examples of those proponents who place great emphasis on human responsibility. As stated above, I will attempt to raise their views of evil to the surface by asking their approaches to healing the searching questions about evil and then critique my findings. I will then apply the same process to those who place great emphasis on God's responsibility for the presence and continuance of evil and suffering. My third section will consist of an examination, by way of the same methodology, of examples of those proponents who attempt to hold the two in tension. I will then conclude this chapter by discussing what the overall positive and negative aspects of these findings might be.

As with the categorization in the previous chapter, rarely is a proponent's position realistically that easy to pigeon hole, and so, there will be overlap between categories. My categorization may cause some debate regarding whether I am justified in its use, however, again, as with the previous chapter, I believe the positives of my methodology far outweigh the negatives regarding the clarity and usefulness of the information unearthed.

---

responsibility" and "human responsibility." The reason for this alteration is that Knight III's approach is concerned more with difference approaches to healing than views of evil and suffering. By changing the poles accordingly, the current work can draw out the respective views of evil and suffering by examining the same material.

A Dramatic Pentecostal/Charismatic Anti-Theodicy

Human Responsibility

The "Word of Faith" Movement

Possibly one of the most well-known yet controversial approaches to healing that comes from within Christianity is what has been termed the "Word of Faith" or "Faith Confession" movement. The most famous proponents of this approach are Kenneth Hagin Sr., Kenneth Hagin Jr. and Kenneth and Gloria Copeland. Others include, Jerry Savelle, Jesse Duplantis, Creflo A. Dollar Jr., Buddy Harrison, Benny Hinn, F. K. C. Price, Jim Bakker, and Reinhard Bonnke. In this section attention will center specifically on the Hagins and the Copelands.

Question 1: Where Did Evil and Suffering Come From?

In attempting to discover an answer to the first of the three questions, what we discover is a response that is in many ways conventional but in other ways controversial. In creation it is believed that Adam was "virtually a replication of God" and that humans were given rule over the world by God for six thousand years before rule was to be returned back to Him.[9] However, due to the fall, humans lose the privilege of being God-like and the world is given to Satan.[10] Humans are now seen to have a "satanic nature" and, as this is all framed in legal terms, God can legally do nothing about any of it.[11] In a common moment of rhetoric, Hagin Jr. proclaims, "who causes all of this world's evil? Who causes sickness and disease? And who causes wars? *The devil does!*"[12] It is clear from this and other statements that the entrance of evil and its continuing presence in the world is the work of the devil. However, due to the covenant that God struck with Abraham, God found a way back in, in order to do something about the mess the fall had caused.[13] In return for allowing him back in, God made a promise to Abraham in which he "promised to care for Abraham and his descendants in every way—spiritually, physically, financially, socially."[14] However, with the re-entry of God into the story, the entrance of evil into the world is understood to come by

---

9. Perriman, ed., *Faith, Health and Prosperity*, 20.

10. Copeland believes that "Adam committed high treason; and at that point, all dominion and authority God had given to him was handed over to Satan. Suddenly, God was on the outside looking in" (*Our Covenant*, 8).

11. See Perriman, ed., *Faith, Health and Prosperity*, 20–21.

12. Hagin Jr., *Basics of Healing*, 16.

13. See Copeland, *Our Covenant*, 9–12.

14. Ibid., 13.

way of one of two curses, both of which have their roots in the work of the devil.[15]

The first of these is understood as the curse the fall brings on all of creation, for which the devil is to blame. The results include hard work for the man and pain in child birth for the woman. The second curse is understood as the curse of the law, which is experienced when one breaks God's rules. Hagin Jr. states that sickness and disease are "part of the penalty for breaking God's law or commandment."[16] Therefore, the curse of the law pre-Christ could be avoided by Abraham and his descendants by obeying God. From this we see that evil *enters* due to Satan and the choice of humans, but that it *continues,* pre-Christ, for Abraham and his descendants, due to disobedience.

Although this is controversial in many ways, it is conventional in that the entrance of evil is blamed upon Satan and the choice of humans.

Question 2: What is Understood by the Term Evil?

Nothing explicit is developed within this approach in answer to the question of how the term "evil" is understood, but, there are a number of things that might point to an implicit understanding. One of the most poignant of these is the idea that humans were originally God-like.[17] What may be deduced from this is that evil can be defined as that which causes or perpetuates the experience of less than God-like being, and that to suffer is to experience this. However, rather than being understood as a lack of goodness, evil in this understanding has agency in the form of Satan.[18] As will be highlighted throughout this chapter, such an understanding sets up a cosmological dualism that is common to Pentecostal/Charismatic approaches to evil.

---

15. Hagin Jr., *Basics of Healing*, 7–12.

16. Ibid., 9. It is interesting that Hagin Jr. does not equate the main forms of suffering and evil with the curse of the fall. See also, Copeland, *Our Covenant*, 16–17.

17. Hagin states that man "was created on terms of equality with God, and he could stand in God's presence without any consciousness of inferiority" (Hagin, *Zoe: The God-Kind of Life*, 35, cited in Hejzlar, *Two Paradigms*, 190).

18. Hagin Jr., argues that Satan is currently the god of this world. See *Basics of Healing*, 13.

A Dramatic Pentecostal/Charismatic Anti-Theodicy

Question 3: What Can Be Done About Evil and Suffering and Who Can Do it?

As stated above, after the fall creation was legally in the hands of Satan. However, as was also stated above, God was able to re-enter the situation by way of his covenant with Abraham. By using texts such as Exod 15:26; 23:25 and Deut 7:14–15 it is suggested that by faith in God and his promises, and obedience to God, freedom from such things as sickness could be experienced by Abraham and his descendants.[19] In the death and subsequent resurrection of Jesus, God unties the legal bind Satan had him in and provides all humans with a way back to the nature which they originally possessed by giving them access to the "blessings of Abraham."[20] "The task of the believer now is to *identify* herself with Christ in order to actualize the full benefits of redemption and to recover the divine nature that Adam possessed in Eden."[21] As well as the traditional belief that the Atonement provides the gift of salvation and the promise of the indwelling of the Holy Spirit, the recovery of the nature of the original Adam also includes the promises of the Old Testament covenant as, "Deliverance from the curse of the Law comes when a person is born again."[22] As Kenneth Copeland argues, "You have a covenant with Almighty God, and one of your covenant rights is the right to a healthy body."[23] It is also believed, in agreement with classical Pentecostalism, that healing is in the Atonement because, "Jesus died for sin and, at the same time, did away with all the effects of sin."[24] However, in order to fully answer the questions of what can be done, and who can do it, we must delve a little deeper.

---

19. Hagin, *Visions*, 94; Copeland, *You Are Healed*, 13–24.

20. See Copeland, *Our Covenant*, 13–15; 18–28. See also Perriman, ed., *Faith, Health and Prosperity*, 21–25; 125–26.

21. Perriman, ed., *Faith, Health and Prosperity*, 26–27.

22. Hagin Jr., *Basics of Healing*, 24.

23. Copeland, *You Are Healed*, 24.

24. Ibid., 19. Although extensive discussion is not possible here due to limited time and space, it is important to clarify the meaning of "healing in the Atonement." By drawing on texts such as Isa 53:4–5 and Matt 8:16–17, proponents of this approach link sickness in the world with sin in the world and therefore suggest that if Jesus defeated sin at the cross he must also have defeated sickness. As Alexander notes, "If the atonement provides not just pardon from the penalty of sin, but power over sin, and if sickness is a result of sin in the world, then the atonement provides for healing from that sickness as well" (*Pentecostal Healing*, 42). Therefore, to experience salvation, and thus sanctification, by faith also means experiencing healing by faith.

Pentecostal/Charismatic Approaches to Evil and Suffering

This approach believes that, "God has built into the universe certain spiritual laws."[25] One of these laws is that when one has faith for a promise God has made, he has no right to hold it back, therefore, "Healing is your right as a born-again child of God."[26] Due to the Atonement, believers can claim the general promise of the removal of the effects of sin and can therefore claim more specific promises God has made. "To stay sick when Jesus has provided healing would be living far below your privileges as a child of God."[27] There is, however, a formula for making these promises into reality, which Kenneth Hagin discovered and later formalized during many supposed visitations by Jesus.[28] The first step is to find the promise in the Bible. With a list of Bible verses containing these supposed promises following, Gloria Copeland advises, "If you have pressing needs for healing in your body, look up the following verses and read them aloud daily . . . And remember: God's Word works!"[29] The second step is to believe that what has been asked for has been received. Early on in his journey Hagin says he realized that "we have to go by faith, not by our feelings. We have to stand on the promises in God's Word and not look at the circumstances surrounding us."[30] The third step is to verbally confess one's belief. Using Isa 55:11 Kenneth Copeland places a strong emphasis on this by advising those seeking healing to, "Put God's Word concerning healing in your heart, meditate and think about it, then speak His Word boldly out your mouth. His word will not return to Him void, but it *will* accomplish what it was sent to do."[31] "The force of faith is released in words."[32] The final step is to act as if it has been received regardless of the immediate circumstances and feelings.[33] During his childhood, Hagin believed that God had healed him and that the Holy Spirit told him to get up, even though he still felt ill, in order to take hold of his healing. This was a key experience

---

25. Knight III, "God's Faithfulness," 67.
26. Copeland and Copeland, *Healing Promises*, 127.
27. Copeland, *You Are Healed*, 9.
28. For a full commentary on these visitations, see Hagin, *Visions*.
29. Copeland and Copeland, *Healing Promises*, 189.
30. Hagin, *Visions*, 19.
31. Copeland, *You Are Healed*, 31.
32. Copeland, *Force of Faith*, 26.
33. In *Exceedingly Growing Faith*, Hagin uses the example of Jesus' encounter with the fig tree in Mark 11:12–14 and 20–22 to demonstrate what Hagin refers to as "the God kind of faith." Hagin then suggests that this is a faith all Christians possess and that when exercised rightly "a man believes with his heart, says with his mouth what he believes, and it comes to pass" (117–20).

for Hagin that led to the development of this formula.[34] The continuance of the effects of sin in whatever form that may take, whether that is to do with health, or poverty, or some other ill, is more often than not blamed upon the believer's failure in one of the steps of the faith formula. "Anytime a believer has a problem receiving healing, he usually suffers from ignorance of God's Word, ignorance of his rights and privileges in Jesus Christ."[35] Hagin even claims that Jesus said to him, "'Many times they beg and cry and pray, but they don't believe. And I cannot answer their prayers unless they have faith, because I cannot violate my Word.'"[36]

With this understanding of the approach of the "Word of Faith" proponents in place we are now in a better position to highlight with clarity their beliefs about what can be done about suffering and evil and who can do it. Their response is very simply to place the emphasis on humans to hold God to the promises he has made. Humans are therefore tasked with identifying those promises, verbally naming what they are and then claiming them as their own.[37] The responsibility that God had has been outworked in him building laws into the universe, making promises, and sending Jesus as an atoning sacrifice to release the legal claim Satan had. In this sense there is a strong use of the classical Pentecostal model of healing being in the Atonement and the usual Scriptural passages are used to support this approach.[38] Living in the era that we do now, the responsibility for the continuance of evil and suffering therefore firmly rests on humans. On rare occasions in this view of evil and suffering there will be statements such as, "There are no magic buttons we can push to operate spiritual gifts; it is only as the Lord leads."[39] Or, "Where the Holy Spirit is in manifestation, anything can happen. I cannot make it happen, however, just because I want it to happen."[40] However, these are extremely infrequent exceptions to the overwhelming rule that it is up to us, not God and are even reduced in authority with state-

---

34. For the narrative of this event in Hagin's life, see *Visions*, 1–35.

35. Copeland, *You Are Healed*, 13.

36. Hagin, *Visions*, 84. Elsewhere Hagin also suggests that in a vision, Jesus gave him Eph 4:27 and highlighted the authority he has over the devil. Hagin claims that Jesus said to him, "'*I have delegated my authority over the devil to you on the earth*. If you don't do anything about it, nothing will be done. And that is why many times nothing *is* done'" (*Believer's Authority*, 43–44). This further emphasizes the power humans are supposed to have according to Word of Faith proponents.

37. Underlying this is the belief that faith is required but, having faith is, again, our choice.

38. The most common texts are: Isa 53:5; Matt 8:17; and 1 Pet 2:24.

39. Hagin, *Visions*, 65.

40. Ibid., 102.

ments such as, "because the Word always works, the manifestation of the gifts of the Spirit do not have to be in operation for you to be healed. You can be healed though [sic] simple faith in God's Word."[41] There is no place for divine mystery or will in this theology as the universe and God are understood more as machines. If used right, the right results will be achieved. Any failing is the fault of humans. There is also a very strong individual aspect to this theology, resulting in the social or corporate aspect being given very little emphasis.

Before entering into a critique of this position I wish to examine two other approaches that may be placed more towards the "Human Responsibility" end of the spectrum, but, that are different to the "Word of Faith" movement in elements of their theology and application. The first of two proponents to be examined is Agnes Sanford.

Agnes Sanford

Question 1: Where Did Evil and Suffering Come From?

Unlike the previous approach Sanford does not develop an understanding of the creation narrative that enables us to glimpse into how she understands the entrance of evil and suffering. The only hints we get are in her description of our state as containing an "inherited drive toward evil" and her belief that "He [God] has given us free will and we are responsible for our own mistakes."[42] However, what she does have in common with the previous approach is that she believes that God has created certain laws in the universe that are there for humans to access. "'But God is omnipotent!' some people say. 'He can do anything He likes!' Certainly, but He has made a world that runs by law, and He does not like to break those laws."[43] "It is for us to learn His will, and to seek the simplicity and the beauty of the laws that set free His power."[44] From this we begin to see that Sanford's approach is one in which God is understood to have set the world going, placing the responsibility for what happens next on humans. And, it would seem that evil and suffering entered due to free will and misuse of these laws and that this drive towards evil has been passed on from generation to generation.

---

41. Hagin Jr., *Basics of Healing*, 48.
42. Sanford, *Healing Gifts*, 127 and 141.
43. Ibid., 16.
44. Ibid., 17.

A Dramatic Pentecostal/Charismatic Anti-Theodicy

Question 2: What is Understood by the Term Evil?

Again, as with the previous approach, a definition of evil and suffering is absent from Sanford's work. But, as the subject under consideration is healing, evil and suffering may be understood as being present when creation is not functioning as it was intended to and when there is disconnection between the sufferer and God. Sanford states, "no one is really healed until he has learned to make his own contact with the Healer."[45] And the reason for this, returning to Sanford's understanding of creation, is because humans are not obeying the laws set down by God, and because we need to put ourselves where God can find us.[46] Alongside this there are also brief mentions of the work of Satan, particularly when considering what one thinks. She suggests that negative suggestions people hear in their minds are the voice of Satan:

> The Bible calls this inner tempter 'Satan,' and suggests that powers of evil beyond the tangible forces of this world battle against us. This is no doubt true. The love-vibrations and the faith-vibrations of God and His saints enter through our thoughts of life and love. In the same way, the destructive thought-vibrations of mankind, and of 'Satan' (whoever or whatever 'Satan' may be) enter through our thoughts of illness, hate and death.[47]

Again a strong impression emerges that evil has agency in the form of Satan, thus enforcing a cosmological dualism. What also becomes apparent is that the mind is the center of focus.[48] As evil begins to permeate human minds it then brings about destruction in their lives and the laws are not obeyed.

---

45. Sanford, *Healing Gifts*, 46.
46. Ibid., 25.
47. Sanford, *Healing Light*, 44.
48. As Knight III notes, a further significant difference between Sanford and the Word of Faith movement is that Sanford "does not understand the believer's words as themselves creative or causal." Instead Sanford's emphasis is more on our "mental imagery" meaning that "one who desires to be a channel of healing or to be healed should picture in the mind a healthy organ or limb or body" ("God's Faithfulness," 72). Negative thoughts therefore prevent healing and this even includes our subconscious where those thoughts are stored. Sanford believed, as Knight III highlights, that "Satan tempts us to have negative thoughts. The subconscious stores these suggestions, making them habitual, and they enter our conscious mind as doubts, fears and resignations. We can, however, dismiss the negative thoughts and learn new thought-suggestions which are more positive, which is Sanford's definition of faith" ("God's Faithfulness," 72).

Pentecostal/Charismatic Approaches to Evil and Suffering

Question 3: What Can Be Done About Evil and Suffering and Who Can Do it?

It has already been established that Sanford believed God created the universe with certain laws in it. She also believed that God wants all people well, "we find no instance of an acceptance of illness as the will of God."[49] According to Sanford, it is up to us to align ourselves with these laws and therefore with God. Sanford refers to this as being like electricity flowing through wires or water flowing through pipes.[50] The continuance of evil and suffering is due to disconnections between humans and God.[51] During one experience of praying for her sick child where healing did not come she wrote, "God could not go through me to heal my baby, for there was a break in the pipe-line that connected me with Him."[52] In this case the "break" was caused by fear and bitterness. The opposite of such things is the presence of love and faith, "For while love is the wiring that connects our souls with His, faith is the switch that turns on the power."[53]

What causes some confusion in Sanford's approach is what difference Jesus' death and resurrection makes. Sanford states, "as He was the Son of God and therefore able to transcend time, He took into Himself all of the sinful thought-vibrations of all humanity, past, present, and future."[54] She continues, "He cleansed the thought-vibrations that surround this globe as a purifying plant cleanses our drinking water, taking it in dirty, throwing it up into the sunlight and sending it forth clean."[55] Although the terminology is questionable—due to it being highly reminiscent of New Age thought rather than Christian thought—from this it is clear she is suggesting that the work of the Atonement is purifying and retroactive. However, what is not clear is whether followers of God, pre-Incarnation, were able to tap into the laws or not. If not, one wonders why, and if so, why was the death and resurrection of Jesus necessary? We shall return to this point in the critique that follows.

Like the previous approach outlined above, what is becoming clear is that, although the proponents place God as the ultimate source, he is always obliged to answer, due to the law. It therefore seems that it is up to humans

---

49. Sanford, *Healing Light*, 48.
50. Ibid., 14–17.
51. Ibid., 22–23.
52. Ibid., 13.
53. Ibid., 39.
54. Ibid., 135.
55. Ibid., 136.

to abolish evil and suffering by connecting better with God. Sanford asks, "why are we not a new creation in any perceptible way? Why do we still walk heavily? Because for this great transformation to take place in our hearts we must *open* our hearts. We must with understanding and faith ask the Holy Spirit to invade and fill us."[56] Based on this, the role of humans is to seek to progress further along in their spiritual development in order to remove more and more of the evil in the world. "One plain fact I dare to state: as more and more of us see God, live in harmony with Him and show forth His perfection in our bodies, minds and spirits, the 'normal' process of growth, maturity, old age and death will be altered."[57] Sanford suggests that this process is achieved by humans training themselves regarding what they think about.

In comparison to the previous approach, Sanford holds many of the same beliefs as the Copelands and the Hagins. These would include the belief that God has put laws in place in the universe that humans are to discover and make use of, that they can claim various things for their lives based on these laws and God's obligation to abide by them, and that receipt of those things they claim does not require initial evidence in order for them to have been received. However, one interesting way in which Sanford's approach differs is that there is a more social, corporate aspect to it. As well as receiving one's own healing through the methodology outlined, she also suggests that she can project healing into others both at close range and from a great distance, and that an essential part of being a pipe for the flow of holy water is passing it on. If one does not pass it on, there is a danger of becoming stagnant. She says to others, "simply call in your mind to me, or to someone else as a human channel for the love of Christ."[58] The result of such a belief is that Sanford aims for the healing of various people she comes into contact with, with the larger aim of making a major contribution to the healing of the whole world.[59] In this sense she is far more outward looking than the Word of Faith proponents. However, a negative point to such an approach is that this belief seems to place sole responsibility for the healing of the world on humans.

Even from this brief outline it may be convincingly argued that this approach, like the previous one, is heavily bent towards human control regarding the existence and continuance of evil and suffering. Humans, therefore, also carry the responsibility for the removal of evil and suffering.

---

56. Sanford, *Healing Gifts*, 128.
57. Sanford, *Healing Light*, 85.
58. Sanford, *Healing Gifts*, 29.
59. See Sanford, *Healing Light*, chapter 15.

Pentecostal/Charismatic Approaches to Evil and Suffering

Morton T. Kelsey

Question 1: Where Did Evil and Suffering Come From?

Under the influence of Sanford whilst at the same time drawing on the psychological insight of Carl Jung, Morton T. Kelsey proposes a position not dissimilar to Sanford's. Kelsey thinks it important to maintain the traditional belief of evil entering creation due to Satan's rebellion against God, but recognizes that this belief still begs the question of why Satan became evil.[60] Kelsey responds to this problem with the question, "Why then is there evil and what is its source?" to which he responds, "there is no final answer."[61]

Question 2: What is Understood by the Term Evil?

In following Jung's rejection of the Augustinian principle of evil being the *privatio boni* Kelsey states, "Evil, a part of the spiritual realm that rebelled against God, is very real and very much at work both in the physical and spiritual realms."[62] In a similar fashion to the two approaches already explored in this chapter, Kelsey sets up a clear cosmological dualism stating, "there are two poles of spiritual reality, a good one, the Triune God, and an evil one, Lucifer or Satan."[63] As well as these two leaders there are also, "angels, demons, both good and evil (or unclean) spirits, principalities, thrones, powers, dominions, authorities, and beggarly elements."[64] Alongside this Kelsey also seems to suggest that evil is some mysterious substance that humans must integrate into themselves or fight against as it is revealed in their subconscious.[65]

Although Kelsey may not be clear on the substance or origin of evil there are a number of things which he is clear on. He states, "all of us are infected with Evil to some degree."[66] He goes on, "Our very unconsciousness of who and what we are contributes to our evil."[67] And further, "The destructiveness—the very reality that we call evil—results in separation and disintegration within the psyche, which leads in turn to emotional ill health

---

60. See Kelsey, *Discernment*, 80, particularly point no. 5.
61. Kelsey, *Psychology*, 295.
62. Ibid., 280.
63. Kelsey, *Discernment*, 97.
64. Ibid., 53.
65. This is particularly apparent in chapter 4 of *Discernment*.
66. Kelsey, *Psychology*, 250.
67. Ibid.

and to physical illness. Healing of either mind, emotions, soul, or body involves throwing back the forces of evil."[68] Evil is thus active and destructive and requires removal for healing to take place.

Question 3: What Can Be Done About Evil and Suffering and Who Can Do it?

Although evil needs to be thrown back, God can only overthrow the evil force as humans begin to connect with him more and more through faith. This throws the emphasis back on to them as the ones in control of whether evil and suffering persist or not. The result of this is that although Kelsey believes God is "dead set against" sickness as a manifestation of evil, and that therefore there is no question over whether its continuation is the will of God or not, ultimately its continuance is due to a lack in human connection with God.[69] In exploring the question of why some are healed and others are not Kelsey states,

> That we do not understand why one person is healed and another is not, is a reflection on our imperfect human knowledge and on our inability to become channels of the power of the Spirit. Our inability to understand the Spirit and use it perfectly does not mean it does not work.[70]

The idea of being a "channel" is reminiscent of Sanford's language and so it is no surprise that Kelsey refers to much of her theology in developing how one should start a healing ministry. Although he goes far beyond Sanford, both in his historical understanding of healing and the emotional and psychological side of it, at the center of his belief system is the idea that evil can be pushed back if humans can just connect better with God and then journey inward and face the evil within themselves in the power of the Spirit. However, the emphasis here is predominantly on their ability to do this. Therefore I would argue Kelsey's approach is rightly placed toward the human responsibility pole of the spectrum.[71]

---

68. Ibid., 283.
69. Ibid., 71.
70. Ibid., 294–95.
71. What I find interesting is that Kelsey refuses to make humans "the original source of evil" as this "destroys any hope of healing and wholeness" (see *Psychology*, 283). However, by placing the responsibility of its removal squarely on human shoulders, one wonders how much hope that generates.

Critique

Regardless of the specific theology and style of these approaches to healing, what is apparent is that they all maintain that the responsibility for the continuance and removal of suffering and evil in the lives of humans ultimately rests with humans. In addition, when humans do all they can to remove evil with everything they know and with all that is available to them and yet it prevails despite their best efforts, these theologies claim that the only one to blame for the prevailing evil and suffering is humans. In the case of the first approach, responding to suffering and evil is not about personal relationship with a mysterious and powerful, intimate creator God but is instead about pulling the right levers to make the right results occur based on some laws God is supposed to have put in place. For those who do see the removal of suffering, the attitude that is encouraged is one of patting oneself on the back for getting the formula right, followed by a consideration of what else can be desired and claimed. The God portrayed in such an approach is one that is bound to these laws and thus powerless to do anything beyond what humans demand. The practical result of this is a worldview that encourages faith in self and in the law rather than faith in God. This becomes problematic when such a worldview is compared to the Biblical narrative in which God is described as being an awesome, omnipotent, omniscient, transcendent, sovereign being who is also all-loving and the personal and immanent creator of all things. By contrast the latter description of God is not one who is bound to respond to our every wish and command but instead is one who, by his very nature, should bring forth a reaction of awe and worship from all creation.[72] If this latter description is indeed a more accurate one of the Christian God then questions must be raised regarding what kind of God "Word of Faith" proponents believe in, and, whether they may retain the label "Christian" whilst maintaining this belief.

---

72. Gordon Fee, as a Pentecostal biblical scholar, argues that in the Bible, "God is revealed to have limitless power and resources; he regularly shows Himself strong on behalf of His people. Yet His people still live out their redeemed lives in a fallen world, where the whole creation, including the human body, is in 'bondage to decay' (Romans 8:21), and will continue to be so until we receive 'the redemption of our bodies' (8:23)" (*The Disease*, 27). Fee then proceeds to highlight the fact that although Scripture testifies to miracles occurring, it also testifies to times when such "successes" were absent. In the light of these absences Fee concludes by asking the rhetorical question: "Why is it, one wonders, that the evangelists do not make *this* Scripture a part of their healing ministry?" (28). In *Itching Ears*, Hagin Jr. seems to show signs of being open to trials and a lack of success, using Paul as his example (see 19–22). However, he then seems to contradict himself and fall in line with the typical Word of Faith approach by stating, "when we are in complete control of our lives through the Gospel of the Lord Jesus Christ, we can go through the mine fields by faith and avoid every explosion" (22).

A Dramatic Pentecostal/Charismatic Anti-Theodicy

With Sanford and Kelsey we find more personal, less mechanistic approaches to the whole subject, but, even they are far from problem free. The central feature for both approaches is that evil will persist until humans connect with the source of goodness, allowing it to flow through them. Although there is more of an emphasis on relationship with this deity than in the previous approach one still gets the sense that behind their various methodologies lies the principle that God is some sort of power source that, if tapped into correctly using the right techniques and living by the right laws, can be used for human benefit. The interesting point about this is that if it is the presence of some sort of evil that is preventing the "flow," and this evil requires God's power to heal it, if it is primarily humanity's responsibility, how do they remove that problem, or even become aware of it in order to attempt to remove it? These approaches rely on humans getting it right first so that they can then use God's power to alleviate all other problems. However, at this point an apparent contradiction emerges. If connecting with and using God's divine power is the way to alleviate evil and suffering, and there is a blockage that prevents that connection, the only way forward would seem to be that either God acts by his own free will—thus contradicting the entire concept that responsibility rests with humans—or humans identify and remove the problem themselves. If this latter solution is employed, then the implication is that humans have some sort of divine capability. In order to solve this problem the only solutions appear to be that, either the approach of placing complete responsibility on humans is relinquished in favor of a more balanced approach that makes space for God's free choice, or, it is acknowledged that humans do have a level of divine capability. If the latter option is selected, the term "Christian" would have to be relinquished as a central tenet of any "Christian" worldview is that humans are not gods.

A further problem with Sanford's approach is the lack of clarity and coherence regarding what was achieved at the cross. As stated above she seems to suggest that connecting with God and using the laws was possible prior to the cross. The result of such a belief is that either the cross becomes redundant—thus forfeiting possibly *the* central tenet of Christianity—or a very serious revision of the internal coherence of the approach is needed. Either way, this is a serious problem.

What is also apparent in all three approaches, although less so in Kelsey, is the extremely poor use of Scripture. Within the theology found in "Word of Faith" approaches is a creation account that adds much to the Biblical accounts without any good reason for doing so, rather than remaining loyal to what the Biblical narrative actually says. Common in Sanford, the Hagins and the Copelands is an approach (whether realized or not) that begins with a particular belief about theology, and healing, evil, and suffering in particular, and then attempts to find, extract and employ specific verses of Scripture to support their beliefs. The result of such endeavors appears to be that the verses or passages used are removed from their context and therefore potentially misinterpreted. Such a technique distorts the full Biblical narrative.[73] Ironically, those in question here who undertake such an approach maintain the importance of the authority of Scripture while the method they use ultimately gives authority to them as the interpreter. The use of and place of Scripture within the worldview of any Christian approach to evil and suffering—and in particular a Pentecostal/Charismatic one—is a fundamental area that must be carefully navigated. What is apparent from what has been explored here is that such a careful navigation has not been undertaken, resulting in poor theology and, no doubt, poor practice as a consequence.

God's Responsibility

Towards the other end of the spectrum regarding responsibility for evil and suffering lie the approaches that place great emphasis on the power, majesty, and freedom of God to act, or not, according to his perfect sovereignty. Two proponents of this approach to be examined here are Kathryn Kuhlman and Charles Farah.

Kathryn Kuhlman

When considering the questions regarding the entrance of evil and a description of what evil is, as would probably be expected, Kuhlman's answers are largely undeveloped due to her emphasis on the present and the future. However, we may be able to gain a possible insight from other topics she did develop.

---

73. Regarding the Word of Faith proponents in particular Fee writes, "[T]he 'gospel' of perfect health is . . . guilty of hermeneutical selectivity. Only those texts are selected which fit the scheme, and a whole series of hermeneutical gymnastics is devised to evade or explain away the texts that are an embarrassment to it" (*The Disease*, 27). Regarding Hagin in particular, Warrington make the argument that, "although he [Hagin] claims to be following the model represented by Jesus, he frequently deviates from it, offering a deviant and defective healing matrix" ("Teaching and Praxis," 128–29). Interestingly, Hagin Jr. berates those who only want to hear parts of Scripture and instead argues "we don't just teach part of it—we don't teach just the part that'll make you feel good—we deal with the whole Word of God" (*Itching Ears*, 18). However, this is clearly a blind spot in his thinking as, both Fee and Warrington highlight, it does not bear out in practice.

A Dramatic Pentecostal/Charismatic Anti-Theodicy

Question 1: Where Did Evil and Suffering Come From?

One of the topics Kuhlman developed was her view of humans. She states, "Man was made to give himself to a higher power than himself. In other words, man is going to be mastered by something. If you are not mastered by God, then you are going to be mastered by things. Or by circumstances."[74] She also went on to state, "when we take our eyes off Jesus, when we refuse to submit to His lordship, His ownership, we gradually turn the control of our lives over to circumstances. Sickness takes over. And we are mastered by things."[75] From these statements we get a glimpse of a central belief within her theology: humans cannot govern themselves well and the best for them is only possible when they are in perfect relationship with God. From this we may assume that Kuhlman believed in a traditional view of the fall whereby humans chose other than God's command, thus bringing forth evil and suffering.[76]

Question 2: What is Understood by the Term Evil?

As Kuhlman understood that humans are made up of body, soul, and spirit, implicit in her theology, I would suggest, is the understanding that evil is anything that is contrary to perfection in all areas of a person, whether this be spiritual, emotional, physical, or psychological.[77] In addition to this, Kuhlman appeared to believe in the traditional view of evil being most poignantly personified in the figure of Satan. This is evidenced in such statements as, "I have no fear of all hell and all the power of Satan . . . As long as I stay crucified, the Holy Spirit will defend me."[78] Yet again this also points to the belief in the concept of two warring parties—God and Satan—who are engaged in a cosmic battle, with God being the stronger party.

---

74. Kuhlman with Buckingham, *Glimpse*, 57.

75. Ibid., 58.

76. Kuhlman's view of the Atonement (see below) as well as the influences on the forming of her theology would also seem to support this assumption.

77. Ibid., 56–57. Kuhlman here highlights her belief that not only are humans made up of body, soul, and spirit, but also that physical illness can have its origin in mental or spiritual illness.

78. Ibid., 119.

Question 3: What Can Be Done About Evil and Suffering and Who Can Do it?

Turning to an examination of how Kuhlman understood the present situation we find ourselves in and what can be done about it, her view of the Atonement comes as no surprise. As would be expected from someone influenced by the Pentecostal movement, Kuhlman held to a traditional view of Atonement that understands Jesus dying for our sins as well as removing the effects of sin in the lives of believers. Put simply, healing in all senses of the word is to be found in the Atonement. "Yes, there is healing in the atonement. Christ died to give us healing—not only in the spiritual area but also for our physical infirmities."[79] In this sense there is common ground between this approach and the extremes of the faith healing approaches, however, this is where the similarities end.[80] Kuhlman does seem to suggest that there is something humans can do and that there are "[spiritual] laws which if followed will bring success."[81] But, these laws must be understood very differently to those used in the Word of Faith movement. Instead of laws used to twist God's arm so we get what we want, Kuhlman seems to suggest that the laws she is talking about are to do with determination, hard work, and perseverance in focusing on God and trusting that he will provide.[82] She states, "Do you want a life of victory? There are three things to follow: hard work, determination, and wisdom. Not your wisdom. No. Lean not to your own understanding. It's *His* wisdom. In all thy ways acknowledge Him, and He shall direct thy path."[83] In conjunction with this are her on-going themes of optimism regardless of the situation, and doing things for others in order to remove focus from your own problems. For Kuhlman then, the responsibility of the person is choosing who or what they will focus on

---

79. Ibid., 40.

80. Particularly noteworthy is Kuhlman's disdain for the "methods" and "performances" she saw when attending meetings held by faith healers. Although Kuhlman does not name anyone in particular, what she describes is reminiscent of that which is found in the Word of Faith movement. See *Miracles*, 224–25.

81. Kuhlman, *Glimpse*, 72.

82. In connection to this Kuhlman also makes clear that she does not believe in restricting the Holy Spirit to working within one particular formula or denomination. In *I Believe in Miracles* she states, "If you believe that I do not acknowledge the sacramental methods of healing, used in many different churches, you are under a misapprehension. The power of the Holy Spirit is not confined to any one place or any one system" (*Miracles*, 5). In addition, in the closing chapter of *God Can Do it Again*, Kuhlman recounts numerous examples of people who have been healed in a variety of different circumstances, thus arguing that one can never fully understand the ways of God. See *God Can*, 251–52.

83. Kuhlman, *Glimpse*, 150.

in any given situation. For her, "The answer lies in fastening your attention not on the thing to be feared, not in the circumstances or the situation around you, not on individuals or personalities—but on Christ."[84] However, this responsibility in Kuhlman's approach must not be underestimated or down played. Although clearly different from the extreme view found in the Word of Faith movement Kuhlman does still place a strong emphasis on the lifestyle choices humans make and what they focus their minds on. This is seen very clearly in chapter titles in *A Glimpse of Glory* that include: "Faith and Gumption," "Hard Work: The Secret of Success," "Determination," "Success and Enthusiasm," "Ambition," "Laziness," "Discipline and Desire," and "Weakness Is No Excuse." It is clear from these alone that Kuhlman places quite a strong emphasis on the choices humans make, however, a key difference between this and the approaches found in the previous section is that doing ones best and focusing on the correct things does not guarantee a specific result. This is left to the sovereign, mysterious will of God. What is therefore interesting about this approach is that Kuhlman believed that what God delivers may not be a removal of the evil and suffering that a person is experiencing, but rather the capacity to handle it and possibly turn it for their good: "no matter what the day holds: if it's sorrow, He'll be the glorious strengthener; if death comes, He'll give you grace; if you're faced with temptations, all you have to do in that moment is call on the name of the Lord, He'll give you the victory."[85] In this way there is a strong belief in the providence of God and also that one is matured in their ability to trust God whilst "in the valleys."[86]

In opposition to so called faith healers, Kuhlman also makes a distinction between different kinds of faith. There is a belief that is human made and there is faith that is God *given*.[87] When one has faith for healing, this is the God given sort. "We can believe in healing. We can believe in our blessed Redeemer and His power to heal. But only Jesus can work the works that will lift us to the mountain of victory. Always remember, faith is a gift—given

---

84. Ibid., 82.
85. Ibid., 87.
86. Ibid., 182.

87. As we will see, like Farah, Kuhlman warns against confusing faith and presumption. Kuhlman states, "There are many who mix the ingredients of their own mental attitude with a little confidence, a pinch of trust and a generous handful of religious egotism. They proceed to add some belief, along with many other ingredients, and mixing it in a spiritual apothecary's crucible, they label the total result *faith*. Actually, the consequence of this heterogeneous mixture is more likely to be presumption than faith" (*Miracles*, 230).

to us by the Giver."[88] And regarding her own ministry she stated, "I'm not a faith healer . . . I have no healing power. I have never healed anyone . . . I'm absolutely dependent on the power of God . . . without the Holy Spirit I have nothing to give. Nothing."[89] Kuhlman also believed that spiritual healing—that is, building a relationship with God—was more important than physical healing.[90] However, as stated above, she did still believe *all* healing is in the Atonement. When considering the question of why some are not healed, Kuhlman reaffirmed that who is healed is God's choice, and why he chooses not to heal some is a mystery.[91] However, even though the effects of the Atonement regarding physical healing are not always manifested, she believed that "all can be healed spiritually."[92]

The upshot of this position is that the responsibility of humans here and now is to make a choice as to how they will live and who or what they will focus on. From then onwards, the responsibility for the removal of evil and suffering seems to rest, at least partially if not fully, with God.[93] Even if evil and suffering persist, according to Kuhlman God will provide everything necessary for his children to carry on through it, and this may even lead to an experience of maturing for the child. To Kuhlman the emphasis is always on the sovereignty of God and the importance of pursuing a loving relationship with Him.

Because of Kuhlman's strong emphasis on the sovereignty of God it seems right to place her approach towards the end of the spectrum that emphasizes his responsibility. However, at this point the necessity of the spectrum as a model becomes most apparent. In contrast to her emphasis on God's sovereignty, the importance she gives to the choice of humans

88. Kuhlman, *Glimpse*, 49.

89. Ibid., 4.

90. Kuhlman states, "A body made whole by the power of God is a great miracle of God's love and mercy, but the greatest miracle of all is a heart made clean by the blood of Jesus Christ—a soul born again by the Holy Spirit, born into the family of God our Heavenly Father, made an heir and joint-heir with our precious Lord and Saviour, Jesus Christ" (*God Can*, 5–6).

91. Kuhlman states, "I have been satisfied to leave the why and the how to Him, for if I knew the answers to those two questions, then I would be God!" (*Miracles*, 227–28).

92. Kuhlman, *Glimpse*, 37.

93. The suggestion seems to be that as long as one chooses to follow God, he will take care of you. However, it remains unclear as to whether God has enough control to remove all evil and suffering and whether the devil has some say in that as, although Kuhlman makes mention of the devil it is too little to draw any solid conclusions from regarding her thinking on the matter. Either way there are problems with this. If God could remove all evil and suffering then why does he not do so? If he cannot, is he as all-powerful as Kuhlman believes him to be? An extended critique will follow below.

to pursue relationship with God means that she therefore places a degree of responsibility on them. The result of this is that her position should be placed *towards* the "God's responsibility" pole but not *at* it, thus reflecting the internal tension.

Charles Farah

A similar approach may be found in the theology of Charles Farah. Being under the influence of the teaching of so called faith healers, Farah tried a formulaic method in his pursuit of healing.[94] However, this did not work, which led to a period of questioning that in turn led to a new and starkly different approach whereby Farah realized "God will not be bound by man's formulas."[95]

Question 1: Where Did Evil and Suffering Come From?

As with Kuhlman, Farah does not present any developed answer regarding the nature or origin of evil. Due to his classical approaches to such things as the Atonement it may be presumed that he held a traditional view of the fall as the origin of evil and suffering. Such a presumption can be supported by Farah's reference to Eden and the temptation of Eve. When writing about the church in Acts, he states, "There was a sense of unity unlike anything since the Garden of Eden."[96] And, when discussing how humans respond to suffering and evil he suggests, "Perhaps it is part of our fallenness from God to question every tragedy, demanding it to yield an answer to us in the same way Eve demanded the knowledge of good and evil."[97] From such references, the presumption about Farah's beliefs appears well founded.

---

94. Farah recalls that in response to a "scalp condition" he had been suffering from, "Every morning I walked into the bathroom where I applied faith formula assiduously" (Farah Jr., *From the Pinnacle*, 9–10).

95. Farah Jr., *From the Pinnacle*, 119. Farah had various experiences that led him to question the approach to healing he had been maintaining—see *From the Pinnacle*, chapters 1 and 2 for Farah's telling of these experiences. Farah's change in view led to him writing vehemently against "Faith-Formula" theology referring to it as "burgeoning heresy." See Farah Jr., "A Critical Analysis."

96. Farah Jr., *From the Pinnacle*, 213.

97. Ibid., 192.

Question 2: What is Understood by the Term Evil?

Regarding the nature of evil and suffering, it is clear from Farah as a microcosm of the larger Pentecostal/Charismatic body of literature on healing, that the emphasis is not on philosophical labeling but, on how one responds to evil and suffering. As is also notable in other Pentecostal/Charismatic literature, Farah understands Satan as the personification of evil and discusses Satan's role in reference to conflict by using phrases such as, "the great arsenal of temptation weapons Satan had to choose from."[98] This is further emphasized when he discusses Paul's thorn and the role of Satan and his agents within that.[99] Farah therefore does seem to suggest that evil has agency, thus placing humans in the midst of a battle.[100] However, where Farah differs from the previous positions is in the confusion over who is held ultimately responsible for the presence of evil and suffering.

Question 3: What Can Be Done About Evil and Suffering and Who Can Do it?

Again, as with Kuhlman, Farah holds to the idea, based on exegesis of Isa 53, that not only is healing from spiritual sickness found in the Atonement, but that healing from physical sickness is found there as well, "it is very clear that healing and the Atonement are bound together."[101] However, he also suggests that spiritual sickness (sin) is worse than physical and therefore believes that it is better to be spiritually healthy and physically sick than the other way round.[102] Although this may be true, it does not answer the problem of why, if both physical and spiritual healing are in the Atonement, all those who come to God in repentance are forgiven and saved, but all those who come for physical healing are not healed. Farah's response to this is an honest signpost into mystery. He states, "Healing is such a complex business that no one but God really has the answers. Humility is the way to understanding and we will never know it all."[103] In keeping with this attitude he further states "Healing is related to the mystery of the kingdom of God. It has to do with the divine mysteries of God's own dispensation. What we

---

98. Ibid., 21.
99. Ibid., 78–85.
100. Ibid., 59.
101. Ibid., 72.
102. Ibid., 61–62.
103. Ibid., 13.

A Dramatic Pentecostal/Charismatic Anti-Theodicy

see now is the kingdom not yet fully restored, not yet fully come."[104] From this we glimpse a number of important points about Farah's approach to evil and suffering. Firstly, this suggests that he believes that humans continue to experience evil and suffering because they live in the tension of the Kingdom partially here but partially still to come. Therefore all aspects of it are not currently accessible.

Secondly, humans are limited in their knowledge of this mystery and it is only God who is omniscient. This understanding points to a more important part of Farah's worldview that has significant consequences for this discussion. In contrast to the Word of Faith movement, he believes that the central concern is to seek God, as relationship with him is key, and that within that relationship, "God is not here for our convenience, we are here for His purposes."[105] There are strong overtones throughout Farah's approach that God is sovereign and humans are very clearly not.[106] Therefore God knows best and they do not. The best thing for them, according to this approach, is to seek to build relationship with the loving God who invites them to join with Him, and in doing so seek to do his will. As with Kuhl-

---

104. Ibid., 74–75. Farah elsewhere critiques Faith-Formula views of the Kingdom suggesting they have an over realized eschatology. He states, "By the blessings of Abraham, they nullify the curse of Adam and thus *hic et nunc* enter into almost all of the Kingdom benefits before the Kingdom has fully come. Thus the dynamic tension between the kingdom here and now and yet-not yet is almost obliterated" ("Critical Analysis," 13).

105. Ibid., 139. Worthy of particular note here is Farah's distinction between the words *logos* and *rhēma*, both of which are translated in the New Testament as "word." In distinguishing between these two words, Farah offers a "theological construct" in order "to see God's truth more clearly, without necessarily having complete scriptural endorsement." The theological construct consists of Farah understanding God's *rhēma* word as a specific word of healing, whereas *logos* is understood as the universal general word of healing found in Scripture. The general word encourages us to pray for healing, but being able to tell someone they are healed is only possible in the light of a *rhēma* word. See *From the Pinnacle*, 47–55. As Hejzlar notes, "The point Farah is making has to do with divine freedom. God can either send his particular word (*rhēma*) and heal us or leave the scriptural promises in their general deactivated form (*logos*)" (*Two Paradigms*, 148). With this construct Farah is here highlighting the point that Word of Faith proponents fail to distinguish between the two and universalize the particular, thus presuming to know the mind and will of God rather than accepting that he is sovereign. See *From the Pinnacle*, 20–21. A fair point though this may be, there is a question mark over the legitimacy of the details of Farah's "theological construct."

106. The importance of defending belief in the sovereignty of God emerges in Farah's critique of Charles Finney's contribution to the rise of the Faith-Formula movement. Farah states, "for Finney the good enjoys an autonomous *ontos* that exists independently of God. It is not whether what God does is good; but rather the good is what God does. This seriously weakened the doctrine of the sovereignty of God and opened the floodgate to humanistic influences. In Finney's theology, the sovereignty of God was down-graded to be displaced by the elevation of man" (Farah Jr., "A Critical Analysis," 5).

man, this approach asks for the kind of faith that will trust in God to deliver, regardless of the situation:

> The Christian whose life is marked by this kind of faith in the midst of death, losses, and ill health, still says, "I trust in God." This is faith that is fidelity no matter what the consequences, this is a faith that outlasts even life itself. It is a fruit of the Spirit. Faith that fixes its object in God himself, and not in what He does.[107]

In contrast Farah states, "Our faith is misplaced if it is placed in faith principles."[108] A principle which is "gimmick-prone."[109] A principle that believes that "All problems dissolve if only you can get the right formula working."[110] Instead what Farah proposes is a relationship with a sovereign, omniscient God whose ways are often beyond human understanding, but, whom they can trust with their lives. The type of theology he promotes, he argues, is rooted firmly in the New Testament and "is an 'in spite of' theology. It simply proclaims that 'in spite of' life's sufferings and hardships, Christ triumphs, Christ reigns, Christ rules."[111]

It is at this point where we really access the hub of why Farah believes evil and suffering continue in his life. He states, "The truth is that God is in control of it all. His hand is on the evil as well as the good. He allows himself to be held ultimately responsible for the evil (not sin) as well as all the good and beautiful things of life."[112] And he continues, "The Lord God permits all these evils to arise in my life and for precisely the reason some teachers disdain. It is to produce Christian maturity, Christian character, and to conform us to the image of Christ."[113] Although we get brief moments of Farah suggesting that humans do have some control over the level of suffering they experience (this is due to their choices relating to food, fitness, and other health related issues, as well as the sins they choose to commit), the overwhelming theme that comes through is one of the control and sovereignty of God.[114] This is even taken to the point of suggesting that it must be God who is held ultimately responsible for the entrance of evil.[115]

---

107. Farah Jr., *From the Pinnacle*, 108–9.
108. Ibid., 126.
109. Ibid., 59.
110. Ibid.
111. Ibid., 136.
112. Ibid., 156.
113. Ibid.
114. Ibid., 203. Farah uses 1 Cor 11:29–30 as an example of sins that result in us dying prematurely.
115. Ibid., 156–57.

A Dramatic Pentecostal/Charismatic Anti-Theodicy

In a similar but slightly more developed way than we see in Kuhlman's approach, Farah proposes a view of evil and suffering in this present age that seems to understand God as being responsible for it. At points Farah also seems to suggest God creates evil, even though he is all-good, and there is therefore a lack of clarity over the free choice of all agents, both human and non, that are involved in the conflict scenario that Farah proposes. As stated above, there appears to be some responsibility on humans in the limited choices that they have, and there also appears to be a level of free choice on the part of Satan and his demons. But, there is an overwhelming sense that control ultimately rests with God.

Critique

There are a number of points to highlight in the approaches of the two representatives of this end of the spectrum. In both cases there is a strong emphasis on relationship between humans and God. Although not stated explicitly, there are references that implicitly suggest that they believe in a traditional view of the fall as the point of entry for evil and suffering and they seem to understand suffering in an existential way rather than developing a philosophical definition. There are also references that suggest belief in a cosmological conflict between Satan and God with God being the stronger and humans being in the middle with some degree of free choice. The emphasis of both approaches is on the here and now and what humans do about it. Because of this, the responsibility of humans here and now is to seek to build relationship with God and in doing this seek to do his will. From there, responsibility firmly rests with God. Although belief in healing being in the Atonement is maintained, both approaches are realistic about the fact that evil and suffering are not fully vanquished now. The reasons for this, they claim, are to do with the belief that the Kingdom is not fully here yet, but, are unknown and ultimately rest in the hands of God. In conjunction with this is the belief that, to a great extent, God is in control of the evil we experience and the provision we get in the midst of the suffering experienced, and, that ultimately, spiritual healing is more important anyway. At this point possible cracks seem to emerge.

Firstly, as hinted at above, if one is maintaining that God is all-loving, and sovereign, whilst stating that God permits the evil and suffering in our lives, the Epicurean trilemma begins to re-emerge, as this approach seems to either question God's sovereignty or his love. If at this point the proponents claim that God permitting evil is different to him causing it, I would argue that the only point worth dwelling on is whether he could have stopped it.

Pentecostal/Charismatic Approaches to Evil and Suffering

If the answer is "yes," then we have the same problem regardless of whether he is first cause or not. If the answer is "no," then we are back to questioning the omnipotence of God. If the proponent continues by suggesting that it is in our best interests for God to permit the suffering we experience because it builds maturity, then the overwhelming historical evidence, regarding horrendous suffering that both Christians and non-Christians have experienced, needs to be brought to bear. In this will be found many cases of suffering that show very little or no sign of maturing for those involved. In such cases difficult questions need to be asked regarding the coherence of an approach that suggests that an all-loving God would allow his children to endure horrendous suffering for the sake of maturity, particularly when there is no evidence that new levels of maturity have been achieved. In the case of Farah, the problem is even more acute as at moments he seems to suggest that God actually creates evil. This may be defended if Farah is claiming that God creates evil by giving humans free choice and therefore the freedom to choose evil.[116] However, even if Farah is explicit about this and develops a coherent rigorous position—such as the Free Will Defense in chapter 2—as can also be seen in chapter 2, even this is far from problem free. But Farah does not even do this. We are therefore left wondering quite what the nature and character of the God Farah believes in is.

Secondly, there is little mention of the presence or actions of the devil and the demonic by Kuhlman or Farah. And again, in Farah's approach, although Satan and his demons appear to have a level of freedom, one is left wondering how much, as Farah does not develop this in any explicit fashion. This area may always be a difficult one to discuss as it holds the potential of attributing too much or too little to Satan, but, in the case of both proponents it seems it is an area that needs examining with more clarity.[117]

Thirdly, as with much of what we have seen so far in this chapter, there is a lack of secure anchorage in Scripture for the basis of what is proposed. As has also been highlighted already, this brings with it an important contradiction for Pentecostal/Charismatic theology. This is so because it has traditionally held to a high view of Scripture yet when approaches to such things as the problem of evil and suffering are proposed, the lack of solid Scriptural foundations becomes blatantly obvious. This issue will be addressed as the study proceeds.

---

116. And also possibly angels.

117. C. S. Lewis suggests that, "There are two equal and opposite errors into which our race can fall about the devils. One is to disbelieve in their existence. The other is to believe, and to feel an excessive and unhealthy interest in them. They themselves are equally pleased by both errors and hail a materialist or a magician with the same delight" (*Screwtape Letters*, ix).

A Dramatic Pentecostal/Charismatic Anti-Theodicy

On the positive side, something this approach seems to do very well is to emphasize the importance of relationship with God instead of appealing to "gimmicks" or formulas. I would suggest this is a great strength that must be embraced. In Kuhlman's approach it is clear that she believes humans have some degree of free choice that must be used wisely in order for this relationship to flourish. However, how this coheres with God's choices and freedom is not very clear—hence the position of Kuhlman's approach nearer the middle of the spectrum.

What is also positive about Farah in particular is the impact on, and mobility of, the community in which he was embedded during the death of his friend Marty.[118] What began to emerge in his account of this episode was the importance of community during suffering. Again, this is something that needs to be embraced and explored further.

Attempts at Striking a Balance

Up to this point we have seen examples, from within Pentecostal/Charismatic theology, of those who place great emphasis on human responsibility for the presence and continuance of evil and suffering, and those who place great emphasis on the sovereignty of God. In what follows, two approaches will be examined that attempt to find a middle ground between these two extremes, thus leading to them being placed near the middle of the spectrum. The first to be considered is that of Francis MacNutt.

Francis MacNutt

Question 1: Where Did Evil and Suffering Come From?

Although, as with all examples given previously, MacNutt's concentration is more on healing than evil and suffering, he does provide a level of backdrop to his practice stating, "the evil in the world has a satanic origin."[119] He further suggests "The scriptural worldview is that there has been a fall and that the human race is broken and wounded."[120] He also seems to reveal elsewhere his traditional view of the entrance of evil and suffering by highlighting that "The traditional Christian teaching is that sickness is an

---

118. Farah Jr., *From the Pinnacle*, chapter 8.
119. MacNutt, *Deliverance*, 32.
120. Ibid., 46.

effect of original sin."[121] What we may deduce from this is that MacNutt presumably holds to the notion of evil entering by way of the temptation of humans by Satan. But what of the nature of evil itself?

Question 2: What is Understood by the Term Evil?

Of the New Testament MacNutt states, "A major theme . . . is the clash between the Kingdom of God and the kingdom of Satan. The climax of human history, in fact, occurs when God, in Jesus, overpowers Satan and frees the human race from Satan's dominion."[122] This view is further supported when MacNutt says of Jesus, "Sickness of the body was part of that kingdom of Satan he had come to destroy."[123] MacNutt also speaks "of that kind of Christianity preached by Christ himself and his apostles—where suffering is seen as an evil—an evil to be overcome when it appears to overwhelm and destroy the inner life of a man."[124] And elsewhere states that evil is "basically supernatural and Satan is behind it."[125] In contrast to the Augustinian view which maintains that evil be defined as the *privatio boni*, MacNutt seems to suggest that evil is a very real entity that is part of the kingdom of Satan, personified by Satan and stands in opposition to the Kingdom of God.[126]

In continuity with his belief in evil having agency, on a larger scale than simply individuals, MacNutt, unsurprisingly, argues for the presence of territorial spirits. What *is* surprising though is that in conjunction with this he also argues for a Winkian understanding of societal evil.[127] "In this view . . . we are all influenced unconsciously toward evil choices because

---

121. MacNutt, *Healing*, 41.
122. MacNutt, *Deliverance*, 32.
123. MacNutt, *Healing*, 63.
124. Ibid., 81.
125. MacNutt, *Deliverance*, 46.
126. In chapters 6 and 14–18 of *Deliverance* MacNutt details the various kinds of spirits and demons that he believes exist and serve the kingdom of Satan.
127. According to MacNutt, this approach understands "invisible evil forces" "not as personal evil spirits but as belief systems with an energy of their own" (ibid., 279). MacNutt draws on Wink's *The Powers* trilogy: Vol. I, *Naming the Powers,* (1984), Vol. II, *Unmasking the Powers,* (1986), Vol. III, *Engaging the Powers,* (1992), particularly *Unmasking the Powers*. See MacNutt, *Deliverance*, 279–83. What is not surprising about MacNutt's engagement with this approach is his disagreement regarding Wink's demythologized rejection of demonic activity per se. Instead, MacNutt aims at a "Both-And" approach that draws on the strengths of Wink's approach whilst also retaining belief in evil spirits. See *Deliverance*, 282–85.

of the evil embedded in the very institutions in which we live."[128] Although there is only brief mention of this, it does seem to suggest that MacNutt believes in a more structural nature to evil alongside the concept of agency. He does not develop this further though.

The view of evil that seems to emerge then is one that understands evil to have agency as well as being embedded in societal structures. And behind it all is Satan, whose weaker kingdom is at war with the stronger victorious Kingdom of God. Furthermore, humans, who are caught in the middle of the struggle, are wished by the creator God who loves them, to be whole, as they were intended, rather than being affected by evil.

Question 3: What Can Be Done About Evil and Suffering and Who Can Do it?

At this point we find ourselves at the more important questions for those in the healing ministry. The answer to these questions for MacNutt is mixed and at times inconsistent.

One thing that does seem clear as a starting point is that "Suffering is a mystery that all of us have had to wrestle with in some form or other."[129] And MacNutt honestly admits, "I do not pretend to have all the answers. Far from it, I bow down, like Job, before the mystery of healing in its connection with suffering: 'And now let us proclaim the *mystery* of our faith.'"[130] Further on he states, "If we really believe that God makes himself responsible for the results of our prayer, we can do our part, which is to pray, and then leave the results to him."[131] MacNutt also maintains a traditional view of the Gospel that emphasizes the saving work of Jesus for all areas of our lives. "In traditional terms Jesus saves us from personal sin and from the effects of original sin which include ignorance, weakness of will, disoriented emotions, physical illness and death."[132] With this comes a view of God that seems to highlight his omnipotence, omniscience, and omnibenevolence and his work at the cross, and thus seems to move towards a position not

---

128. MacNutt, *Deliverance*, 279.
129. MacNutt, *Healing*, 84.
130. Ibid., 120.
131. Ibid., 122. MacNutt, in a similar way to Farah's *rhēma/logos* distinction (MacNutt actually includes an essay by Farah on this subject in Appendix I of *Power to Heal*), suggests that there is are two different kinds of faith: that which is given generally to all Christians in order for them to trust in God, and that which is given as a specific gift, of which the two should not be confused. MacNutt suggests that no faith at all need necessarily be present for healing to occur though. See *Healing*, chapter 8.
132. *Healing*, 49.

Pentecostal/Charismatic Approaches to Evil and Suffering

too dissimilar from that proposed by Farah and Kuhlman.[133] The only thing required of humans is that they pray: "our part is to ask; any healing that takes place is God's responsibility."[134]

To further emphasize this view MacNutt highlights the shortcomings of the formulaic approaches to healing and warns, "God teaches us over and over again that he is beyond our limitations and will not be boxed into our neat compartments."[135] Humans are right to ask God for relief from evil and suffering as this is his general will for them, but, they have no right to stipulate how and when this prayer is answered, "I try to find out, when possible, what it is that God is doing—or wants to do—rather than to approach a sick person with my own prejudging notions of how God should work."[136] At this point it seems clear that apart from simply asking, responsibility for the removal of suffering rests with God. However, MacNutt is not finished.

Even though he maintains the mystery and sovereignty of God he also proposes different kinds of sickness and relevant healing methods with which to meet them, and in some cases in quite a detailed manner.[137] Although these are proposed as suggestions, the underlying belief seems to be that there are actually certain formulas one can use to cause healing, thus putting the emphasis back on humans. This is further compounded when highlighting the various ways in which humans block the healing power of God. This may be due to someone being unwilling to forgive,[138] "not ready to be healed,"[139] or due to "lack of faith."[140] How long one is prayed for may also affect healing, "The longer the sick area is held in the healing light of God, the more the germs or tumors have to wither up and die."[141] Our own weakness can play a part as well if we are the one

---

133. A key difference here, though, is that, as Hejzlar highlights, "MacNutt is a stranger to the Holiness-Pentecostal doctrine of healing in the atonement" and "never posits healing side by side with forgiveness of sins as the twofold benefit of the atonement we have a legal entitlement to" (See *Two Paradigms*, 78–79, for an evaluation of MacNutt's understanding of healing and the atonement).

134. MacNutt, *Power to Heal*, 38. Ibid., 90n1, MacNutt recounts an incident of healing in which the person healed was not even prayed for.

135. MacNutt, *Healing*, 137.

136. MacNutt, *Power to Heal*, 50.

137. See chapters 11, 12, 13, 14, and 15 of *Healing*.

138. Ibid., 173.

139. Ibid. 196.

140. Ibid. MacNutt lists "Eleven Reasons Why People Are Not Healed" in chapter 18. Some of these, such as "lack of faith," "faulty diagnosis," or "not praying specifically," clearly place the reason for continued suffering at the door of humans.

141. MacNutt, *Prayer That Heals*, 61. In *Power to Heal*, MacNutt tells a story of a cancer patient whose cancer came back, he believes, because they were not prayed for

praying. MacNutt argues that God's life and power "is filtered through your weakness and your brokenness. So, naturally, it takes time for it to take effect."[142] Elsewhere he states, "There is also an element of *more or less power*, more or less authority in me."[143]

Although cautious about the demonic, MacNutt also believes humans can be oppressed and possessed by all sorts of demons ranging from a spirit of homosexuality to a spirit of lust, and that humans can be bound by curses.[144] Deliverance from these causes of suffering weaves a similarly contradictory path between divine and human responsibility.

As a final point, MacNutt also highlights a stronger sense of human responsibility for the removal of evil and suffering in areas relating to healthy diet and social and environmental choices. How humans respond to these choices will also affect the amount and type of suffering they experience.

Critique

The foremost question this approach encourages is: how do we make sense of its mixture? In one sense the principle that God wants us to join him in the battle against the forces of evil, meaning we must co-operate to a certain degree for him to work in our lives, is a valid point with much Biblical support. However, the constraints MacNutt puts on God by way of the actions of humans may not be as valid. Concepts such as failure of healing due to "faulty diagnosis" seem to contradict the power and sovereignty that God is supposed to have.[145] MacNutt also seems quite formulaic in suggesting what kind of evil we may encounter and how to deal with it, which again contradicts his dislike of formulas. It is difficult to see how this formulaic approach coheres with his view that "God teaches us over and over again that he is beyond our limitations and will not be boxed into our neat compartments."[146] On the one hand MacNutt seems to suggest there are formulas, but on the other, he also seems to suggest that God is beyond formulas. This makes his approach somewhat unclear. One is also unclear on how he understands

---

enough. See ibid., 29–30.

142. Ibid., 62. This is reminiscent of Sanford's theology and clearly shows her influence on MacNutt.

143. MacNutt, *Power to Heal*, 33.

144. See MacNutt, *Healing*, chapter 15—"Deliverance and Exorcism," and *Deliverance*, chapters 6–8 and 14–18.

145. Ibid. See chapter 18—"Eleven Reasons Why People Are Not Healed," reason number 6.

146. Ibid., 137.

Pentecostal/Charismatic Approaches to Evil and Suffering

faith with regard to evil and suffering. At times the impression is that the amount of faith that is present is irrelevant whereas at other times he suggests that a lack of faith is to blame for the continuance of suffering.[147]

Along with this is the lack of clarity one finds regarding the definition of evil. There is the cosmological dualism that is common to Pentecostal/Charismatic theologies that sees some suffering as being sent by Satan and his minions. But, there is also the belief in the presence of societal structural evil as well as some suffering being caused by poor use of creation by humans. The problem with this mixture is not that any of it is necessarily completely false but, as with most of what is being examined in this chapter, there is a lack of clarity regarding the basis for such beliefs. This brings with it a lack of coherence in belief that in turn leads to a lack of coherence in practice. There seems to be a mixture of Biblical foundations and experiential foundations—a problem common to us all. However, what seems apparent in MacNutt's theology is that his use of Biblical texts is more often than not for the support of his experience. This poor use of Scripture means that when texts are used as support they are often taken out of context. And, because texts are used in this manner, it is not the text that holds authority anymore but the one using it, as it is they that have selected the appropriate text to support their experience. This again raises the reoccurring paradox of claiming a high view of Scripture and yet contradicting such a belief in practice. This issue will be addressed in the next chapter.

The second position to be examined in this section is proposed by John Wimber and associate Ken Blue.

John Wimber and Ken Blue

Question 1: Where Did Evil and Suffering Come From?

Unlike most of the proponents examined in this chapter, Wimber and Blue are much clearer on their understanding of the origins of evil and suffering. Wimber states, "God created human beings . . . to experience everlasting communion with him. That relationship with him was lost when sin entered the race," thus "inclining us towards evil."[148] The fall is therefore understood as the point of entry for evil into the world by way of Adam's rebellion against God. Blue suggests that when this rebellion occurred, "Adam delivered himself and his descendants into the hands of Satan who became the

---

147. It is worth noting that MacNutt places "lack of faith" as reason number 1 in his "Eleven Reasons Why People Are Not Healed" in chapter 18.

148. Wimber and Springer, *Power Healing*, 76.

false king of the earth."[149] And therefore, "Because of Adam's original sin we are all born into the service of Satan."[150] The kingdom Satan has allegedly set up on earth is referred to by Blue as a "pseudokingdom."

Making the origin and the reason for the continuance of evil clearer still, Blue states, "the good and sovereign God has willed that angels and human beings be free to choose and therefore also be free to choose evil."[151] This approach combined with the belief that "God is all-loving, all-knowing, all-powerful,"[152] and the rejection of the belief in the impassibility of God, begins to set up the possibility that it could be accommodated in the Openness camp explored in chapter 2, as it has many of the same characteristics.[153] However, any further development of a more rigorous approach ends there with Blue claiming, "We have not been given intellectual answers to the problem of evil; rather, we are given authority and power over it."[154] This leads us back to the true heart of this approach, which is a practical one.

Question 2: What is Understood by the Term Evil?

At this point, based on their view of the origins of evil and suffering we can begin to examine how Wimber and Blue define and understand the nature of evil. However, as is common in this chapter, there is more than a hint of mystery about this. Wimber suggests, "until Christ's return we are still in a battle with the world, the flesh, and the devil and his demons" thus setting up three sources of evil.[155] But, he goes on, "Satan is the mastermind, the manipulator, of the flesh and the world."[156] What may be gleaned from this is that ultimately, although humans have free choice, the source of evil is the devil and he attempts to gain rule over creation and place it in bondage by all necessary measures. Wimber elsewhere re-emphasizes his point by stating, "we know Satan attacks on three fronts: through the flesh, through the world, and by direct assault."[157] Evil thus seems to be understood both as a force, but also anything that goes against God, with suffering being the result. Wimber confirms this by stating that even "unbelief *is* the kingdom

---

149. Blue, *Authority to Heal*, 65.
150. Ibid., 65–66.
151. Ibid., 90.
152. Wimber and Springer, *Power Healing*, 61.
153. Blue, *Authority to Heal*, 74–78.
154. Ibid., 94.
155. Wimber and Springer, *Power Healing*, 115.
156. Ibid., 121.
157. Wimber and Springer, *Power Evangelism*, 38.

of Satan, albeit a far less visible form of him than demons or illness."¹⁵⁸ He also lists "demons, disease, destructive nature, and death" as key areas in which Satan works.¹⁵⁹

Up to this point it is clear that the worldview being presented here is one in which there is "a confrontation between two worlds—Satan's and God's."¹⁶⁰ Humans are somewhere in the middle, being not completely good, but far from pure evil, and having the power to choose who they will fight for.

Question 3: What Can Be Done About Evil and Suffering and Who Can Do it?

Blue states, "Human history, as the Bible reveals it, is determined not simply by the decrees of a sovereign God but to a large extent by the choices of people."¹⁶¹ This belief combined with the belief about Satan's aims and power and that there is a war going on, moves us towards a complete answer to Question 3. Wimber states, "we have been thrust into a war with Satan and, as in any war, there are casualties."¹⁶² Borrowing from George Eldon Ladd, Wimber and Blue hold the position of living between times.¹⁶³ God's Kingdom is breaking in as a sign of the future, but, it does not yet fully rule on earth. Humans are therefore in the now-not yet tension. Although by his death and resurrection Jesus has won the ultimate victory, "Freedom from sin and sickness is eschatological—that is, it comes finally and fully only with the eschaton."¹⁶⁴ "Between these times, the effectiveness of the

---

158. Ibid., 52.
159. Ibid., 165.
160. Ibid., 35.
161. Blue, *Authority to Heal*, 37.
162. Wimber and Springer, *Power Healing*, 58.
163. Ibid. See also ibid., 169.

164. Blue, Authority *to Heal*, 108. It is worth noting that Wimber, following the thought of Baxter and Brown, believes in healing *through* the Atonement rather than *in* it (see Wimber, *Power Healing*, 164–67). The distinction here concerns differentiation between forgiveness of sin, which they claim is *in* the atonement and presently available to all, and healing, which is possible *through* the atonement but not necessarily presently available to all. The latter is therefore eschatological in nature. By making this distinction Wimber claims to avoid the difficult question of why forgiveness of sins is universally available now to those who accept it, but healing is not. This idea is not unlike the concept of "inaugurated eschatology" suggested by Wright (see chapter 2 above) in that a victory is won at the cross but the implementation of that victory will be an ongoing task prior to the Eschaton. However, I find Wimber, Baxter, and Brown's language on this issue unhelpful as the difference between "in" and "through"

A Dramatic Pentecostal/Charismatic Anti-Theodicy

kingdom of God against evil is in part contingent on the obedience of the church."[165] "In the present age . . . the victory over Satan needs to be applied in the lives of people still under his power."[166] We can therefore say that this view sees evil continuing due to the war that is in progress—and therefore the influence of Satan—and also due to the choices of humans and angels.

Joint responsibility seems to exist regarding what can be done and who can do it. Humans have choices to make as to how they will act and whose side they will fight for and God has a responsibility to respond to the obedience of his children. For humans, seeking after right relationship with God, and therefore discovering and doing his will, is of utmost importance. Wimber states, "good health and wisdom, though greatly to be desired, are pointless unless we are rightly related to God."[167] He also believes, "In any evil circumstance God blesses us when we trust and rely on him."[168] However, as Blue recognizes, "God does not have to heal"[169] and "there will always be mystery in what God does and why. He does not answer to us for his actions nor does he always explain them."[170] In this there is a recognition that God is sovereign and cannot be made to act in the way humans want, contra Word of Faith proponents. This is joined to the concept that God is trustworthy and is working for humanity's best. But, in the area of healing specifically, Wimber and Blue both suggest that God's will can be thwarted to some degree by human actions. Similar to MacNutt they point to such things as misdiagnosis, sin and unbelief. Wimber states, "There are many reasons why people are not healed when prayed for. Most of the reasons

---

when examined, is not all that clear. Instead I would prefer to speak of the possibility of inaugurated eschatological healing made possible by the Atonement. This phrase picks up Wright's point about the inauguration of that which will be completed at the Eschaton, it focuses specifically on healing, and it highlights the fact that this inauguration is brought about by way of the Atonement. Because it is inaugurating that which will only be completed at the Eschaton, it also allows for the possibility that experience of it now may only be partial and may not even be experienced at all. This phrase would thus seem to convey what Wimber intended without the lack of linguistic clarity.

165. Ibid., 94.

166. Wimber and Springer, *Power Evangelism*, 57–58. Again this resonates with Wright's "inaugurated eschatology."

167. Wimber and Springer, *Power Healing*, 175. Kay notes that, "in Wimber's thinking, healing became paradigmatic of salvation; in a sense to be saved *was* to be healed, for everyone was thought to be harmed by sin whether they knew it or not" ("Introduction," 51).

168. Ibid., 34.

169. Blue, *Authority to Heal*, 104–5.

170. Ibid., 159.

involve some form of sin or unbelief."¹⁷¹ Wimber also seems to suggest that how we see the world will affect whether we see miracles or not. However, having said this, he then continues to tell a story of how "God healed *in spite of*" a wrong worldview.¹⁷² We see from this approach then, that some sort of middle way between the poles is attempted. However, the success of it is questionable as it seems to bring contradiction.

Critique

In its attempts to integrate the free will of humans and angels, the actions of Satan, and the actions of an omniscient, omnipotent, all-loving, sovereign God in its understanding of evil and suffering, this approach if developed more rigorously may be accommodated within the camp of Open Theism. I suggest specifically this camp as both also believe that God is affected by our choices and that his plans can be thwarted by ours and Satan's choices. In this sense Wimber and Blue clearly have a lot in common with Open Theism proponents. However, with such an approach come all the problems that were explored in the previous chapter regarding the Openness Theodicy. How sovereign and omnipotent is a God that can be thwarted, even if just in the short term, by Satan and humans? And if he can be thwarted in the short term why not in the long term? Also, although Blue claims to believe "There is no absolute dualism between God and Satan," the picture of the cosmic battlefield that is being painted, seems to suggest otherwise.¹⁷³ Nigel Wright asks, "do we need to see all the sickness as in integral unity with Satan and therefore calling forth only uncompromising hostility?"¹⁷⁴ In answering his own question he responds, "much if not most sickness can best be understood as the consequence of the world's disorder and alienation arising out of resistance to God."¹⁷⁵ The point being that there seems to be quite a strong overemphasis by Wimber and Blue on the work of Satan.

Overall this approach seems to make a good attempt at trying to balance the role of humans, Satan, and God in understanding suffering and evil, and the highlighting of the now/not yet tension is something we shall return to. However, there is a clear lack in theological rigor, an overemphasis

---

171. Wimber and Springer, *Power Healing*, 164.
172. Wimber and Springer, *Power Evangelism*, 152.
173. Blue, *Authority to Heal*, 94.
174. Wright, "The Theology of Signs and Wonders," 41.
175. Ibid. Wright throughout this essay offers a particularly insightful examination and critique of Wimber's theology and practice, especially, in the light of what is being discussed here, with regard to the apparent dualism within it (see ibid., 40–42).

A Dramatic Pentecostal/Charismatic Anti-Theodicy

on the work of Satan, and thus a lopsided approach to an attempted Biblically anchored view of evil and suffering. This is evidenced by the lack of work that has been undertaken in producing coherent, Biblically grounded definitions of such things as the nature and character of God, humans, Satan and evil, and how these entities relate to one another. And again, as with much of what we have seen in this chapter, experience plays a heavy role in defining what texts are used to support the theology being proposed and how those texts are to be used.

Conclusion

From the various views outlined above it appears that Pentecostal/Charismatic approaches to evil and suffering seek to be practical and can be best characterized by where emphasis is placed regarding who can do what about evil and suffering. There are those who place great emphasis on the laws that God has built into the universe and in the certainty and necessity of God adhering to those laws. The natural consequence for such beliefs is to place great responsibility for the removal of evil and suffering on humans. On the other hand there are those who place great emphasis on the sovereignty of God and thus place the responsibility for the removal of evil and suffering in the hands of God. And finally there are those who attempt to position themselves at near equal distance from the two poles. In the first case, the experience of seemingly innocent, meaningless suffering must be the fault of the sufferer or the one praying for the sufferer—therefore muddying the waters regarding being able to ever define suffering as "innocent." In the second case, the experience of seemingly innocent, meaningless suffering may either have meaning that we have not discovered yet, or, it should simply lead us to shrug our shoulders and bow before the mysterious sovereignty of almighty God. Donald Gee takes this approach stating, "If no apparent reasons for failure to receive supernatural healing are made clear to the conscience or mind of the sufferer we have no recourse but to leave the case in the hands of our heavenly Father—without condemnation of ourselves or others."[176] The third approach provides grounds for the first and second responses. Perhaps sometimes it is our fault and at other times we must leave it to the sovereign will of God.

What is a common theme throughout all approaches explored in this chapter is the high *view* of Scripture that is foundational and yet the contradictory *use* of Scripture. A high view is claimed, thus suggesting that Scripture is the authoritative foundation for worldview and practice, and yet

176. Gee, *Trophimus*, lines 55–56.

in practice, Scripture is simply used as a source of proof texts to support the view of the proponent whose real authority is their experience. This is not to say that all uses of the various texts appealed to are purely abuses of those texts by these practitioners, as this is not the case. Neither am I suggesting that the role of experience in the construction and modification of worldviews should be devalued. The issue is more to do with the authority given to experience and the selective reading of Scripture that is undertaken to support this experience. The result of this is a lopsided and distorted use of Scripture in the development of an approach to evil and suffering. This may be most blatantly observed in the cosmological dualism that emerges when the work of Satan is overemphasized. It would be foolish to dismiss the work of Satan *per se* but it is equally as foolhardy (and, more importantly, un-Biblical) to see demons behind every experience of suffering.

It is important to here re-emphasize that the aim of this study is to provide Biblically rooted, systematic guidance for the production of a fitting Pentecostal/Charismatic performance in the face of seemingly innocent, meaningless suffering when God appears to be absent. In order to achieve this aim and retain a high view of Scripture, we must re-examine what Scripture has to say about evil and suffering and how God and humans are called to respond to it. However, in order to do this, we must first make sure we have in place a hermeneutical method that retains a high view of Scripture, but that also provides space for the experience of the individual reader and community of readers. And further, this method must be conducive to Pentecostal/Charismatic theology. This is the task of the next chapter.

4

A "Dramatic" Pentecostal/Charismatic Hermeneutic

Introduction

So FAR IN THIS study, an overview of Christian views of and responses to evil and suffering has been provided (chapter 2), which was then followed by an exploration of Pentecostal/Charismatic views of and responses to evil and suffering (chapter 3). Having completed these explorations a number of points emerged. Firstly, to be Pentecostal/Charismatic is to maintain both a high view of Scripture and a practical outworking of one's faith—particularly when faced with experiences of suffering. However, secondly, there is often a misuse of Scripture when practically seeking to respond to suffering. This has meant that thirdly, when relief from suffering does not come and the suffering appears innocent and meaningless, there is a void in one's theological tools as to how to respond, which has led to either unhelpful, potentially destructive responses, or, no response at all. Fourthly, as was noted in chapter 2, Scripture affirms a practical response and potentially provides guidance for occasions when the suffering is seemingly innocent and meaningless—most notably in the lament tradition. However, fifthly, in order to begin to construct an answer to the central research question, and therefore provide guidance for right performance that is systematic and Biblically rooted, it is necessary to have the correct tools with which to build this answer. Before being able to suggest how direction may be given by God through Scripture as to how to respond to the experience of suffering in question here, it is necessary to have in place a clear method as to how

A "Dramatic" Pentecostal/Charismatic Hermeneutic

Scripture is to be read, and how the community of readers is to interact with it. The development of a hermeneutical method, that is conducive to Pentecostal/Charismatic theology, is the aim of this chapter. Once achieved, this tool can be put to use to enable construction of an answer to the central research question.

The subject of hermeneutics is a notorious minefield that is guaranteed to cause controversy and discussion whenever and wherever it arises, and this is no less the case within Pentecostal and Charismatic theology. It is therefore a subject that to cover exhaustively (if indeed this is ever possible), would require, at the very least, an entire book dedicated to it, which is not the aim of this particular work. Instead, what follows in this chapter is, firstly, a short account of the history of Pentecostal hermeneutics in order to provide a background and context for the ensuing discussion. This will be followed, secondly, by the exploration of two Pentecostal scholars' recent work on hermeneutics. The two scholars to be examined here are John Christopher Thomas and Kenneth J. Archer. These particular scholars have been chosen because, as will become clear, their methodology, to a great extent, is some of the most developed in Pentecostal theology and wrestles with the desire to interact with Scripture in an existential way whilst maintaining a high view of Scripture. The first section of this chapter will therefore briefly look at the history of Pentecostal hermeneutics, with the second section being dedicated to Thomas and Archer.

However, as will also become clear, I suggest that Thomas and Archer's approaches are not without problems and so, rather than being purely descriptive, my aim will be to critically engage with them by way of dialogue between their work and the work of Kevin Vanhoozer. Vanhoozer's "dramatic," "post-conservative" approach to doctrine and Scripture has been selected as a dialogue partner because I believe it holds great potential for fruitful results in the continuing evolution of Pentecostal hermeneutics—as noted in the introduction. By offering a corrective to the problems that will be highlighted in Thomas and Archer's approaches, my suggestion is that dialogue with Vanhoozer will provide a more rigorous hermeneutic that will remain conducive to Pentecostal/Charismatic theology. The third section of this chapter will therefore examine Vanhoozer's hermeneutics followed by a dialoguing of the three partners in section four. What will emerge from this will be a working methodology that can be applied in the following chapters.

A Dramatic Pentecostal/Charismatic Anti-Theodicy

A Brief History of Pentecostal Hermeneutics

Early Pentecostal Hermeneutics

French Arrington writes, "Classical Pentecostals embrace the principle of the Protestant Reformation that the Scriptures are the only rule for faith and practice. This principle is foundational to Pentecostal hermeneutics."[1] In this sense then both early and current Pentecostalism holds Scripture in high view believing it is the norm by which belief and practice must be measured. To early Pentecostals, this high view of Scripture was affirmed by maintaining the belief that it was actually the substance of God speaking, and so, in many ways it was believed to be as revelatory as the Incarnation and the Holy Spirit. Arrington continues, "It is a primary witness to God because it is the speech of God recorded in the biblical text through the inspiration of the Holy Spirit."[2] However, this creates somewhat of a grey area regarding the place of humans in the creation of the texts. Earlier Pentecostals initially resolved this issue by resorting to the concept of dictation whereby all human authors of Scripture are believed to have had the words dictated to them by God. A view such as this made the study of context of those authors irrelevant. At this point "Pentecostal interpretation placed little or no significance upon the historical context of Scripture nor would it be concerned with the author's original intent (the historical critical method)."[3]

Pentecostalism from its outset placed a great deal of weight upon the experience of the believer and the believing community, which had a telling influence on how interpretation was conducted. At this point we are faced with the question of which comes first, experience or interpretation? This is a particularly difficult question to resolve (as we will see shortly) and this was no less the case for early Pentecostals. Although the claim was always that Scripture was normative, it also appears that it was always approached through the experience of the believer and the community. Behind this approach was the belief that God was still active in the same ways now as he

---

1. Arrington, "Hermeneutics," 379. It is worth noting that whereas in the rest of this book the term "Pentecostal/Charismatic" is used (for reasons discussed in the Introduction), in the present chapter "Pentecostal" will be the dominant term. This is so because predominantly, it is specifically classical Pentecostalism from which Pentecostal hermeneutics has emerged and it is this tradition within the Pentecostal/Charismatic family that continues to dominate in Pentecostal/Charismatic hermeneutics. However, the hermeneutical method generated in this chapter is applicable to all those included in the term "Pentecostal/Charismatic."

2. Ibid., 380.

3. Archer, "Pentecostal Hermeneutics," 66.

A "Dramatic" Pentecostal/Charismatic Hermeneutic

was in the first church in Acts and that this was confirmed through the testimonies of believers. In conjunction with this the texts were read through a "Full Gospel" Christology that understood Jesus as Savior, Sanctifier, Baptizer in the Holy Spirit, Healer, and soon coming King. This was done within a "Latter Rain" narrative that controlled the worldview and hence the engagement with and use of the texts.[4] At this point one has to ask whether there is a contradiction between the claim to see Scripture as normative, and the apparent experiential, extra-Biblical factors that seem to determine how they interpreted and used Scripture. I shall return to this point below.

At the same time, early Pentecostals dismissed "man-made" creeds and approaches to Scripture by the academy and those who treated it as an archive, as this was not seen to be Spirit led but instead led by men. The rise of Liberalism had meant that those under its influence followed the dual paths of both redefining theological doctrines based on the supposed universal human experience and culture of the day, and, applying supposedly objective, scientific, rational methods and findings to the study of Scripture. Gerald Bray suggests that to Liberals, "The Bible was a human book written within a given historical and religious context" and the route used to separate truth from fiction was the historical-critical method.[5] Such a low view of Scripture was unacceptable to Pentecostals.

Fundamentalism was dismissed, on the other hand, because it saw "Scripture as a static deposit of truth that the interpreter approaches through his/her rational faculties alone."[6] For Fundamentalism, Scripture is true because it is the Word of God and is therefore historical, and "biblical interpretation demonstrated that the Bible is objectively and historically true."[7] This approach privileged those with better "rational faculties" as well as ignoring the role of the Holy Spirit in illuminating the Scriptures for believers—an important belief for all Pentecostals.

Both Liberalism and Fundamentalism privileged a positivistic, objective approach to truth and history. The rational Biblical studies strand of the

---

4. Of the "Latter Rain" motif Archer states that it "is based upon the typical weather cycle in Palestine and the biblical promise that God would provide the necessary rain for a plentiful harvest (the former and latter Rains) if Israel remained faithful to their covenant with Yahweh" (Archer, *Pentecostal Hermeneutic*, 101). This motif was then appropriated by Pentecostals who suggested that the first Pentecost and the early church could be equated with the "first" or "early rain," and the outpouring of the Holy Spirit from which the Pentecostal movement emerged was to be equated with the "Latter Rain." Texts that are usually cited to support this view are: Deut 11:10–15; Job 29:29; Prov 16:15; Jer 3:3, 5:24; Hos 6:3; Joel 2:23; Zech 10:1 and Jas 5:7.

5. Bray, *Biblical Interpretation*, 272.

6. Arrington, "Hermeneutics," 381.

7. Cargal, "Fundamentalist—Modernist Controversy," 168.

Liberal approach got to the "truth" of Scripture by way of critical methods, whereas Fundamentalism, which was more pre-critical, said Scripture was true because it was historical, and defended this with critical methods. As Cargal points out, the common factor of these two approaches was that "only what is historically and objectively true is meaningful."[8] How they outworked this theory in practice, however, was very different.

Although early Pentecostalism rejected the two approaches brought forth by the influence of the Enlightenment on western theology, they did have some aspects of their approach in common with Fundamentalism. They held to Scripture as infallible, like Fundamentalism, and they used the pre-critical "Bible Reading Method" that was adapted from the "Proof Text" method of reading Scripture, used by Fundamentalism. This method "encouraged readers to trace out topics in Scripture and then synthesize the biblical data into a doctrine."[9] Anyone with a concordance could take this approach, but, for Pentecostalism there were a few added twists. Firstly, although on one level they did believe that anyone could read the text with rational faculties, they also believed "that there is a deeper significance to the biblical text that can only be perceived through the eyes of faith" and therefore with the aid of the Holy Spirit.[10] Secondly, for Pentecostals there is a canon within the canon through which the rest of Scripture is read. Because Pentecostalism is restorational in approach, it seeks "experiential continuity with the NT church."[11] The canon within the canon therefore came to be Luke-Acts, but particularly Acts. The desire to restore the experiences of the first church combined with the "Latter Rain" motif and the doctrine of the "Full Gospel" meant that although there were crossover points with the approach of Fundamentalism, there were also distinct differences. In this way then, Pentecostalism emphasized the importance of experience characteristic of Liberalism, but the authority and infallibility of Scripture characteristic of Fundamentalism. Archer aptly describes the situation:

> The Pentecostals said yes to both the authority of Scripture and the authority of experience. This put Scripture and lived experience into a creative dialectical tension. Pentecostalism's lived experience was coloring their understanding of Scripture and Scripture was shaping their lived experiences.[12]

---

8. Ibid., 171.
9. Archer, *Pentecostal Hermeneutic*, 82.
10. Arrington, "Hermeneutics," 382.
11. Ibid., 383.
12. Archer, *Pentecostal Hermeneutic*, 63.

A "Dramatic" Pentecostal/Charismatic Hermeneutic

With this potentially irresolvable paradox we see again a central problem for Pentecostal hermeneutics regarding where final authority actually lies.

Before we press on to look at more contemporary Pentecostal approaches to hermeneutics, a further point that needs to be highlighted is the importance for Pentecostals of the community setting. Richard Allan suggests that early Pentecostalism "places specific emphasis upon the use of narrative and the communal participation in establishing meaning."[13] Whereas much Biblical interpretation took on a strong individualistic bent following the Enlightenment, Pentecostalism maintained a strong community orientation. With regard to interpretation, this was probably because, rather than intellectual expertise dominating the use of Scripture, experience of God through signs and wonders, as in the early church, was a dominating factor, and everyone is open to experience. Being a strongly oral community, testimony of various experiences was placed in dialogue with the rest of the community and with Scripture, since experience of the Holy Spirit needed to be verified by the community and preceded by Scripture. This trialectic of the work of the Holy Spirit, the Community and the Scriptures, as we will see, goes on to be a defining factor in Pentecostal hermeneutics.

Contemporary Pentecostal Hermeneutics

As Pentecostalism spread and grew it could not help but be affected by the academy and the higher criticism methodology of the Biblical scholars within the academy. Early Pentecostals believed "that there was one truth and therefore one correct interpretation of Scripture."[14] The issue that higher criticism took with this was not so much to do with the belief itself but rather how it was substantiated. Pentecostals held to a pre-critical positivism of believing that this truth could be accessed by anyone with a concordance and the illumination of the Holy Spirit. Higher criticism, weighed down with the dualism of objectivity and subjectivity carried over from the Enlightenment, bracketed such an approach as naïve and subjective and held that only via its objective, rational methodology could the "truth" be obtained. The issue then was more epistemic at root than hermeneutic.

One result of this was a polarizing amongst Pentecostals. On the one hand there were those who held to early anti-intellectual beliefs and chose a more "fundamental" approach. On the other, there were those who succumbed to the criticism and sort to find ways to apply this to

13. Allan, "Contemporary Pentecostal Hermeneutics," 8.
14. Arrington, "Hermeneutics," 382.

their Pentecostalism.¹⁵ The result of this was that Pentecostal academics ultimately began to emerge and enter institutes where higher criticism was the norm, and so, they began to take on board the methods used by Modernity, particularly the historical-critical and historical-grammatical methods for reading the Bible.¹⁶ These approaches are founded on the false claims that the texts can be accessed objectively and that truth can be extracted from the texts objectively in order to generate universal principles. The belief posited is that the author's intended meaning is the correct meaning and that this can be recovered by these "behind the text" approaches, and therefore, "a neutral and objective description of 'what it meant' is . . . possible."¹⁷ Any approach that gives space or credence to the experience of the current situation or reader is seen to be impure and subjective and therefore not authoritative.

The difficulties that were to be faced by those who would maintain both their Pentecostalism and the rationalism of higher criticism Biblical scholarship are obvious. Pentecostalism, known for its experience driven, Holy Spirit guided approach, appears to contradict the neutral, objectivity demanded by the academy. This problem has brought forth a plethora of responses from Pentecostal scholars who have attempted to overcome it.

A significant helping hand for Pentecostalism has come in the form of the post-modern turn. As Vanhoozer writes, "The postmodern challenge is simply stated: every attempt to describe 'what it meant' is in fact only an assertion of *what it means to me*, or worse still, *what we will it to mean*."¹⁸ Although, as we shall see below, such nihilistic relativism is avoidable, Archer states a more conservative revision of the problem: "any hermeneutic cannot be reduced to a static, distinctive exegetical methodology but must include the important element of the social location of the reader and their narrative tradition."¹⁹ The point of this turn in hermeneutics and epistemology is that there is no neutral ground in how one interprets texts. Everyone is embedded in a particular context, community and culture, with a particular background and set of presuppositions, and when an individual or a community attempts interpretation, they cannot divorce themselves

---

15. See Cargal, "Fundamentalist—Modernist Controversy."

16. Bray makes the point that "Grammatico-historical criticism relied heavily on exegetical principles which had been worked out since the time of Erasmus and which continue to be regarded as valid today" (*Biblical Interpretation*, 354). Thus, although employed by Modernist scholars, historical-grammatical methods have their origins in the fifteenth–sixteenth centuries.

17. Vanhoozer, "Exegesis and Hermeneutics," 54.

18 Ibid., 55.

19 Archer, *Pentecostal Hermeneutic*, 133.

from this, and so some level of subjectivity is impossible to avoid.[20] In addition to this, Grant Osborne highlights another problem with the higher critic's approach: "while the original authors had a definite meaning in mind when they wrote, that is now lost to us because they are no longer present to clarify and explain what they wrote . . . Therefore . . . the author's intended meaning is forever lost to us."[21]

For Pentecostals, these criticisms of post-Enlightenment hermeneutics and epistemology mean that they no longer have to answer to the supposed superiority of the rationalism it brought forth. It also means that one would appear valid in acknowledging the importance of experience when doing interpretation. But, where does this leave Pentecostal hermeneutics? How does one negotiate and maintain the combination of validity of experience in the community *and* the role of the Holy Spirit as guide, whilst maintaining a high view of Scripture? In the next section I will explore how two prominent Pentecostal scholars have responded to this question.

Two Contemporary Approaches to Pentecostal Hermeneutics

In this section we shall examine the work of John Christopher Thomas and Kenneth J. Archer. We begin with John Christopher Thomas.

The Hermeneutical Methodology of John Christopher Thomas

As a prominent Pentecostal New Testament scholar, Thomas has obvious interest in how one does hermeneutics as a Pentecostal. At the center of his methodology is an approach that he has developed from the paradigm of the Jerusalem Council doctrine making process found in Acts 15:1–29, which, he argues, follows the three fold pattern of community, Spirit, text.[22]

---

20. In reality "subjectivity" is somewhat of a myth with the situation perhaps being better described with the term "inter-subjectivity." The reason for this redesignation is due to the fact that the term "subjective" suggests that a view being held has been constructed purely by the perceiver. However, in reality few of us live in isolation and so our views are co-constructed in community and thus shared by others. There is, therefore, common ground in our views, meaning that "inter-subjectivity" more accurately describes the situation.

21 Osborne, *Hermeneutical Spiral*, 7.

22. This approach is developed in: Thomas, "Women," and in a slightly shortened format in Thomas, "Reading the Bible."

A Dramatic Pentecostal/Charismatic Anti-Theodicy

A key part of this paradigm for Thomas is that it seems to begin with experience, particularly the experience of the church, and the testimonies from within that community, which as stated above, resonates with Pentecostals. Thomas states, "Of the many things that might be said, perhaps the most obvious is the role of the community in the interpretive process."[23] This brings together two important aspects of interpretation: the role of the community—as opposed to individuals—and the importance of experience in interpretation—as opposed to the rationalism of higher criticism. From here Thomas moves to another important part of the interpretation process for Pentecostals—the role of the Holy Spirit.

In reflecting on modern hermeneutical approaches Thomas writes, "It is, indeed, one of the oddities of modern theological scholarship that both liberal and conservative approaches to Scripture have little or no appreciation for the work of the Holy Spirit in interpretation."[24] By contrast, the opposite is true for Pentecostal scholars and Thomas in particular. Referring back to the role of the Holy Spirit in the Acts paradigm, Thomas is aware that this particular pericope shows that the role of the Holy Spirit "in the interpretive process clearly goes far beyond the rather tame claims regarding 'illumination' which many conservatives (and Pentecostals) have often made regarding the Spirit's role in interpretation."[25] Instead, the Spirit seems to be involved in the experience of the community, the decisions over use of Scripture, and the final doctrinal decision.

Thomas' third voice in this hermeneutic is that of Scripture. However, "the methodology revealed in Acts 15 is far removed from the historical-critical or historical-grammatical approach where one moves from text to context."[26] Instead, Thomas argues that the move is actually in the other direction. The council observes what the Spirit is doing in the community and then is guided to a particular text that affirms this. Scripture is thus seen to be authoritative, as it provides guidelines for how to move forward in this particular situation, but, is used in dialogue with the community and the Spirit.

In the light of the evaluation of this methodology Thomas uses discussions regarding the role of women in the church as a test case. In doing so he begins with the experience of the community stating "It would be a community whose shared experience of the Spirit would allow for testimony to

---

23. Thomas, "Women," 49.
24. Ibid., 42.
25. Ibid., 49.
26. Ibid., 50.

be given, received and evaluated in the light of Scripture."[27] He therefore suggests that the experiences of the community must be the starting point and that these experiences are accessed via testimony. From this testimony it is hoped that the work of the Holy Spirit in the community is made known in order to be brought into dialogue with what Scripture says on the matter. As with the case of the Gentiles in Acts 15, an important question to address is the problem of contradiction in Scripture on the relevant subject. In response to this problem Thomas states: "Simply put, it would appear that given the Spirit's activity, those texts which testify to a prominent role for women in the church's ministry are the ones which should be given priority in offering direction for the Pentecostal church on this crucial issue."[28] For Thomas this is based on his belief that the evidence from the testimonies in the community shows that women should have a more prominent role.

Although Thomas argues that his approach maintains the view of Scripture as authoritative, one wonders how authoritative it is, as the community seems to have a higher level of authority in the way it determines how Scripture is used. Also, although it may be argued that it is a mystery, I am left wondering if more clarity is needed regarding what the Holy Spirit's activity is and how it is defined. This is so because the activity of the Holy Spirit ultimately has to be mediated by those who experience it and thus it is interpreted in the process of testifying about it. There is no pure phenomenological experience of the Holy Spirit and so, as with the interpretation of Scripture, this leads to the community having authority as to what is, or is not, correct interpretation of the work of the Holy Spirit.

A further query that this methodology provokes is, how, if at all, Thomas uses any historical-critical methods. In a 1998 Presidential Address in *Pneuma*, Thomas explored how the New Testament should be taught from a Pentecostal point of view. In his proposal he lists five sections to a suggested methodology, with the third being the "Original Context." He states: "This is not to say that behind-the-text concerns are unimportant, nor is it to say that they are without their own distinctive contributions. It is to acknowledge, however, the provisional and hypothetical nature of much historical critical work on New Testament documents."[29] In a review of Max Turner's *The Holy Spirit and Spiritual Gifts* in the same year, Thomas again highlights what he perceives as a problem, stating of Turner's methodology, "instead of taking one's lead from the clues given in the text, one is

---

27. Ibid., 52.
28. Ibid., 54.
29. Thomas, "Pentecostal Theology," 15–16.

always reading through the lens of the historical-critical construct."[30] His main critique of Turner is that he focuses too much on the unknown world behind the text to discover meaning, and in so doing, uses unknowns as a foundation, which is no foundation at all.[31]

In contrast, the approach that Thomas seems to take is one that opts for "a careful reading of the text on its own terms."[32] This is a reoccurring theme for Thomas, as, number one on the list in his presidential address is "Content, Structure and Theological Emphases," followed by "Canonical Context" at number two.[33] In *The Devil, Disease and Deliverance*, Thomas states of his methodology, "The . . . approach employed in this investigation is primarily that of literary analysis, with some utilization of historical studies at points where such seems appropriate."[34] In his more recent *Pentecostal Commentary on 1 John, 2 John, 3 John*, he emphasizes the importance of starting from the experience of the reader and asking how the commentary can speak to that. To support this there are provocative questions at various points in the commentary to try and connect the reader with the text.[35] In addition Thomas again refers to reading the text "on its own terms," further supporting his literary emphasis.[36]

What causes some confusion, however, is the fact that, firstly, one is left wondering what it means to read the text on its own terms. We have

---

30. Thomas, "Max Turner's *The Holy Spirit and Spiritual Gifts*," 14.

31. Turner responds to the criticism by firstly suggesting that "there is an equal and opposite danger of assuring that the meaning of a discourse can be read from the text *alone*" (Turner, "Readings and Paradigms," 24). He continues, stating, "Much or most of the meaning we convey in discourses (whether written or spoken) is *not actually articulated* at all, but lies in the shared presupposition pool of the speaker and hearer, or writer and intended readers" (24). Elsewhere he also states, "The content of 'presupposition pools' is . . . a matter of what is in the public context of a speaker's utterances, and so may be taken to count as part of the utterance meaning" ("Historical Criticism," 50). Therefore, in order to understand the text better, exploration is needed into what constituted the presupposition pool of the speaker/author. Doing this guards against simply reading our own presuppositions into the text and ignoring the intent of the speaker/author. However, Turner also recognizes the danger of behind-the-text approaches dominating interpretation and states, "The 'background' material should not be used as a sceptre to rule the text, but as a lamp to illuminate it. Such material offers 'possibilities' to be explored in relation to the text, not a Procrustean bed on which to stretch texts or cut off their developing limbs" ("Readings and Paradigms," 26). For further explanation of the concept of "presupposition pools," see Cotterell and Turner, *Linguistics*, particularly chapters 3 and 8.

32. Thomas, *Devil, Disease and Deliverance*, 16.

33. Thomas, "Pentecostal Theology," 14–15.

34. Thomas, *Devil Disease and Deliverance*, 15.

35. Thomas, *Pentecostal Commentary*. See particularly the "Editor's Preface."

36. Ibid. See the "Introduction."

A "Dramatic" Pentecostal/Charismatic Hermeneutic

already pointed to the downfall of the so called objective, rationalism of Modernism, so how does one read the text on its own terms without bringing something of oneself to it, which begs the question as to whether it is still on its own terms? In his exploration of why the Amos text is used at the Jerusalem council, Thomas suggests that James "shows a decided preference for the LXX's more inclusive reading."[37] Surely this suggests that Thomas thinks that James chose that rendering because it fitted better with the situation. In which case, James does not seem to be reading the text on its own terms. Instead, he seems to have selected a particular text and a particular rendering of that due to his own interpretative needs—which is exactly what Thomas appears to be doing in his use of, and interpretation of, texts that support the place of women in Pentecostal ecclesiology. This problem is further drawn out by Thomas suggesting that another reason why this text is chosen to be recorded by Luke is because it fits the Davidic theology that Luke is trying to highlight, "It would appear . . . that part of the reason for the choice of this particular text from Amos is to continue the emphasis on the continuity between David and Jesus."[38] This compounds the contradiction by highlighting Thomas' belief that Luke used a certain text and perhaps recorded a certain situation in a certain way to highlight a theological point. How can Thomas argue for reading a text on its own terms when his understanding of the event on which he is basing his hermeneutical strategy shows that he does not think that James or Luke read the texts on their own terms? This seems incongruous.

Secondly, how do we read the text on its own terms primarily without bringing something of the historical-critical methodology to the table to help us? Again there seems to be some confusion here as to what Thomas is doing as again in his commentary on John's epistles he seems to show a great deal of interest as to the author's meaning, whilst claiming to be text centered.[39] Drawing on the point made above about the James/Luke selection of the Amos text, Thomas justifies the use of this text by James and Luke by employing historical-critical methods, therefore making use of such methods integral to *his* engagement with the text.[40] By showing the potential discrepancy between the Hebrew and LXX texts he also, inadvertently, highlights the fact that language is embedded within cultural and historical

---

37. Thomas, "Women," 47.
38. Ibid., 48.
39. Thomas, *Pentecostal Commentary*; see particularly the "Editor's Preface" and the "Introduction."
40. Thomas, "Women," 46–48.

contexts. Being able to understand this and attempt a reading of the text on its own terms is only possible by way of historical-critical methods.[41]

In sum, it seems that Thomas is right to emphasize the reality of the experience of the reader/s as being an important part of doing hermeneutics. However, it would appear that for all the protests to the contrary, there is a serious danger that this results in Thomas giving the community authority over Scripture, thus removing the high view of Scripture that he claims the community has. As Arrington points out, "the problem is that personal experience can displace Scripture as the 'norm' against which all proposed revelation is to be tested."[42] In addition, the claim to read the text "on its own terms" seems fraught with difficulty as this seems firstly, to ignore the subjectivity of the reader, and secondly, to ignore the importance of the use of at least some historical-critical tools to contextualize the text in its original setting. What is more, Thomas seems to contradict himself, as, it appears, when doing textual work, he is very interested in the author's meaning. As stated earlier, a further point of contention is how we know it is the Holy Spirit at work in interpretation, as its activity is also mediated and interpreted by the community.

It seems then that Thomas raises some important points in his methodology and there is much that is positive to work with in it. However, it appears that there are also a number of problems that perhaps need to be addressed. Before pressing on to look at these further, we turn to examine the hermeneutical methodology of Kenneth Archer.

The Hermeneutical Methodology of Kenneth J. Archer

In an article in the *Journal of Pentecostal Theology* in 1996, Archer surveyed the Pentecostal hermeneutical landscape in order to ascertain what the future may hold for such endeavors.[43] The conclusion he came to was:

> if Pentecostalism desires to continue in its missionary objective while keeping in tune with its classical ethos, then Pentecostalism must have a postmodern accent; an accent which is both a protest against modernity as well as a proclamation to move beyond modernity; or better, after the modern.[44]

---

41. Ibid., 46–47.
42. Arrington, "Hermeneutics," 384.
43. Archer, "Pentecostal Hermeneutics."
44. Ibid., 80.

A "Dramatic" Pentecostal/Charismatic Hermeneutic

At that point he flagged up John Christopher Thomas as someone whose Acts 15 paradigm may suggest a way as to how that task might move forward. However, what Archer went on to do was construct his own version, and it is this we will explore below.

Although Archer is aiming to construct a new Pentecostal hermeneutical methodology, in doing this he is also aiming to retrieve and reappropriate much of the essence of early Pentecostal hermeneutics. Like early Pentecostalism, Archer places a great deal of emphasis on the role of the community and the experiences of that community in the interpretational process. With this comes the narrative tradition that the respective communities have been a part of. Archer states, "the narrative tradition of a community becomes an essential part of any hermeneutical strategy, for the making and explaining of meaning is inherently communal."[45] He argues that, although Pentecostalism is part of the bigger Christian metanarrative, it "exists as a distinct coherent narrative tradition within Christianity."[46]

Looking specifically at the Pentecostal narrative, he defines it as, "an eschatological Christian story of God's involvement in the restoration of the Christian community and God's dramatic involvement in reality and the Pentecostal community."[47] The overarching theme that Archer appeals to is that of the "Latter Rain," which is taken from seasonal expectations in the Old Testament.[48] Used in a metaphorical way by Pentecostals this has come to be understood as the new outpouring of the Spirit to bring unification and perfection of the church, where the early rain was understood as the initial outpouring on the first church in Acts. The period in between is understood as when the church became apostate—particularly the Roman Catholic Church—prior to the fall of the "Latter Rain." This narrative provides what Archer refers to as the "Central Narrative Convictions" (or CNCs) of the community.[49]

Within this narrative is the message of the "Full Gospel," which is then brought into dialogue with Scripture and the experience of the community voiced through testimony, as it is these on-going testimonies that continue to shape the community story. In short, "The Pentecostal story brought together the Full Gospel message and extended the past biblical 'Latter Rain' covenant of promise into the present Pentecostal movement."[50] In conjunc-

---

45. Archer, *Pentecostal Hermeneutic*, 96.
46. Ibid., 97.
47. Ibid., 98.
48. Ibid., 100–110.
49. Ibid., 114–18. See also Archer's "Pentecostal Story."
50. Archer, *Pentecostal Hermeneutic*, 110.

A Dramatic Pentecostal/Charismatic Anti-Theodicy

tion with this approach, "The Holy Spirit is viewed as both the one who inspires Scripture as well as the one who illuminates Scripture; therefore, the Holy Spirit plays a vital part in elucidating the contemporary meaning of the Scripture."[51] In this sense then, in Archer's methodology, there emerges a similar community, Spirit, Scripture dialogue that Thomas opts for, but with a more robust metanarrative that forms the story of the community.

However, at this point Archer takes his approach several steps further by discussing at length how we are to understand and develop meaning. By using semiotics Archer suggests, "Comprehension of a written text involves both a discovery and a creation of meaningful understanding."[52] Following in the footsteps of Umberto Eco, Archer proposes a text-centered approach whereby one seeks to access the "intention of the text" by examining the cultural-linguistic context of that text (thus establishing the rules for how meaning is conveyed), as well as what the signs are referring to in the socio-cultural context.[53] This is done by a community that realizes it brings its own historical socio-cultural context into the process and seeks to ask afresh "what does this mean to us?" Meaning is both found and made by maintaining "a dialectical link between the reader and the text."[54] However, Archer is quick to downplay the role of the historical-critical methodology and dismisses any reference to authorial intention, but, is keen to impress the positives of the internal evaluation of one text against another within the canon.

In conjunction with this use of semiotics, Archer combines the method of Narrative Criticism, which "reads the story as a coherent piece of literature that invites the reader's participation in the creation of meaning while also recognizing that narratives can shape the perception of the reader."[55] The focus for this is, again, the text itself and trying to respond to the direction in the text in the correct way rather than trying to discover how the original audience responded.[56] The intention here is to fuse the two horizons of the story world of the text and the story world of the reading community, in order to collapse the historical distance and create meaning for the reader, and therefore inform praxis.

51. Ibid., 144.

52. Archer, "Pentecostal Story," 37.

53. See Eco, "Interpretation and history"; Eco, "Overinterpreting texts"; and Eco, "Between author and text."

54. Archer, *Pentecostal Hermeneutic*, 162.

55. Ibid., 167. Archer draws largely on the work of Powell for this. See Powell, *What is Narrative Criticism?*

56. The term for the correct response is the "implied reader" and it is the implied author that is giving direction. Archer, *Pentecostal Hermeneutic*, 169–70.

As a final twist, Archer's employs a reader-response methodology developed by Wolfgang Iser.[57] Iser's approach maintains that there are guides and directions as to how the text should be read, but, they are limited. Combined with this is the belief in "latent potential meaning" in the text that can only be actualized by the reader.[58] As Iser states, "it is in the reader that the text comes to life."[59] Thus, although the idea of the implied reader can be maintained to some degree, it seems that it has multiple personalities because only when the reader interacts with the text and fills in the gaps can meaning be actualized. And how this is done will in turn depend on the reading individual/community and their spacio-temporal location. How one derives meaning from a particular text can therefore shift with each changing moment in perspective. The employment of this approach seems to highlight the criticism post-modern scholarship makes regarding the supposed objectivity of any historical-critical methods, as well as showing the importance of the community in the making of meaning.

If this is Archer's vision of the role of the community in conversation with the text, the next port of call for him is the role of the Holy Spirit. His view of the Holy Spirit's role is to "lead and guide" by way of manifestation within the community.[60] However, Archer argues that there must be a level of discernment in identifying the work of the Holy Spirit stating, "The individual's claim of being led by or speaking in behalf of the Spirit will be weighed in light of Scripture and other individual testimonies."[61] And, in conjunction with his view of the interaction between community and text, he also suggests that as well as the Holy Spirit guiding interpretation of Scripture, Scripture will guide interpretation of the work of the Holy Spirit.

Archer sums his approach up by stating, "The purpose of interpretation of Scripture is to hear God's voice through the Scripture guided by the Holy Spirit in order to obey the will of God in the present context."[62] In doing so one must evaluate one's current narrative in the light of the larger metanarrative of the Christian story and, "the validation of meaning should be open to the scrutiny of academic communities both non-Christian and Christian."[63]

---

57. Iser, *Act of Reading*.
58. Archer, *Pentecostal Hermeneutic*, 176–77.
59. Iser, *Act of Reading*, 19.
60. Archer, *Pentecostal Hermeneutic*, 182.
61. Ibid., 183.
62. Ibid., 192.
63. Ibid., 190.

A Dramatic Pentecostal/Charismatic Anti-Theodicy

What Archer seems to develop then, is, like Thomas, a methodology that attempts to maintain a high view of Scripture and place a strong emphasis on the role of the community, whilst also dismissing much of the historical-critical methods. Unlike Thomas, Archer seems to go into more depth regarding how this interpretation is done and what the roles of the Spirit, community and text are within it. However, what Archer develops still seems less than problem free.

Although many of the points made about the role of narrative and the contribution of the reader in the construction of meaning appear valid, there still seems to be too high a level of emphasis on the inter-subjective nature of the reading community for a position that holds to such a high view of Scripture. In what seems an attempt at having the best of both worlds, Archer maintains a traditional high view and seems to give some credence to the original context of the Scriptures, yet dismisses the real author and gives a seemingly equally high view to the reader. The protection against pure subjectivity is, allegedly, the guides "in the text" that prevent infinite meanings, but these guides are only attainable by some cultural-linguistic work, which is somehow detached from historical-critical methods. One wonders how it is possible to do any meaningful cultural-linguistic work whilst dismissing any substantial historical-critical work, and, how it is possible to dismiss the presence of a real author who is trying to communicate something in the speech-act.

Like Thomas, Archer speaks of maintaining a high view of Scripture, but in reality favors the contribution of the community in the making of meaning. In the same way, the validity of the work of the Holy Spirit is described as being discerned by way of Scripture and community, but in reality, it seems that authority may rest solely with the community. This then begs the question, which community?

At this point it seems fair to say that both Thomas and Archer, in attempting to realistically incorporate the community and the Holy Spirit into the interpretation process, over-emphasize the role of the community. The result of this is that it is the community that ultimately controls "correct" interpretation of both Scripture and the work of the Spirit. The question remains then, is it possible to successfully navigate a course that gives space for the inter-subjectivity of interpreting communities, and the work of the Holy Spirit, whilst also maintaining Scripture as the authoritative Word of God? And if it is possible, how are we to do this whilst maintaining a Pentecostal identity and narrative? At this point I wish to suggest an approach taken by Kevin J. Vanhoozer that may provide direction as to how we answer these questions.

The Hermeneutical Methodology of Kevin J. Vanhoozer

Following the "cultural-linguistic" turn—most famously explored by George Lindbeck—and the rise of narrative criticism, Kevin Vanhoozer has attempted to respond to the emphasis on subjectivity in interpretation that these changes have brought forth.[64] His overarching method for doing this involves viewing the unfolding Christian story not simply as narrative, but instead as drama or rather, "theo-drama."[65] Embedded within this view of salvation history is a particular way of doing hermeneutics, and therefore, a particular view of the places of Scripture, community and the Holy Spirit within it. In the preface of *The Drama of Doctrine* Vanhoozer writes, "The present book sets forth a post conservative, canonical-linguistic theology and a directive theory of doctrine that roots theology more firmly in Scripture while preserving Lindbeck's emphasis on practice."[66] My suggestion is that this approach may be able to present a way of reframing Archer's and Thomas' approaches in such a way as to suggest a more favorable methodology for Pentecostal hermeneutics.

We have noted already the conversation in Vanhoozer's approach with that of Lindbeck's, but, the crux for Vanhoozer is about where authority lies. "Both agree that meaning and truth are crucially related to language use; however, the canonical-linguistic approach maintains that the normative use is ultimately not that of ecclesial *culture* but of the biblical canon."[67] Lindbeck argues, "What is taken to be reality is in large part socially constructed and consequently alters in the course of time."[68] In this sense Lindbeck's cultural-linguistic approach seems to give more weight to the idea of "intra systematic" truth claims that are to do with the inner "coherence" of a system rather than "ontological" truth claims that are about "correspondence to reality."[69] "Meaning is constituted by the uses of a specific language

---

64. Central to this was the "Yale School," which included Frei and Lindbeck. Lindbeck's key contribution, to which Vanhoozer responded, was *The Nature of Doctrine*. Possibly Frei's most famous contribution was *The Eclipse of Biblical Narrative*.

65. Influenced particularly by Balthasar and Barth, amongst others, Vanhoozer uses the term "theo-drama" to describe the self-revelation of God—primarily in the Gospel accounts of the incarnation—and the interaction with his creation, as a divinely initiated unfolding drama in which the actors in the current act have been provided with direction for performance in the form of Scripture as Script. See Vanhoozer, *Drama of Doctrine*, 30; 37–56.

66. Vanhoozer, *Drama of Doctrine*, xiii.

67. Ibid., 16.

68. Lindbeck, *Nature of Doctrine*, 82.

69. Ibid. See chapter 3 in particular.

A Dramatic Pentecostal/Charismatic Anti-Theodicy

rather than being distinguishable from it."[70] In observation of Lindbeck's approach Alister McGrath suggests, "This grand retreat from history reduces doctrine to little more than a grammar of an ahistorical language, a language which—like Melchizedek—has no origins."[71]

From the outset it seems clear that a key aim for Vanhoozer is to follow McGrath's criticism of Lindbeck and root doctrine, and more importantly truth, in something more historically grounded than a particular community. For Vanhoozer, canon is to be preserved as authoritative over any community, but, consideration must also be given to the practice and language games of any specific community. Before we examine this further, it is important to understand the metanarrative that Vanhoozer is using.

As he appeals to the concept of drama to understand salvation history, Vanhoozer divides that history into five acts. Act One is Genesis 1–3—creation and the fall. Act Two is the rest of the Old Testament—the creation of the nation of Israel as God's chosen people set with the task of helping to bring healing. Act Three is the life, death and resurrection of Jesus. Act Four is the sending of the Spirit, and Act Five is the Eschaton. In terms of our current position, we are located in Act Four.[72] For Vanhoozer, his approach is Evangelical in the sense that it is gospel centered (or more specifically Christocentric, a point we will come to below), and it is catholic as it involves the whole church in dialogue. He states, "The *one* gospel is best understood in dialogue with the *many* saints."[73] In addition, Scripture is therefore understood as the script to be performed, and tradition is understood as the performance so far. "Canonical-linguistic theology gives scriptural direction for one's fitting participation in the drama of redemption today."[74] More specifically, "the task of theology is to ensure that we fit into the action so that we are following rather than opposing Jesus Christ."[75]

If this gives us a basic outline of Vanhoozer's approach, let us delve a little deeper by examining, firstly, how he understands Scripture, secondly, how that is used in the community, and thirdly, what the Holy Spirit's role is in that.

In his understanding and subsequent use of Scripture, Vanhoozer has at the core of his method "Speech-Act" theory, thus his statement that

---

70. Ibid., 114.

71. McGrath, *Genesis of Doctrine*, 34.

72. Vanhoozer, *Drama of Doctrine*, 2–3. Vanhoozer acknowledges "borrowing this image of salvation history as a drama from Tom Wright, as adapted by Samuel Wells" (see ibid., 2n4).

73. Ibid., 30.

74. Ibid., 22.

75. Ibid., 57.

A "Dramatic" Pentecostal/Charismatic Hermeneutic

"The proper starting point for Christian theology is *God in communicative action*."[76] Following J. L. Austin and John Searle, Vanhoozer argues that a text is a communicative act that consists of locution/s, illocution/s and perlocution/s.[77] The locution is the utterance or text itself, the illocution is the act undertaken in the saying or writing, and the perlocution is the intended result produced by the communicative act. The author, in this view, is understood to be doing something in writing and therefore must not be detached or overlooked.[78] Vanhoozer is aware that the author's consciousness cannot be accessed, but, this does not have to result in infinite meanings. "A text is a complex communicative act with *matter* (propositional content), *energy* (illocutionary force), and *purpose* (perlocutionary effect)."[79] The text therefore has a "determinate nature" that is determined by the author and "the author is the one whose action determines the meaning of the text—subject matter, its literary form, and its communicative energy."[80]

In order for us to grasp the meaning that the author is trying to convey, we must understand the rules of the "game" of which the author is a part. In a distinctly Wittgensteinian way Vanhoozer argues, "To define meaning in terms of author's intention ultimately involves us in a search for the constitutive rules and the institutional facts that make movements or marks *count* as communicative action."[81] On the surface this appears a straightforward approach to a text, but, the issue becomes a little more confused with the question: who is the author of Scripture? Vanhoozer negotiates this question with a "both and" approach. Although the various books are authored by humans, Vanhoozer understands "inspiration" to mean that while the locutions and illocutions of individual books in the Bible are that of the respective human authors, ultimately the locutions and illocutions within the whole canon are God's. "To speak of divine canonical discourse is to highlight the role of *God as the divine playwright who employs the voices of the human authors of Scripture in the service of his theo-drama.*"[82] Any single piece of Scripture must therefore be read in the light of the whole canon in order to fully appreciate it as God's communicative act.

---

76. Ibid., 62.
77. Austin, *Things with Words*; and Searle, *Speech Acts*.
78. See Vanhoozer, *Is There a Meaning*, in particular, chapter 5.
79. Ibid., 228.
80. Ibid., 230.
81. Ibid., 245.
82. Vanhoozer, *Drama of Doctrine*, 177.

In addition to this, Vanhoozer maintains that "Interpreting . . . is properly basic" and so is a belief in an exterior world.[83] He employs Alvin Plantinga's defense of warranted belief in other minds to support the belief in the existence of the author.[84] Built into this approach is the basic belief that what we are told is true—there is a level of trust at work in order for communication to take place. Testimony is therefore a vital way of gaining information, and the Bible should be taken as testimony. A problem comes when the views on the reliability of the interpretation polarize into those that believe we come to the text as neutral and can objectively extract propositions, and those that drift into nihilism and believe that we can do what we like with the text. Vanhoozer does not slip to either of the poles but instead, in a similar way to N.T. Wright, suggests a position entitled "Critical Realism."[85] "Critical realism maintains both that theories describe things that exist (hence 'realism') and that theories can be true or false (hence 'critical')."[86] In line with this approach, Vanhoozer therefore maintains belief in the existence of a right reading of the text, but also acknowledges that, "In the final analysis, the ideal of the single correct interpretation must remain an eschatological goal; in this life, we cannot always know that we know."[87] In the task of reading, we must therefore read to gain what Vanhoozer refers to as a "thick description" of the text, whilst living in the belief that there may always be room for revision, as none of us can approach a text from a neutral perspective.[88] This approach "does not mean that we

83. Vanhoozer, *Is There a Meaning*, 289.

84. Ibid. 288–90.

85. See Wright, *New Testament*, particularly chapters 2 and 3; and Meyer, *Critical Realism*.

86. Vanhoozer, *Is There a Meaning*, 322.

87. Ibid., 303.

88. Vanhoozer states of "thick description": "*A description is sufficiently thick when it allows us to appreciate everything the author is doing in a text*" (*Is There a Meaning*, 284; emphasis original). The aim of achieving thick description is thus to understand the communicative action of the author in the text by way of all available tools. In his use of this term Vanhoozer cites Geertz and Geertz's use of the term in cultural anthropology as an important source and influence for Vanhoozer's application in literary interpretation. He also notes Ryle as a source that was prior to Geertz in the use of this term. See Vanhoozer, *Is There a Meaning*, chapter 6, nn6 and 13. In addition to this, Cotterell and Turner speak of "discourse meaning." They suggest that the meaning of any particular discourse can only be achieved if one understands the context in which the discourse is set. In unearthing this, greater clarity can be obtained regarding the authorial intent and, therefore, the discourse meaning (see Cotterell and Turner, *Linguistics*, 61–72). Cotterell and Turner's understanding of obtaining "discourse meaning" appears to be one of the aims of Vanhoozer's use of Speech-Act theory, Wittgensteinian languages games and the achievement of "thick descriptions." However, Vanhoozer takes this

will know everything there is to know about the text, but that we will know *enough* to be able, and responsible, to respond to its subject matter."[89] With this as a brief overview of Vanhoozer's approach to the Biblical texts we need now to look at how the community is to engage with them.

With his metaphor of the unfolding "drama," Vanhoozer continues to press the point that to be a Christian is to participate, which is what the community must do. In response to the question, "of what do we participate?" the answer is simply, the unfolding drama. Here we must follow Vanhoozer into the etymology of the word "drama" in order to grasp why this metaphor is of such importance to him.

At its root, the English word "drama" is derived from the Greek verb *draō* meaning "to do." As Vanhoozer points out, "A drama is a *doing*, an enactment."[90] He continues by stating that *The Drama of Doctrine* "insists that God and humanity are alternately actor and audience. Better: life is divine-human interactive theatre, and theology involves both what God has said and done for the world and what we must say and do in grateful response."[91] Whereas narrative—a currently popular method in theology— only covers a single genre, a genre of *telling*, drama encompasses multiple genres that comprise the interaction between the divine playwright and the human actors—of which narrative is one of these genres. Drama is about what has been *done*, and what the Script and the playwright are directing the current actors to *do*. Based on this view, to participate in the drama is more than just telling stories about it, it involves the whole plethora of activity that makes up human-human and human-divine relationships. This makes the use of speech-act theory even more powerful since even to speak, from such a viewpoint, is to *do*.

This excursion into Vanhoozer's use of drama leads to the question of "how exactly do we participate?" The answer to this for Vanhoozer begins with the view of "Scripture . . . as a script that maps out the way of truth and life."[92] For the community then, they must learn to look in two directions at

---

beyond a single text or book within the Canon and seeks the Canonical discourse meaning of any particular text. He does this by asking what the meaning of that text is in the light of the whole Canon, and in particular in the light of the performance of Jesus as revealed in the Gospels. In this sense of obtaining "discourse meaning," the author is understood as God, thus making the text authoritative as the divine speech-act, and the meaning obtains "transcultural significance" that allows it to offer direction to the reader. The concept of "transcultural significance" will be drawn out further below.

89. Vanhoozer, *Is There a Meaning*, 317.
90. Vanhoozer, *Drama of Doctrine*, 37.
91. Ibid., 37–38.
92. Ibid., 121.

A Dramatic Pentecostal/Charismatic Anti-Theodicy

once. They must be able to look back and decipher the communicative acts of God portrayed in Scripture, but they must also be able to look to their own contexts and ask how to apply what they learn in order to continue the drama in a relevant way in the present. The aim is *"nonidentical repetition,"* which I shall return to shortly.[93]

In their use of Scripture, the community must first think canonically. Vanhoozer argues, "We begin to speak, see, judge, and act canonically when we learn to interpret the history recounted in the Bible, as well as our own ongoing history, as part and parcel of the drama of redemption in Christ."[94] To engage with the canon is to engage with the covenant that God communicates through it, where "To covenant is to enter into a personal relationship structured by solemn promises to behave in certain ways and to do certain things."[95] For Vanhoozer, reading of the text to gain as thick a description as possible must ultimately involve reading canonically with a typology that has Jesus as the central key. An example found in Scripture where he argues this is put to good affect is the "Gaza experience" in Acts 8:30–31 where we see Philip acting as the translator to the Ethiopian. In doing so, Philip uses a typological methodology that allows Jesus to shed light on the Isaiah passage and the Isaiah passage to shed light on Jesus.[96]

As mentioned above, in the reading of the "Script" the community must also pay close attention to such things as the genre of individual texts, rather than reducing them down to fit into a single system. Vanhoozer is thus pluralistic in the sense that he suggests that the various voices and genres of Scripture must be heard for what they are. As stated above, included in this suggestion is that one of the genres is narrative and so, therefore, precaution must be taken against reading all texts narratively, as this is only one genre among many. The argument for this plurality is that different people need to hear different things at different times and in different ways, but rather than the plurality getting too wide, there remains "unity in diversity" as long as a canonical, typological, Christocentric approach is maintained.[97] Of course all this must be done by the community with a critical realist approach in view.

As this is dramatic for Vanhoozer it does not end for the community with them simply examining the texts to see what God has said and done. Instead, the other direction for the community to look is to how to

93. Ibid., 125.
94. Ibid., 224.
95. Ibid., 136.
96. Ibid., 116–20.
97. Ibid., 275.

A "Dramatic" Pentecostal/Charismatic Hermeneutic

perform the Script. As with Vanhoozer's use of the drama metaphor, it is again crucial, in understanding his method, to take a deeper look at what he means by the term "performance," before we explore how this performance is achieved.

He states, "The overriding imperative in performance is, as the etymology of the term itself indicates, 'to carry the *form* through (*per*).' In the case of theology, *the commanding form to be carried through is the form of Jesus Christ: the communicative act of God.*"[98]

In the beginning, the creation texts at the start of Act 1 tell us that humans were created in the image of God (*imago dei*) and that they were placed upon the cosmic stage to "subdue" and "have dominion" over it (Gen 1:26–28). Greater insight into this task is given in chapter 2 of Genesis where we are told that Adam was placed in the Garden of Eden to "till it and keep it" (v. 15). The role cast for humans here is one of stewardship. Ultimately this is God's good creation of which humans are a part and our role within that is to look after it, cultivate it, and help it to grow. Walsh and Middleton note, "The twofold original human task is to *develop* and *preserve* our creational environment."[99] And, as it is God's creation, humans are therefore answerable to the creator for what we do.

Further reflection on the idea of being made in the image of God opens up more definition to this role. As a part of creation, humans are made to look to and worship their creator. In the same way, by being made in the image of God, they are made to be God's representative on earth. "Human beings are God's ambassadors, his representatives, to the rest of creation."[100] By worshipping anything else in creation they both dedicate their lives to something less than God, and give up their place as the image of God in creation to the new image that they now worship. We see from this that to be made in the image of God is to share responsibility and power with God for what happens in his creation. Like the rest of creation, humans are in covenantal relationship with God, but, they have the added task of being in relationship with, and tending to, the rest of creation. We may say then that humans were originally created to perform *imago dei* on the cosmic stage, as they were tasked with carrying through the image of God into creation.[101]

---

98 Vanhoozer, *Drama of Doctrine*, 253.

99. Walsh and Middleton, *Transforming Vision*, 54.

100. Ibid., 64.

101. Vanhoozer notes, "Being human . . . involves both indicative and imperative dimensions: what we should do follows from the kind of creatures we are" (Vanhoozer, "Human Being," 183). Elsewhere he states, "A person is a situated communicative agent—an author—in dialogical relation to others and, ultimately, to God" (Remythologizing Theology, 319).

A Dramatic Pentecostal/Charismatic Anti-Theodicy

As will be discussed in chapter 5, in the event of the fall, humans begin to produce a less than fitting performance for the part in which they are cast, a problem that begins in Act 1 but carries on through into the present act. At this point we can return to the Vanhoozer quote that began this section. In losing sight of how to perform the role cast for us originally, God communicates this role afresh to us in the form of Jesus Christ. Hence why Vanhoozer argues that we should be "performing *Christ* in the power of the Spirit, speaking and acting as a *persona* 'in Christ' should speak and act."[102] This does not, as yet, give us a definite understanding of the concept of performance, but, it gives us examples of what is and is not a good performance from which one can be derived.

In his understanding of performance Vanhoozer follows the acting method of Constantin Stanislavski.[103] The hub of this method runs contrary to the concept of simply displaying externally what this particular part looks like whilst internally not embodying it—this way hypocrisy lies. Vanhoozer sees such an approach as "play-acting" and states, "'Hypocrisy' thus indicates a dichotomy between one's outer appearance or action and one's inner reality or 'heart.'"[104] He further suggests that this approach is opposite to the "integral selfhood" that the Stanislavski method adapted for this drama requires. Instead "we have to learn not simply how to play-act as a role but rather to become the role we play."[105] With this in mind, following the fall hypocrisy reigns supreme in the life of humans as they fail to perform fully the part for which they were cast. Conversely, what we see in the life of Christ is a perfect performance, as there is no sign of play-acting or hypocrisy.

However, to carry the form of Christ through into current contexts, the community must first understand the culture in which it finds itself situated, where "'Culture' refers to the beliefs, values, and practices that characterize human life together at a particular place and time."[106] Vanhoozer continues, "Culture sets the stage, arranges the scenery, and provides the props."[107] And it is this that the community must understand. From Vanhoozer's perspective then, as stated above, the aim is "non-identical repetition" of a performance of Christ, which Vanhoozer seems to approach in three different ways.

---

102. Vanhoozer, *Drama of Doctrine*, 373.
103. Ibid., 369–74. Vanhoozer draws particularly from Stanislavski, *Actor Prepares*.
104. Vanhoozer, *Drama of Doctrine*, 366.
105. Ibid.
106. Ibid., 129.
107. Ibid.

Firstly, drawing on Ricoeur, he contrasts "*idem*" identity with "*ipse*" identity. The former of these describes "hard identity" in the sense that there is no change in repetition. The latter of these however, describes "soft identity" in which the character remains reliable and stable, but, there is growth and change.[108] The employment of this idea leads on to the second idea of "improvisation" where, "The directions drawn by Scripture's normative specification of the theo-drama enable the church to improvise, as it were, with a script."[109] The key to improvisation is translation into a relevant format for the particular culture, whilst maintaining the "*ipse*" identity. Drawing on the world of music, Vanhoozer explains the improviser as one that knows the rules of the music being played but is not limited by them. They must not pre-plan or adlib, which Vanhoozer understands as doing one's own thing with no regard for the rules. On the contrary, "The true improviser is the one whose actions appear neither prescribed nor cleverly novel but fitting, even obvious."[110] Previous situations/actions open up "offers" for improvisation, but, in order to recognize these it is important that the community has a memory of the "performance history" of the theo-drama.[111] The community must also know how to "overaccept" the offer, which involves placing the improvisation within the bigger picture.[112]

This links in to Vanhoozer's third approach to non-identical repetition—fittingness. In the same way that N. T. Wright uses the idea of "*innovation and consistency*," here the understanding is that the present performance must not be a carbon copy from previous performances (and is therefore innovative),—as the situation is inevitably different to some degree—but, neither must it be authored anew (meaning that there must be a high level of consistency with what has gone before).[113] Instead the performance must fit the whole, in a way relevant to the particular context. It "is a matter of transposing biblical modes of speech and action into their contemporary counterparts."[114] Vanhoozer states, "We are to *fit* into some-

---

108. Ibid., 127–28.

109. Ibid., 129.

110. Ibid., 338.

111. An "offer," in the sense of the dramatic, is when an actor creates an opportunity for an improvised response from the interlocutor within the rules of the "game" in play. The receiver then has the opportunity to "accept" or "block" the offer. A good improviser will accept whereas a bad one will block. Vanhoozer, *Drama of Doctrine*, 338–39.

112. Vanhoozer states, "Overaccepting neither accepts offers on their own terms nor blocks them but rather incorporates them into a broader narrative, thus allowing the actor to retain both her identity and her relevance" (*Drama of Doctrine*, 340).

113. See Wright, "How Can The Bible Be Authoritative?," 18–19.

114. Vanhoozer, *Drama of Doctrine*, 260.

A Dramatic Pentecostal/Charismatic Anti-Theodicy

thing that is already there: There is both a structured stage (creation) and determinate plot (the history of salvation)."[115] He continues, "'Fittingness' makes sense only on the assumption that there is a state of affairs—God's action in the world, the drama of redemption—against which one can measure the rightness or wrongness of a course of action."[116] Again using Stanislavski's method, Vanhoozer refers to the "super-objective" of a drama where this is understood as the overarching aim of it.[117] "The ultimate point of a performance is to communicate what he [Stanislavski] called the play's main idea or 'super-objective.'"[118] In the case of the drama in question, the super-objective is "the eschatological project of forming a new world, a new creation, a new 'house' of God with Jesus Christ as the cornerstone (Eph. 2:20)," or what we may term "eschatological consummation."[119] To perform fittingly, again to follow Stanislavski, is to have in mind one's "through-line" in the performance, which is that which directs the performance rightly in order to convey the super-objective, and so perform in such a way as to aid in moving the drama towards that super-objective.[120] To perform fittingly is therefore to perform in such a way as to enable the inauguration of eschatological consummation. "The ultimate aim of canonical-linguistic theology is to achieve fittingness—cross-cultural modal similarity—between Scripture and the contemporary situation."[121] And this is built on the view that "Scripture governs theology not by providing the field from which we harvest abstract universals but *by embodying truths of transcultural significance in particular contexts*."[122] Anthony Thiselton refers to such a system as "transcontextual" because the principles at the heart of the system are thought to be able to be applied in a "fitting" way within any given context, and thus operate at a metacontextual level.[123]

---

115. Vanhoozer, "Voice and Actor," 100, italics mine.

116. Ibid. 100.

117. Ibid. 95. See also, *Drama of Doctrine*, 371ff.

118. Ibid. 95.

119. Vanhoozer, *Drama of Doctrine*, 374.

120. Vanhoozer, "Voice and Actor," 96. See also Vanhoozer, *Drama of Doctrine*, 371–74. Although the term "super-objective" fits within the dramatic paradigm, it seems unnecessary to use it as a substitute for "eschatological consummation." This is so because, as this latter term is well used and understood in the Christian tradition, to replace it with a less familiar, and therefore potentially confusing term, for the sake of continuation of the dramatic language, seems counter-productive, as such a change would not appear to add anything to this discussion, but may instead create an unwanted distraction.

121. Vanhoozer, *Drama of Doctrine*, 260.

122. Ibid., 348.

123. See Thiselton, *New Horizons*, particularly in reference to "Socio-Cultural" and

A "Dramatic" Pentecostal/Charismatic Hermeneutic

We can see from this that for the community to produce a non-identical, repetitive, improvised, fitting performance, they must be aiming to read the Script to grasp the nature of eschatological consummation. In doing so they are also aiming to ascertain the identity of the performance that they will repeat with an *ipse* identity through improvisation, in order that they carry on their through-line in a way that is fitting both to the drama so far, and the current context. From what we have seen of Vanhoozer's approach, the ultimate aim is to improvise on the performance of Jesus in order to produce a fitting performance in our current contexts that seeks to carry on our through-line towards eschatological consummation.

This is all good and well regarding the task of the church in following Jesus, but, a significant issue in the drama from the fall onwards is that humans are incapable of performing *imago dei* on their own. In response to this problem, Vanhoozer, in a thoroughly Trinitarian fashion, explores the role of the Holy Spirit in the performance of the travelling company of actors.

Vanhoozer is traditional in the sense that he believes in the "inspiration" of Scripture as "*a matter of the Spirit's prompting the human authors to say just what the divine playwright intended.*"[124] The Spirit was thus at work both in the writing of the "Script" and in the formation of the canon. Following on from this, the Spirit then hands on the Script to the next generations as well as aiding them in attempting to perform it correctly. Thus, in the same way that the Spirit ministered to Jesus in his embodiment of the temple of God, post-ascension, the Spirit ministers Christ to his followers as they become the temple where the Spirit of God dwells.

Vanhoozer is quick to guard against the idea that the Spirit may add to the Script when he argues, "The Spirit is active not in producing new illocutions but rather in *ministering* the illocutions that are already in the text, making them efficacious."[125] Later he states, "The drama of doctrine consists in the Spirit's directing the church rightly to participate in the evangelical action by performing its authoritative script."[126] Based on this we may say that the Spirit's role is to aid in the translation of the Script and to give vision and inspiration for a right performance by the church in whatever context it finds itself in. It is therefore the aim of the Spirit to enable the continuation of *ipse* identity, whilst inspiring improvisation that leads to a fitting perfor-

---

"Socio-Pragmatic" "strands" of hermeneutics, in chapter 10. Although the context of Thiselton's discussion here is not identical with that of Vanhoozer's, the way in which Thiselton refers to "transcontextuality" would equally fit with Vanhoozer's system.

124. Vanhoozer, *Drama of Doctrine*, 227.
125. Ibid., 67.
126. Ibid., 102.

mance. From a Pentecostal perspective, what is worth noting is Vanhoozer's opinion that "The Jerusalem Council (Acts 15) surely ranks as one of the highlights in the history of the church, and of contextualization."[127] He thus seems to affirm it as a good example of how the church was open to the prompt of the Spirit whilst seeking to perform in a new context.

From what we have briefly explored above, Vanhoozer attempts a hermeneutical methodology that maintains a high view of Scripture by viewing it as God's speech-act to be taken as the script for the church to follow. In doing so he also maintains a critical realist approach to this Script that negotiates between pure objectivism and nihilism. The community, and in particular the theologian, is thus tasked with both looking at the Script for direction, as well as being aware of the way the Script has been performed in the past, whilst enquiring how it may be performed afresh and become meaningful in the present context. In addition to this, rather than being distant and abstract, Vanhoozer maintains that God is working via his Holy Spirit to inspire, and guide the actors as to how to understand the Script and how to perform it fittingly in their present context.

The question remains then, what is there to be gained from a dialogue between this approach of Vanhoozer's and the approaches of Thomas and Archer? It is to this question we now turn.

A "Dramatic" Pentecostal Hermeneutical Methodology

We may recall that both Thomas and Archer were aiming to navigate a path that maintains a high view of Scripture, whilst giving significant weight to the experience of the reader and reading community in its interpretation of Scripture. We may also recall that both seemed to favor (explicitly or implicitly) placing final authority with the community. What then does Vanhoozer's approach have to say to this?

Primarily, my suggestion is that Vanhoozer's use of speech-act theory and the critical realist approach that he maintains towards the text, shows the importance of maintaining authorial intent, and using all necessary methods to gain as thick a description as possible of what that may be.[128] Although the accusation of Thomas and Archer in response may be that this just supports the outdated historical-critical model, Vanhoozer's critical realist approach navigates around this issue by allowing for the subjectivity of the reader, but not allowing this to rule. Nor does it attempt to second guess what was going on in the mind of the human author. The

---

127. Ibid., 319.

128. This therefore also involves examining the "discourse meaning."

result is that a high view of Scripture as "script" can be maintained, whilst allowing for the fallenness and subjectivity of the community as it seeks to perform *imago dei*.

A further important feature of this approach is that rather than collapsing the distance between the text and the community into a single point of meaning, the two contexts are maintained, something that Archer seemed reticent to do. This upholds the importance of the context of the reading community, whilst allowing space for the original context to be acknowledged, thus reducing the chance of misinterpretation and misperformance. Two big challenges that this poses to a Pentecostal hermeneutic—Archer's in particular—that affirms an overarching "Latter Rain" narrative are, firstly, the legitimacy of such a narrative, and secondly, the rather narrow view of tradition on which it is based. We shall deal with these in turn.

To maintain a Latter Rain motif involves reading into the Script something that the community may like to believe and something that they think provides meaning for their experiences but, ultimately, something that I do not think the Script substantiates. To take such a position simply reinforces the point about the community being the center of authority regarding understanding and directing right living and belief as a Christian. My suggestion is that such a view cannot be maintained by those who claim a high view of Scripture and look to the revelation of Christ in Scripture to provide direction for right belief and practice. Instead, what I am suggesting here is that Vanhoozer's dramatic hermeneutical method can place authority back where it belongs, but take into account the experience and contexts of the reader and reading communities. To do this though also requires a wider view of tradition.

As Vanhoozer highlights, the term "tradition" stems from the word "*tradere*" meaning "to hand on."[129] Tradition is thus about examining the reception and performance of the Script in church history to determine those performances that are more authentic than others, and to learn from those performances—Catholic and none. It is, after all, reception after reception that has led to the beliefs currently maintained, as none of us exists in a vacuum. In the light of this, if Pentecostalism can adopt a hermeneutical approach such as Vanhoozer's, then a study of the performances that follow the closing of the canon may provide fresh insight into how their performances should look, as well as re-framing their place within that history. This latter point is particularly relevant to Archer as he sees the importance of understanding the place of Pentecostalism within the unfolding narrative (or in this case, drama) of salvation history.

---

129. Ibid., 152.

A Dramatic Pentecostal/Charismatic Anti-Theodicy

Many Pentecostals, including Thomas and Archer, may be reticent to take such suggestions as are presented here on board, as it risks crushing the importance of experience and the work of the Holy Spirit within that. However, a further suggestion is that the concept of drama may fit well within the Pentecostal camp. The reason for this is that the dramatic view advocated here can, I suggest, do many of the things found in Thomas' and Archer's hermeneutics, whilst avoiding the pitfalls.

Firstly, a dramatic approach is an extremely helpful metaphor for living as a Christian, as it is not a dry, cerebral approach that crushes experience. In fact, as has been emphasized above, there is great emphasis on understanding the context and the Script and *doing (draō)* Christianity, albeit it in a *fitting* manner. The following of Christ is something to be performed, and the stage on which we find ourselves has to be examined and placed in conversation with the Script, other actors and the Holy Spirit so that we can ascertain what a fitting performance looks like. A dramatic approach can value experience and the living out of Christianity whilst maintaining a high view of scripture. Both Thomas and Archer place a high level of importance on involving the community in the interpretation process, and the dramatic model maintains that by listening to the experience of the community in order to develop what a fitting performance will look like in specific contexts. With regard to Archer's hermeneutics in particular, having the community involved in working out what a fitting performance is, means that they are involved in bringing latent meanings to life. The difference is that the dramatic approach does not have to compromise the authority of Scripture in doing so, or, collapse the distance between the community and the text.

Secondly, as the plurality of genres in the Script is respected and maintained, cold propositionalism is avoided and instead, a script that caters for all moods of life and all types of performance is used. This enables a greater interaction between the cast and the Script as there is always a section of script, and previous acts in the drama, that provide a sense of direction and empathy for current actors. This means that current actors do not have to see the Bible as just about rules, but about a drama, of which they are a part, that a script is in existence for, and of which previous performances have been done and can be learned from.

Thirdly is the point that the form to be carried through in the performance of our own through-lines is Jesus Christ. The dramatic approach has Jesus as central and demands that those who wish to take part in the drama seek to improvise on the performance of Jesus in their current contexts, as the action moves towards eschatological consummation. Whether a "Fivefold" gospel is maintained within that is a discussion that rests outside this study, but, there would certainly be room for it with such a central place for

A "Dramatic" Pentecostal/Charismatic Hermeneutic

Jesus being maintained within this approach. In conjunction with the previous point, this does however question the Luke-Acts emphasis on entry into the text. With Christ as the performance we are to learn from and improvise on, a canonical reading method with a Christocentric entry into the text are the order of the day, rather than privileging one particular human author over the others. It would be expected that both Thomas and Archer can sympathize with this notion, as both are seeking to give credence to a canonically contextualized approach, and both hold a high view of Jesus. A Luke-Acts approach appears as further evidence for a community based authority on Biblical hermeneutics rather than a divine one, for the same reasons as the Latter Rain motif is suggested to be, above. And so, perhaps Vanhoozer's model can produce a revision of that practice.

A fourth point that potentially provides a connection is the work of the Holy Spirit within the dramatic hermeneutic. The Holy Spirit is still very much active in this methodology as the one who helps us to understand the Script and how to perform on the various stages, and the one who connects us to God in prayer. The Holy Spirit is also the one who ultimately ministers Christ to us to enable the performance of *imago dei* that we have been tasked with as the actors in the theo-drama. However, because the Holy Spirit cannot add anything to the Script, it is the Script as the divine speech-act that functions as that which all alleged manifestations of the Spirit are tested with, in order to discern the authentic from the false.[130]

As this chapter draws to a conclusion, what I am proposing is a Vanhoozian, dramatic, Biblical hermeneutical methodology that, due to the details of how it is practiced, resonates with and can be employed by Pentecostals without compromising central features that comprise what it is to be Pentecostal. I have sought to argue this point by showing that key features of the dramatic model run parallel to key features of John Christopher Thomas and Kenneth J. Archer's approaches, but, at the same time supersede such approaches by overcoming the highlighted pitfalls of them.

---

130. Vondey suggests that Vanhoozer's approach is "in essence a cognitive-linguistic performance of the canonical script that lacks an explicit kinesthetic dimension" and thus leaves little room for "the unexpected, unscripted, unutterable, and transforming work of God's Spirit" (Review of *the Drama of Doctrine*, 366). However, the point being made in this chapter is that if one is to maintain a high view of Scripture, then Scripture becomes the norming norm. To proceed with Vondey's approach is to replace the authority of Scripture as God's speech-act with the authority of a particular (which?) community, as the work of the Spirit (as noted above) must be interpreted, and thus determined as authentic or not, by the community. Vanhoozer's approach does not rule out a kinesthetic dimension per se, but instead puts in place guides for determining whether "unexpected" moments in performance really are the work of the Spirit.

A Dramatic Pentecostal/Charismatic Anti-Theodicy

With this methodology firmly in place we must now turn our attention back to the aim of this study: to provide Biblically rooted, systematic guidance for the production of a fitting Pentecostal/Charismatic performance in the face of seemingly innocent, meaningless suffering when God appears to be absent. This chapter has provided us with the hermeneutical tools with which to begin construction of this guidance. The task ahead of us is to apply these tools as we press on to achieve our aim.

5

Humans, Evil, and Suffering—A Theo-Dramatic Perspective

Introduction

IN FOLLOWING ON FROM the previous chapter, there are four steps that remain in order to answer the central research question and fulfill the aim of developing Biblically rooted, systematic guidance for the production of a fitting Pentecostal/Charismatic performance in the face of seemingly innocent, meaningless suffering when God appears to be absent. And, all of these steps are dependent on the hermeneutical method developed in the previous chapter. The first step is to clarify which act we currently find ourselves in, in order to bring to the fore the situation we are faced with regarding the existential realities of the problem of evil and suffering. This will provide clarity regarding the nature of the current context in order to assist in making the guidance for fitting performance, being constructed in this study, relevant.

The second step is to examine the divine perspective of, and response to, evil and suffering, as revealed in Scripture. The third step, of examining Jesus perspective of, and response to, evil and suffering, can then be developed in the light of this, as step two will provide the context that will enable the possibility of step three. In examining Jesus' perspective and response, we will be able to establish how he performed in situations comparative to the type of situations in question in this study, and thus provide a performance on which we can improvise. In the light of this we will then be in a

A Dramatic Pentecostal/Charismatic Anti-Theodicy

position to undertake the fourth step of providing guidance for our own fitting performances, and thus answer the central research question.

However, the second step brings with it a particular complexity—which also needs to be explored. This complexity is found in the fact that, part of God's response to suffering and evil involves drawing humans in to aid him in this. And further, it is only by examining the human response—particularly to seemingly innocent, meaningless suffering when God appears to be absent—that we will be fully able to examine Jesus' response, as I suggest that Jesus improvises on the performance of Israel in his performance.

These four steps are too great a task for the current chapter alone so the focus of this chapter will be firstly, clarifying which act in the drama we currently find ourselves in, and secondly, examining the divine perspective of and response to evil and suffering in Acts 1 and 2 of the drama. This second focus will also include examining God's intended role for humans in response to evil and suffering, looking particularly at how Israel—as the divinely appointed cast members—perform in times when the suffering seems innocent and meaningless and God appears to be absent. Exploring how Jesus improvises on such performances, and the provision of guidance for fitting performance in the current act, will have to wait until chapter 6.

In order to view evil and suffering from the divine perspective we must, according to the method laid out in chapter 4, return to the Script as God's speech-act. We must also interpret canonically, typologically and Christocentrically. However, in order to do that we must first look at Acts 1 and 2 of the drama before revisiting them again through the Christocentric lens provided by Jesus' performance in Act 3 (the task of the next chapter). In doing so it seems fitting to pick up and dialogue with some threads that were exposed in the "Anti-Theodicy" section of chapter 2, particularly those of Wright, Vanhoozer, and Brueggemann. In the cases of Wright and Vanhoozer, this is so because they appear the approaches most intent on taking a high view of Scripture in determining their understanding of evil and suffering. In the case of Vanhoozer the particular focus will be on his examination of evil in *Remythologizing Theology*. In the case of Brueggemann the focus will be on his exploration of the practice of lament in the life of Israel. We begin, however, by making ourselves familiar with where we are in the drama in order to fully appreciate the scenes for which we seek guidance for a fitting performance.

Humans, Evil, and Suffering—A Theo-Dramatic Perspective

The Drama We Are to *Fit* Into

We can recall that in the previous chapter the concepts of performance and fittingness were explored in order to enable the production of guidance for a fitting performance in the face of seemingly innocent, meaningless suffering in the current act of the drama. The aim is to *fit* into the action as it is unfolding using the Script to help us both understand the nature of eschatological consummation, and provide us with direction for our through-line. We must also read the Script canonically, typologically and with a Christocentric key, but, as Vanhoozer quite rightly points out, "To fit in rightly with the action, of course, one must first have some sense of what is going on."[1] We must further recall then that this is a five act drama of redemption. Humans, cast in Act 1, to perform *imago dei* on the cosmic stage in covenant with God, fail to give a fitting performance. From here onwards, the theo-drama follows plot twist after plot twist as the divine playwright keeps faith with his human actors and authors a drama in which they fail to overcome the hurdles that they encounter, and ultimately, fail to remove the evil and suffering entrenched in creation. As we reach Act 3, divine author turns divine actor in human form as he enters the stage to show and tell how the human actors should be performing, as well as remove the obstacles that prevent them from doing what they were cast to do. However, the overcoming of the obstacle that prevents fitting performance is completed, we are told, but the implementation of the defeat of that obstacle is firstly, part of the performance for which we are currently cast, and secondly, therefore as yet incomplete. We may add at this point that, following the Easter event, and therefore in the light of the Way of the incarnate Christ, part of our performance of *imago dei* is to perform, as we noted in chapter 2, what N. T. Wright has labeled an "inaugurated eschatology." By this he means, the inauguration of the redemption of creation, the arrival of the Kingdom in which the divine author will be all in all. Here in lies a problem and the crux of this study—what kind of performance are we to give when instead of experiencing the "now" of the inaugurated Kingdom, we innocently experience the "not yet" of the obstacles that, although defeated, have not had that defeat implemented upon them yet? And, in the light of chapter 3, what performance are we to give when healing does not work, Satan and his minions do not appear to be primarily behind the suffering, and the sufferer is bereft of meaning for their suffering? To return to our central research question: *What does it mean to produce a fitting Pentecostal/Charismatic performance*

---

1. Vanhoozer, *Drama of Doctrine*, 53.

A Dramatic Pentecostal/Charismatic Anti-Theodicy

in the face of seemingly innocent, meaningless suffering when God appears to be absent?

The Script and Evil

In order to begin to move towards answering this we must look afresh at how the Script describes evil and suffering, and how the divine playwright faces them. In chapter 2 we examined the various general approaches that have been made to evil and suffering by Christians in the scenes of the current act. In chapter 3 we examined the spectrum of Pentecostal/Charismatic responses. We also noted in both, the importance of a high view of Scripture and, apart from some notable exceptions, how most failed to actually maintain this in the outworking of their approaches. However, if we are to call this a *theo*-drama we must begin our approach by examining the divine perspective of, and response to, evil and suffering, in order to give us direction for our performances. To do this we look to the Script and to those scholars who have managed to maintain a high view of Scripture in their explorations regarding the problem of evil—in this case Vanhoozer and Wright.

The Drama of Evil

Vanhoozer states, "God does not author evil, yet evil nevertheless infiltrated the text of his world, and his hero."[2] He also claims that, "The biblical accounts suggest that there is a species of personal opposition to God that predates the human hero's revolt."[3] Following his approach laid out in *The Drama of Doctrine*, Vanhoozer describes God as a triune "being-in-communicative-activity" and as such is a being who does things through communication.[4] Of particular interest here is his belief that God authors his

---

2. Vanhoozer, *Remythologizing Theology*, 342. In reference to the concept of "hero" Vanhoozer writes "By 'hero,' Bakhtin has in mind a person 'about whom a story could be told'" (324). Vanhoozer is thus drawing on the work of Mikhail Bakhtin in his understanding of a hero. However, Bakhtin states, "A given human being is the condition of aesthetic vision; if he turns out to be a determinate object of that vision (and he always tends, and tends essentially, toward that), he constitutes the hero of a given work" ("Author and Hero," 230). For Bakhtin then, a hero is thus the human being who is the aesthetic focal point for the author. In this sense, Vanhoozer's use of Bakhtin does not do justice to Bakhtin as, for Bakhtin, it is not that a story *could* be told about a hero but that the hero is the focal point of the story. It is Bakhtin's understanding of hero that is employed in the present work.

3. Ibid., 343.

4. See chapter 4 of *Remythologizing Theology*, in particular 198–222. where Vanhoozer outlines what he has labeled a "post-Barthian Thomism."

heroes through speech and that via dialogue with them, which he initiates, the opportunity is placed before them to respond in such a way that will disclose and "consummate" their character—"dialogical consummation."[5] Also, following his Christocentric entry into a canonical, typological reading of Biblical texts, Vanhoozer reads the fall texts in the light of Jesus' statement about the devil being the "father of lies" (John 8:44), where "A lie is a misbegotten communicative act whose birth in words (what one claims as true) contradicts what one conceives (what one knows as false) and consequently misleads the one who hears it."[6] Thus, a contrast emerges between how God works and achieves his goals, and how Satan works. God communicates truth in such a dialogical fashion that his heroes can do nothing but disclose the truth of who they are in their response, whereas Satan manipulates via corrupt communicative agency to attempt to achieve his ends. "Liars do not communicate in the strict sense of the term ('making common'), then, for they take back with the left half of their forked tongue what they proffer with the right."[7] Where truthful dialogue shines light and discloses reality via response, a lie orients someone towards pretense, falsity and ultimately nothingness. With this in mind Vanhoozer states, "Satan has no positive communicative or causal force of his own. The serpent cannot compel Adam or Eve to disobedience but merely provide the occasion."[8] To return to the rules of speech-act theory, perlocution for the liar is impossible due to the lacking in aptness of the illocution.[9] This means that, "Satan can *do* nothing with words but gesture vainly."[10] But, Vanhoozer warns that, "One should no more dismiss Satan's pathological communicative agency, however, than ignore evil. For though it lacks positive being, nevertheless it is (paradoxically) there."[11]

As Satan "gestures vainly" under the guise of the serpent, Adam and Eve respond by doubting God's word, beginning their path towards nothingness and falsity under the delusion that they can be God-like. Sin is

5. Vanhoozer, *Remythologizing Theology*, 324–27.
6. Ibid., 343.
7. Ibid., 344.
8. Ibid.
9. Austin notes six conditions that need to be met in order for a speech-act to be "happy." However, by lying, Satan fails to meet the last two of these and so his speech-acts fall under the categories Austin labels as "Abuses" and "Insincerities." See Austin, *Things with Words*, 12–24.
10. Vanhoozer, *Remythologizing Theology*, 344. It is worth noting that Vanhoozer follows this comment with a footnote in which he points out that his position concurs with the idea of evil being the privation of being.
11. Ibid.

therefore opposition to the truth revealed through God as being-in-communicative-act and "a matter of using God's image (communicative agency in covenantal relation) to deface the original."[12] With the fall of humans a chain reaction begins in which the effects of this fall ripple throughout the creation that humans were scripted to tend and care for. "Satan is the key antagonist in the drama from beginning to end."[13] "What we see, at every level of creation, is Satanic powers attempting to subvert the Authorial intention."[14] Vanhoozer here follows the path of suggesting that it is not that anything that God creates is bad in itself, but more a case of, due to the entrance of sin and evil, what is good can and does get corrupted. This includes politics, ecology, biology etc. Nothing is left untouched by the fall of humans. However, central to the drama is who humans will choose to listen to and to who or what they will orient their heart, minds, souls and actions.

What is also important to note at this point is that Vanhoozer continues his call for allowing the canon to have multiple perspectives on subjects—in this case evil and suffering—and for the reader to "give a thick, multi-level description"[15] of the subject under investigation. His aim in his discussion on evil and suffering is to "take up the task not of solving the problem of evil but of deepening its mystery,"[16] as he suggests that "[a] theodicy provides a monological, theoretical view that does not solve but inadvertently contributes further to the problem of evil by remaining on the theoretical level."[17]

What is apparent from Vanhoozer's approach is that, firstly, the definition of evil must be anchored in the canon, as only God can objectively instruct on what (who?) evil is and does. Secondly, there is a reticence in Vanhoozer's approach to define evil too tightly. He is correct in suggesting that we are not told of origins or why evil came to be, and, that there is something very elusive and mysterious about the Satan figure and his minions. It is hard to place this character in the drama as, Vanhoozer seems to suggest, Satan *is*, in some sense but what he *does* is create opportunities for creation to tend towards non-being. There is then a sense that sympathy is to be had with the Augustinian concept of evil being the privation of the good, whilst not denying that Satan is a figure of some sort that stands behind it—as this is how Jesus seems to face Satan.

---

12. Ibid., 343.
13. Ibid., 354.
14. Ibid.
15. Ibid.
16. Ibid., 342.
17. Ibid., 350.

Humans, Evil, and Suffering—A Theo-Dramatic Perspective

The issue of free will is an important part of Vanhoozer's "Remythologizing" but time and space do not allow for a full discussion of this here. However, noteworthy is his apparent suggestion that the influx of evil and suffering into creation is due in part to the voice that the human actors *choose* to listen to, thus crediting its spread to some sort of free will on the part of the human actors. What is baffling, however, is that further along in his project Vanhoozer claims that God can make an effectual call (illocution) that has propositional content and is aimed at a particular perlocution of communion with the triune God, and that that perlocution can be guaranteed by the Holy Spirit. This seems to suggest that an actor who is met with an "effectual call" cannot say no. Is this really free will and why was this not the case with Adam and Eve? There are echoes here of the problems with the free will defense outlined in chapter 2, which suggests that although Vanhoozer, on the one hand, has wisely maintained some distance from attempting to "solve" the problem of evil, on the other, there are moments when this does not seem the case.

As stated in chapter 2, solutions are not my aim here as I do not think one would help even if it were achievable. However, what Vanhoozer suggests in the rest of his understanding of evil and suffering, outlined above, does seem helpful, if a little sparse in places. At this point we can draw on the work of N. T. Wright to add a little more substance.

Wright refers to three forms or levels of evil in the Old Testament in particular: "evil seen as idolatry and consequent dehumanization; evil as what wicked people do, not least what they do to the righteous; and evil as the work of the 'satan.'"[18] At the first level is what may be termed, the evil within. All humans from the moment of the fall experience the desire and consequent choice not to respond correctly to the voice of the divine actor—which is what evil is—and so there appears to be an absence of goodness where the image of the creator in the created is slowly defaced and removed. In connection to this first level, Wright states, "When we humans commit idolatry, worshipping that which is not God as if it were, we thereby give to other creatures and beings in the cosmos a power, a prestige, an authority over us which *we*, under God, were supposed to have over *them*."[19]

At the next level, there is systemic or corporate evil. Pushing Wright's definition further, not only is there evil experienced in what people do, in amongst a *group* of people that are experiencing a lack in goodness, there begins to emerge a lack of goodness that is somehow greater than the sum lack in the individuals. At this point it almost seems as if evil can take on

18. Wright, *Evil*, 23.
19. Ibid., 71.

A Dramatic Pentecostal/Charismatic Anti-Theodicy

a life of its own even without it necessarily consisting of anything. Thus the external evil experienced by way of suffering seems to come from both systemic evil and a created order with a wrongful distribution of power and authority. We can say that on set, the characters are either not following the Script, or, have exchanged parts with others, meaning that the drama does not play out as it was authored to do.

This leads to a third form that Wright refers to as "quasi-personal" and "supra-personal." It is beyond the personal and is neither fully personal nor apersonal. He states,

> The biblical picture of the satan is . . . of a non-human and non-divine quasi-personal force which seems bent on attacking and destroying creation in general and humankind in particular, and above all on thwarting God's project of remaking the world and human beings in and through Jesus Christ and the Holy Spirit.[20]

Like Vanhoozer, and in following that which is revealed in the canon, Wright stops short here of saying how this force appeared, or explaining the seeming crescendo in appearance throughout the Script.

Drawing these perspectives together we can say that the plot began to twist when the mysterious (anti) character called Satan began to try and bend and complicate it and drive the direction of the drama away from the divine author's intended path for it. We know not who authored this character, but, we know his chief weapon is a lie of which he authors many to tempt the heroes from the path that the divine author is calling them to. We can also say that the disobedience that the actors perform begins to corrupt them in such a way that an honest performance of their intended parts becomes impossible. The voice of the divine actor in the drama consummates this fact in dialogue, and as the drama speeds along the corruption builds.

As the rest of the set, background, and props depend on the human actors performing fittingly in their assigned roles, the inability of the actors to perform these roles sets the whole drama off balance, and nothing and no-one is left unaffected by this. As the human actors can no longer perform their parts correctly, a systemic level of corruption emerges. Behind it all stands the eerie figure of Satan, who created the opportunity for this corruption to emerge and continues still to create more opportunities for the corruption to continue.

If this is how the Script displays the emergence of evil and suffering in the drama, the natural progression from here is to ask what the divine author does in response.

20. Ibid., 70.

Humans, Evil, and Suffering—A Theo-Dramatic Perspective

A Divine/Human Response to Evil[21]

We must begin this section by restating the point that humans, prior to the fall, had been cast in the role of *imago dei*. We noted in the previous chapter that part of this role involved stewardship of creation. We also noted that as covenant partner with God, performing the role of *imago dei* involved being God's image bearer and representative to creation, which entailed both worshipping him—and him alone—as well as sharing with him power and responsibility for the future of the rest of his creation. To worship something other than him would lead to corruption in the created order. All this is said to prepare the ground for the fact that God's response to evil and suffering in the drama includes a role for those cast to perform *imago dei*.

As the results of the fall take effect, we approach Genesis 6 and discover that evil had reached such a level that, "the Lord was sorry that he had made humankind on the earth, and it grieved him to his heart," (v. 6). His attempted resolution at this point was to start the process again by wiping out "all flesh" with a flood, saving one family—Noah's—and a pair of all creatures. However, this too fails as, following the flood narrative, what we discover is that this attempted resolution seems not to have achieved the goal of destroying all evil (Gen 8:21). We are essentially at a near identical place in the drama as we were when Adam and Eve were banished from the Garden of Eden. The divine playwright's response to this is to re-establish a covenant with humans in a parallel way to that which was established with the original humans, with the added promise of never flooding the earth again. Essentially, Noah and family have become the new Adam and Eve and so take on the role of God's agents—it is they that are now tasked with performing *imago dei*.

As the drama moves on and the evil and suffering again rises, due to the promise God has made to Noah, a resolution must be found within humanity. The resolution that unfolds in Genesis 12 involves the creation of a nation through Abraham that will be chosen and blessed by God, that they might pass this blessing on (Gen 12:1–3). Abraham, followed by Israel, becomes the new agent as God affirms the covenant promise with each of Abraham's descendants (Gen 18:17–18; 22:17–18; 26:4–5; 28:14). As Middleton states, "The task entrusted to Abraham and his descendants is, narratively speaking, to aid in reconciling humanity to God and thus

---

21. In this section much credit needs to be given to both Wright and Middleton for their appropriations of Propp's and Greimas's work on plot analysis as both Wright and Middleton's work have proved exceedingly helpful in the development of this study. For further details see Wright, *New Testament*, chapter 3, and Middleton, "New Heaven," 77–86.

restoring humanity to its original purpose, by helping to remove or overcome the impediment of sin/violence."[22] The drama is one in which Israel, as agent, has been sent by God to remove all evil and corruption—both within herself, and, in the rest of creation—in order that humanity may carry on unimpeded to complete the objective it was set in the main story.[23] In dramatic terms, rather than draw the drama to a close as a disastrous tragedy, the playwright scripts a revised part for some of his human characters that not only involves them performing *imago dei*, but, also now involves combating the evil and destruction that seeks to subvert the plotline as part of that performance.

Throughout the rest of the Old Testament, Israel remains the chosen heroes to carry out the task at hand, but fails to produce a fitting performance. In order to aid her, God sends various helpers onto the stage throughout Act 2 in order to try and bring Israel back to the task with which she was commissioned. This begins with the performance of Moses, followed by the Judges, then the kings, who are also joined by the prophets—who attempt to bring failed kings, and the corrupt Israel under them, back into line.[24]

A pattern that emerges in the drama from the moment of the fall is one in which God seems to allow evil to go so far before he confronts it, judges it, stops it and sets about a new method for plot resolution, which always involves the human cast.[25] As Wright states, "The overarching picture is of the sovereign creator God who will continue to work within his world until blessing replaces curse, homecoming replaces exile, olive branches appear after the flood, and a new family is created in which the scattered languages can be reunited."[26] However, as the curtain falls on Act 2, it is clear that the actors are simply incapable of performing fittingly in their respective parts.[27] But, before we can move on to examine the divine actor's response to suffering and evil, we must examine a little closer the relationship between the company of actors known as Israel, and the divine playwright, particularly during times when Israel experienced seemingly meaningless, innocent suffering and God appeared to be absent. The reason for this examination is that it is the performance of Israel, in this relationship, that I will suggest Jesus improvises on in a non-identical repetitive manner when

22. Middleton, "New Heaven," 82–83.

23. Ibid., 82–84.

24. Ibid., 80. Middleton, in "Figure 2," offers a helpful diagrammatic explanation of the unfolding of the plot.

25. Wright, *Evil*, 25–29.

26. Ibid., 29.

27. Satan is perhaps the only character throughout the whole of the drama, excluding the divine actor, who manages to fulfill its part as expected.

Humans, Evil, and Suffering—A Theo-Dramatic Perspective

producing a fitting performance of his own, particularly in the midst of innocent suffering.

Innocent Suffering and the Performance of Lament

What may be noted from the previous sections in this chapter is that, in facing the evil and suffering in creation, God authored a script in which both he and his chosen company of actors had responsibilities as part of their relationship. These responsibilities, up to this point, have been subsumed under the phrase "covenant." It has also been noted that Israel, far from innocent, had evil dwelling within her, and so, did not always honor her side of the covenant. In these cases it is understandable as to why suffering was experienced. However, to focus again on the main point of this study, there were also times when Israel, or individuals within Israel, innocently experienced suffering, for no good reason. This experience was often further compounded by the apparent absence of the covenant partner who seemed not to be upholding his side of the relationship. What follows in this section examines how Israel responded when these instances occurred.

The primary focus here will be that of the Psalms, and the lament psalms in particular, as the sections of Scripture that most explicitly present Israel's responses to the situation of suffering in question. In an article entitled "Psalms and the Life of Faith: A Suggested Typology of Function," and then later in *The Message of the Psalms*, Walter Brueggemann, drawing on the work of Paul Ricoeur, developed a specific categorization or lens through which he viewed and grouped the Psalms in order to provide a way of understanding them.[28] His method involved grouping them into psalms of orientation, psalms of disorientation, and psalms of new-orientation/re-orientation.[29] This linear movement from orientation through disorientation to re-orientation, will be the categorization that I will use in what follows as an illustration of how Israel, more generally, transitioned through the times of suffering in question, and, how it maintained relationship with God in the midst of them.[30]

---

28. Brueggemann, "Psalms and Faith" and *Message of the Psalms*.

29. Brueggemann makes the point that "[t]he reorientation has both continuities with and discontinuities from what has been. But the accent is on the new. It is a surprise" ("Psalms and Faith," 6). Brueggemann, in his designation of this stage, seems to switch between "re" and "new," and from this statement one can see why. However, for the sake of clarity in my use of this paradigm, I will use "re-orientation," as I think that it best represents the dis/continuity tension that I agree is present, whilst removing the confusion that comes with swapping between two seemingly different terms.

30. Elsewhere, in a discussion surrounding the book of Job, Brueggemann splits

A Dramatic Pentecostal/Charismatic Anti-Theodicy

Based on this, I will explore the subject matter of this section in three sub-sections followed by a summary of the findings. In the first sub-section I will briefly look at "orientation." Lament as a part of the performance does not appear from nowhere, but is an intrinsic part of the covenantal relationship that the hero has with the playwright. Therefore, a brief account of the nature of this relationship and the place of the partners within it when it is functioning as it should, is necessary. This is before "the first move" takes place, which is the move from orientation to disorientation.[31]

The second sub-section—"disorientation"—encompasses the first move and the performance of lament that springs forth from this move when disorientation is realized and faced. I propose that it is within this performance of lament that a level of dialogical consummation takes place regarding the human actor's true view of his relationship with the Author. What will become clear as this chapter progresses is that the performance of lament as viewed from a Biblical perspective is pointless unless there is an end to it at some point, or at least belief on the part of the sufferer that a positive conclusion is possible. As will also become clear, its key function is to enable the actor/s to carry on their through-line as the drama is moved towards eschatological consummation.

Exit from any particular period of suffering is signified by way of "the second move," which brings forth hope and leads to "re-orientation." When the second move takes place within the various scenes in the drama, I suggest this provides a foretaste of the final move towards eschatological consummation.

Sub-section three—"re-orientation"—will look at the process of moving out of disorientation into re-orientation and how the performance of lament transitions to a performance of praise. What will become clear is that, although the process explored here is primarily understood as a linear movement, there is a sense in which it may, prior to arrival at eschatological consummation, also be understood as cyclic. This is so because whilst there is still evil within creation and epistemic distance between humans and creator, it is inevitable that periods of re-orientation will, at some point, give way to further periods of disorientation. However, rather than this simply becoming a vicious circle, it is hoped that there is movement forward in

---

Job into three sections (Job 1–2; 3:1—42:6; 42:7–17) and states, "This sequence nicely reflects the sequence of orientation/disorientation/new orientation that I have suggested for the Psalms some time ago" (*Theology of the Old Testament*, 489). As will be seen in what follows in this chapter, I concur with the wider use of this paradigm and also draw on Job in my examination of and use of it.

31. For diagrammatic illustration of the linear movement of Brueggemann's process, see *Message of the Psalms*, 21.

the relationship in the completion of each cycle. That said, a spiral acts as a better model of what actually occurs, since the drama is moved closer to eschatological consummation with each turn.[32] This spiral will be discussed further below and in the next chapter. We begin with "orientation."

"Orientation"

As stated above, the performance of lament does not exist in a vacuum and does not appear outside of a specific socio-historical context. In reference to the "Psalms of Orientation," Brueggemann writes, "Life . . . is not troubled or threatened, but is seen as the well-ordered world intended by God."[33] In this world we find a settled life in which God is known and trusted and relationship with him is clear. Belief that the system works is affirmed by the circumstances, and the parts to be played by the actors are clear and are performed in a fitting manner. According to Brueggemann, this structure of life is affirmed by such psalms as the "Songs of Creation" and "Songs of Torah."[34] Within these songs is reflected a faithful, sovereign, powerful God of love who was able to bring forth creation and provide Torah with which to give direction for Israel to follow in its performance. In his *Theology of the Old Testament*, Brueggemann describes the content of these and other descriptive, testimonial texts as "Israel's Core Testimony." This "is the speech to which Israel reverted when circumstance required its most habituated speech" and it is this testimony which dominated Israel's description, and understanding, of creation and its creator.[35] At this point it is necessary to clarify the understanding of covenant being used here.

Brueggemann appears to offer two aspects to his concept of covenant. On the one hand, it is deeply relational. It is "a relationship that matters intensely to both parties"[36] and as the initiator, "God . . . *wills* covenant, *makes* covenant, and *keeps* covenant."[37] Terence Fretheim emphasizes this relational aspect by arguing that, "Covenantal texts reveal that the relationship,

---

32. This concept is based on an idea by Goldingay suggested in a response written to Brueggemann. See Goldingay, "Dynamic Cycle"; and for Brueggemann's response, Brueggemann, "Response."

33. Brueggemann, *Message of the Psalms*, 25.

34. In the bracket "Songs of Creation" Brueggemann places Pss 145, 104, 33, and 8, and under "Songs of Torah" he places Pss 1, 119, 15, and 24. See *Message of the Psalms*, 28–42.

35. Brueggemann, *Theology of the Old Testament*, 122. See part 1 of this work generally for a more detailed description.

36. Brueggemann, "Prayer as Dance," 135.

37. Brueggemann, "Covenanting as Human Vocation," 153.

indeed an elective relationship, between God and Israel (or an individual) precedes the establishment of any covenant."[38] In this sense a relationship forms between the two parties before any formal, boundary clad "covenant" is established.

However, on the other hand, "this relationship, marked by awe and gratitude for its inexplicable generosity, brings with it the expectation and requirements of the sovereign who initiates it."[39] As James Dunn notes, in this sense "'Covenant' means simply 'agreement,' or, more formally, 'treaty' or 'contract.'"[40] Brueggemann concurs with this view and in one particular article has emphasized the "contractual theology" at the heart of Israel's covenant with Yahweh.[41] This contractual aspect involves adherence to Torah, which is given as guidance, thus providing direction and shape to what the covenant partner is to do. "The Torah . . . is the way in which creation has been ordered."[42] More than a mere human rule book, it describes the way the whole of life hangs together and therefore how to live in harmony with creation and its creator—it provides divine direction for fitting performance. "As Israel (and the world) is obedient to torah, it becomes free for praise, which is its proper vocation, destiny and purpose."[43] In Deut. 11, one of many notable examples within Scripture, there is a clear cause and effect philosophy present whereby application of the laws brings forth blessing and breaking of the laws brings forth curses.

In the light of these two aspects of covenant, which are to be held in tension, Brueggemann concludes that,

> if this relationship is indeed one of passionate commitment, as it surely is, it is undoubtedly the case (by way of analogy) that every serious, intense, primary relationship has within it dimensions of conditionality and unconditionality that play in different ways in different circumstances.[44]

He thus opts for what E. P. Sanders has termed "covenantal nomism" as "it subsumes law (*nomos*) under the rubric of covenant."[45]

---

38. Fretheim, *God and World*, 15.
39. Brueggemann, *Theology of the Old Testament*, 417.
40. Dunn, "Judaism and Christianity," 35.
41. Brueggemann, "Shape for Old Testament Theology I."
42. Ibid., 39.
43. Brueggemann, *Message of the Psalms*, 167.
44. Brueggemann, *Theology of the Old Testament*, 419.
45. Ibid., 419.

Robin Gill has aptly drawn parallels between this concept of covenant, and marriage—an analogy found throughout much of Scripture. He states, "whereas marriages lacking contracts can lead to injustice, marriages based solely upon contracts and without any covenantal love can result in joyless relationships."[46]

This covenant is also dialogical. "It is like an ongoing conversation: God speaks and Israel responds, Israel speaks and God responds."[47] As noted earlier, it is via communication that God consummates his hero. Brueggemann has described the relationship between these two parties as being like a dance where there is a deep trust that must exist between the two parties and where the choices and movements of one party will affect the other.[48] As well as trust there is also a freedom experienced. In this great dance, this view of life and creation, to experience true freedom is only possible if one is bound to God and his ways, as this is how humans were made, and is therefore what is best for them within God's creation. According to this core testimony, it is poor performance of the part in which one is cast that causes suffering to emerge.

The picture being painted here, although briefly and with broad strokes, is one of scenes in the drama where the Script is clear and the cast is performing as they were intended to. It is a picture of harmony. As can be noted in the creation texts, the divine playwright brings forth order from chaos, and there is order and structure to creation and a way scripted to perform fittingly in relation to God and his creation. To experience this is to experience "orientation."

However, what happens when the experience of those in covenantal relationship with God is one whereby this status of orientation slips away? There are, of course, multiple examples where individuals, and Israel as a nation, experienced this slippage due to what was very clearly their own fault.[49] However, this study is concerned with seemingly innocent, meaningless suffering. So, a reframing of the question should perhaps be: what happens when the experience of those in covenantal relationship with God is one whereby the status of orientation slips away, for no obvious reason, resulting in seemingly innocent, meaningless suffering? And further, what

---

46. Gill, "Health Care," 112.
47. Billman and Migliore, *Rachel's Cry*, 25.
48. See "Prayer as Dance" for more detail.

49. In the case of the Psalms this is most famously reflected in the so called "Penitential Psalms" (6, 32, 38, 51, 102, 130, and 143). For further details regarding prayers of confession and penitence, both inside and outside the Psalter, see Miller, *They Cried*, chapter 7.

do they do when the other partner in the covenant appears to be absent?[50] It is in answering these questions that we can make significant headway regarding constructing an answer to the central research question. This is so because the answer to these questions will provide details of the performances on which Jesus improvises. This, is turn, will provide details of the performance on which we are to improvise, and therefore enable the production of guidance for a fitting performance.

The issue central to these questions is the emergence of an apparent contradiction between belief and experience. To return to the paradigm that Brueggemann uses in *Theology of the Old Testament*, what is Israel (or an individual within the covenant community) to do when experience does not match up to the "core testimony"?

Examples of this existential question abound in the Old Testament, of which the book of Job is perhaps the archetypal one. Upon experiencing the various loss, pain and trauma that he does, Job's initial reaction, in the face of experience to the contrary, is to maintain the core testimony (Job 1:21; 2:9–10). Such a response does not last long however, and Job soon begins to question it whilst the part of its advocate is taken up by his friends. The concept of a contractual theology comes to the fore and Job is repeatedly encouraged to confess the sin that he clearly must have committed to deserve such punishment, so that sacrifices can be offered and forgiveness can be received. Job's response, however, is to point out that he has committed no sin worthy of such punishment. On the subject of the theology of Job's comforters, Gustavo Gutiérrez writes, "It is . . . a convenient and soothing doctrine for those who have great worldly possessions, and it promotes resignation and a sense of guilt in those who lack such possessions."[51] To return to the contradiction of belief and experience, it is easy for those, whose experience seems to match their belief, to ignore the testimony of one who may question this congruence, or worse, try and close such a voice

---

50. In conjunction with this question it is worth noting that non-penitential psalms significantly outnumber penitential ones. Fredrik Lindström has argued that in the "Individual Complaint Psalms," there is a distinct lack of evidence for linking sin and sickness. He also argues that it is in fact the absence of God, or God's hiddenness, that is the problem in these psalms. See *Suffering and Sin*, chapter 4, and 454–60.

Samuel Balentine, in his consideration of the hiddenness of God, also highlights the point that this hiddenness is not necessarily due to sin or disobedience. He notes, "God's hiddenness is not primarily related to his punishment for disobedience. It is not basically a reflection of man's inability to understand or even to perceive God's presence in the world. It is manifest in both these ways, but it is not restricted to them. It is rather an integral part of the nature of God which is not to be explained away by theological exposition of human failures or human limitations" (*The Hidden God*, 175).

51. Gutiérrez, *On Job*, 22.

down. One of the themes of Job is that he refuses to accept this approach and the oppression it brings but instead seeks relationship with God in spite of the clash between belief and experience. As Ellington notes, "In lament Job draws together what is and what should be, offering both to God in prayer."[52] In contrast, "The friends believe in their theology rather than in the God of their theology."[53] The result of this is that they try "to insulate and distance God (and themselves) from Job's pain by speaking correctly *about* God" but never *to* God.[54] This leads them to wield their theology as an oppressive battering ram rather than asking afresh what God is doing. The contractual element is thus given preference over the relational element of covenant to the point of idolatry, as the God they talk about is, as they discover, not an accurate representation of Yahweh.[55]

In a similar way, but on a much larger scale, there were occasions when the experience of Israel clashed with its beliefs at the hands of those outside her community. When in Egypt Israel was at the mercy of a "common theology" that sociologically defined justice in a certain way, and thus worked out the structures of its society accordingly.[56] Middleton states of the Egyptian system, "This oppressive social order, understood as the eternal expression of universal cosmic order, was legitimated by a pantheon of static gods of state and was mediated by the divine pharaoh, their son and image."[57] The core testimony said that Yahweh was the only true God and that Israel was his people. And yet, as the innocent party, they were suffering at the hands of the Egyptians for no good reason, whilst their all-powerful and all-loving God seemed absent. Orientation had slipped away begging the question:

---

52. Ellington, *Risking Truth*, 127.
53. Gutiérrez, *On Job*, 29.
54. Ellington, *Risking Truth*, 118; emphasis mine.
55. Brueggemann states, "The Much greater and more pervasive problem in ancient Israel is not a refusal to speak of Yahweh—that is, not a practical readiness to dismiss Yahweh as a factor in life, but the temptation to engage in *wrong* speech about Yahweh, which amounts to idolatry." He continues, "To speak wrongly about Yahweh—to bear false witness, to provide an inadequate construal of Yahweh—is to treat Yahweh as though Yahweh were one of the impotent, irrelevant idols that were all around Israel" (*Theology of the Old Testament*, 136). In a footnote connected to this, Brueggemann further adds, "what the canonical representation regards as false is an attempt to domesticate Yahweh, or to make Yahweh compatible to social control, i.e., to produce an idol" (ibid., 136n32).
56. For Brueggemann's definition of "common theology" and a discussion of Israel's interaction and wrestling with it, see Brueggemann, "Shape for Old Testament Theology I."
57. Middleton, "Creation Theology," 260.

A Dramatic Pentecostal/Charismatic Anti-Theodicy

does one turn a blind eye to the situation and continue to profess the core testimony with a level of denial and incongruence, or, is there an alternative? Ellington writes,

> When our beliefs collide with contradictory experiences, those experiences may be radically reinterpreted or even ignored entirely in order to sustain our beliefs. But there is a price to be paid for such alterations to experience, as cognitive dissonance grows between what we believe about God and the ways that we have access to him through experience.[58]

When the drama that is unfolding all around the actors is incongruent with the parts they are cast to perform, ignoring the chaos and suffering and carrying on regardless is not an option. As Ellington highlights, this kind of performance begins to drive a wedge between playwright and actor, and that, is unacceptable. Rejection of the covenant may not be an option, but highlighting and protesting about the incongruence between belief and experience is. It is in this slippage that the "first move" occurs. Orientation has given way to this incongruence, and as the first move proceeds, it can only lead to a state of disorientation.

"Disorientation"

With the state of orientation feeling like a distant memory, the transition away from it brings the first move to a halt in a state of disorientation. In what follows in this sub-section, we will begin by examining the context in which disorientation occurs. Having already had a glimpse of it in the breakdown of orientation and the first move, here we will clarify it further. Following on from this we will then examine the concept of memory, specifically its importance in periods of disorientation, as both a point of anchorage and fuel for lament. Thirdly, we will then examine the actual expression of the sufferer during this period, particularly looking at what form that takes and its justification.

Context

The context for the eruption of lament always involves suffering. We may define this suffering as the experience of some sort of pain or discomfort that indicates this is not the way life was intended to be. Of Israel's view of suffering in the Old Testament, James Crenshaw writes, "They understand

58. Ellington, *Risking Truth*, 13.

suffering as retributive, disciplinary, revelational, probative, illusory, transitory, or mysterious."[59] No matter which one of these is relevant to the specific situation, what is apparent is that it is not about theory but is about lived reality. What is also apparent from what we have seen of Israel's relationship to God so far is that, with a cause and effect style of relationship, if it were as simple as cause and effect, the cause of the suffering would be explored and discovered in order that a solution might be found to alleviate the suffering. However, with Job as an example, when one party suggests that suffering is due to a certain cause, presumption can be a dangerous trap that leads to misdiagnosis and further suffering. The point being made here is that although Crenshaw may be right, and I am sure he is, about the variety of ways that suffering was understood by Israel, what I suggest is more important to note is that such categorization is really only possible in retrospect.[60] Claus Westermann notes, "For the poet of the Book of Job there is no such thing as thoughts about suffering, or reflective suffering; for him there is only real, experienced suffering."[61] What we are considering here, in examining the context of disorientation, is this real, experienced suffering, and it is a suffering which appears to be innocent and meaningless in which belief and experience contradict one another.

Brueggemann writes that "The entire literature of the Old Testament, since the Exodus narrative, concerns the interface of God and social justice."[62] This, to Brueggemann, therefore involves the question of theodicy as theodicy in his understanding is about the sociological, context specific, manifestation of God's person and justice amongst his people. Brueggemann argues, "that every theodic settlement (including its religious articulation) is in some sense the special pleading of a vested interest."[63] The point being that everyone maintains and lives out a theodicy. The theodical view within the social structures of periods of orientation was a stable, ordered, cause and effect one that maintained order in the world of Israel and was reflected in the core testimony. With the move into disorientation there is much to be questioned about this model. If the core testimony is true, then surely the sufferer must have done something wrong. If the sufferer is innocent, is the core testimony reliable? If it is not reliable, has the covenant been misunderstood, or worse, has the nature of the divine partner been misunderstood?

---

59. Crenshaw, "Introduction," 4.

60. And even then knowledge of whether correct categorization has been applied is limited due to the general limited knowledge of humans.

61. Westermann, *Structure of Job*, 32.

62. Brueggemann, "Theodicy," 5.

63. Ibid., 7.

A Dramatic Pentecostal/Charismatic Anti-Theodicy

Referring back to the story of Job, the former of these approaches is offered by his alleged friends, whilst Job pursues the questions surrounding the trustworthiness of the covenantal God he believes in.[64] His friends begin to categorize the situation, claiming to know the mind of God via the now static, absolutized, contractual theology and Job questions the legitimacy of that particular theodic stance. The result of this is that, "The ancient equation between blessing and good fortune, which is fundamental to the Old Testament, is shattered for Job."[65]

In the lament psalms, as with Job, "*Israel is profoundly aware of the incongruity between the core claims of covenantal faith and the lived experience of its life.*"[66] At this point of disorientation, "The issue of theodicy in Israel is the acute awareness that the promises of the covenantal sanctions were not kept."[67] Not only is the suffering innocent and meaningless but the one with who Israel is in relationship, the all-powerful, all-loving, faithful God, seems to have neglected his side of the covenant and mysteriously hidden himself from the sufferer. As we will see below, this not only brings forth questions of trust but also suggestions that God is someone who may be an enemy.

What is apparent from this brief exploration is that the context of the disorientation being discussed in this study is one in which the faith of the sufferer, which is expressed in the core testimony, is being questioned by their experience. There is neither rhyme nor reason for the suffering. It is unrelenting and worse, the covenant partner appears to be absent and potentially untrustworthy. The irresolvable issue of theodicy hangs in the air and a context emerges that demands questions be asked of all parties involved, including enemies and, primarily, God.[68] This is the context in which lament erupts. Rather than always being silently on the receiving end, lament "shifts the calculus and *redresses the distribution of power* between the two parties, so that the petitionary party is taken seriously and the God who is addressed is newly engaged in the crisis in a way that puts God at risk."[69] The "embrace of pain" that Brueggemann notes, interrupts the idolatry of "contractual theology," and the mismatch between the dominant core testimony and the painful experience of the present is brought to the fore with a view to opening up new possibilities for the sufferer and the future of

---

64. Mjaaland notes, "According to the principle of retribution common in the Near East, Job's suffering must have been a result of sin, either his own or that of his ancestors" ("Fractured Unity," 102).

65. Westermann, *Structure of Job*, 89.

66. Brueggemann, *Theology of the Old Testament*, 378.

67. Ibid,. 385.

68. As noted above, sometimes God is addressed as the enemy.

69. Brueggemann, "Loss of Lament," 101.

the relationship.⁷⁰ This embrace of pain, resulting in a vocalized challenge to the core testimony, is what Brueggemann has labeled "countertestimony," and leads to a "cross-examination" of the core testimony.⁷¹

Before we can examine the expression of countertestimony and cross-examination in the form of lament that pours forth from this context, we need first examine the concept of memory in the life of Israel due to its importance in providing fuel for lament and anchorage during lament.

Memory

We have already seen that the presence of covenant is of the utmost importance to Israel and in particular to understanding the state of disorientation and the ensuing performance of lament. Covenant becomes prominent once again when we explore the place of memory in periods of disorientation. Brueggemann suggests, "When we have completely forgotten our past, we will absolutize the present and we will be like contented cows in Bashan who want nothing more than the best of today."⁷² Whereas the dominance of the core testimony and, in particular the contractual aspect of covenant, were used by Job's friends in attempting to close down his protests of innocence, loss of the story of the relationship between Israel and Yahweh, that is embedded in the core testimony, results in present experience becoming the dominating factor. The way that this is allowed to occur is through the loss of memory. Brueggemann's point is that when we forget where we came from, we lose sight of where we were going, and what is present becomes all there is.

As we have seen, the drama that is unfolding has a past in which a plot was developing, and this plot centered on the ever evolving relationship between the divine playwright and all that he created within his drama. And further, this plot is going somewhere. It has an aim of eschatological consummation, which will be brought about by the actors and the playwright in their carrying on of their through-lines. Therefore, to prevent absolutization of the present, which causes the drama to grind to a halt, what is encouraged is a dialogue between the memory and tradition of the history of the covenant, and the full experience and acknowledgement of "the present reality of pain."⁷³ As Brueggemann states, "It is the interaction of remembered text

---

70. Brueggemann, "Shape for Old Testament Theology II."

71. See Part II of *Theology of the Old Testament* for an in depth discussion regarding the use of countertestimony in the process of cross-examining Israel's core testimony.

72. Brueggemann, *Hopeful Imagination*, 102.

73. Ibid., 99.

and the present pain that form the matrix out of which comes new speech."[74] As we will see below, memory serves to create new possibilities within the performance of lament that mean lament is not the end but is instead a vehicle through the period of pain and suffering. But how does it do this?

The primary reason why memory is so important is because it situates those that remember in the present within a particular view of history. It acts as an anchor. To remember is to acknowledge one's place in an unfolding narrative that has a past and will have a future. Memory of this past, combined with the concept of the unfolding of the drama of salvation that Israel was so rooted in, meant that as memory was awakened of the past acts of Yahweh, and the promises of what Yahweh would do in relationship with Israel to unroll the future of the drama, Israel could draw on this to provide fuel for lament and for hope. In contrast to this, "People without historical sense and a proper practice of tradition are so bound in the 'eternal now' that they finally end in despair."[75]

In an article entitled "The Formfulness of Grief," Brueggemann compares and contrasts the Old Testament lament tradition with the approach of a leading expert on grief, Elizabeth Kübler-Ross.[76] In this comparison Brueggemann highlights the point that Israel's approach is embedded in a history that has a future, whereas Kübler-Ross's approach is not so well anchored: "Israel's speech presumes a history of interaction, of speaking and hearing which gives life. In urban consciousness, loss must be faced without history and so instead of covenantal address there is denial."[77] Israel's memory of the story so far provides the promise of a hope-filled future as the grounding for lament and a healthy path through grief. Kübler-Ross's approach can provide no such grounding.

As we will see below when we explore the details of the expression of lament, once memory is in place as anchorage, it then provides fuel for the lament and encourages a sense of power in the one who feels powerless. Writing about Ps 22 Cynthia Rigby argues, "It is because he [the lamenter] recognizes himself as a subject in relation to God and subsequently in

---

74. Ibid.

75. Ibid., 123. In his work on memory and liturgy, in which he draws on modern science to explore how the brain works, Atkins states, "Without a memory there can be no liturgy. Without a liturgy there can be no memory of God for the people" (*Memory and Liturgy*, 24). His research appears to affirm the importance of repetitive liturgy in order to anchor one in the story that the liturgy provides a memory of. This therefore supports the emphasis placed on memory and liturgy in Israel's history.

76. Brueggemann, "Formfulness of Grief." For Kübler-Ross's approach, see Kübler-Ross, *Death and Dying*.

77. Brueggemann, "Formfulness of Grief," 269.

relation to his context of oppression that the psalmist has power even when he perceives himself to be powerless."[78] In this and many other lament psalms the sufferer reminds God of past acts and in doing so brings memories into the present. By doing this the sufferer becomes aware of a God who has moved in a salvific way previously and therefore can move in a salvific way again. The interruption of the suffering of the present with this salvific memory gives the lamenter energy and hope to press on in their cries to God in the belief that the God who has heard and acted previously, can and will hear and act again. Johann Baptist Metz refers to such memories as "dangerous memories" and describes them as an "expression of eschatological hope."[79] This is so, he argues, since a dangerous memory "threatens the present and calls it into question because it remembers a future that is still outstanding."[80]

In spite of the positive value of memory when in the state of disorientation, there is also the danger of memory being used wrongly, which in turn can lead to further suffering. Paul Hanson, in his exploration of Second Isaiah, highlights in particular how the misuse of memory by Israel had done just this.[81] In this period of exile Yahweh commanded that Israel should remember their history whilst forgetting the old things, as Yahweh was doing something new (Isa 46:8–9; 43:18). Hanson negotiates this apparent contradiction by suggesting that Israel was to remember their "historical ontology"—the unfolding of their being and becoming—but not ritualize for the sake of rituals, as this brings stagnation.[82] In this sense they should forget and be ready for Yahweh to do something new. Hanson states, "The past is to inspire openness to new inbreakings of grace, not slavish imitation of past forms removed from their ontic roots and vulnerable to regressive, elitist myths and ideologies of domination."[83] What Hanson is suggesting here, can link with the dangers of presumption highlighted by Farah in chapterchapter 3, and the concept of improvisation and non-identical repetition proposed by Vanhoozer in chapter 4. The quest was for Israel to seek to remember who Yahweh is, who they are in relation to Him, and the promises made regarding how they would interact with one another. And all this could only be done by recounting previous acts in the drama, and looking for ways to improvise on those performances whilst allowing room for Yahweh to do likewise. To do

78. Rigby, "Someone to Blame," 96.
79. Metz, *Faith in History*, 184.
80. Ibid., 200.
81. Hanson, "Divine Power."
82. Ibid., 182–83.
83. Ibid., 183.

this is to anchor oneself in the drama, be open to fresh action by God, and to navigate away from presumptuous attitudes that can blind one to what God wants to do. In this sense care must be taken regarding how memory can be absolutized in the present.

If we transfer this theme into the context of lament that comes forth from a period of suffering experienced by an individual, the same theory holds true. Remembering that God moved in the past during periods of suffering, that he can do it again, and that he has promised covenantal faithfulness, whilst also being free from presumption regarding what the fresh move of God may look like, opens the future up to new hope. The removal of presumption, and the openness to improvisation regarding what the next move in the relationship between God and the sufferer may entail, enables maintenance and continuation of the relationship whilst opening up space for fresh, salvific acts of God.

With the importance of context and memory when in the state of disorientation in place, we can now move on to examine the actual performance of lament that pours forth in this state.

Expression

The single most important point to be noted about the expression of lament is who the lament is expressed to. As can be gathered from the content of this chapter so far, the context for lament always involves the covenantal relationship between actor and playwright, and therefore the sufferer always addresses God. Linking in with the importance of memory Brueggemann notes, "Prayer is direct address to and conversation and communion with, an agent known from a shared, treasured past."[84] From the time of oppression in Egypt that brought forth a cry to God from the people, "the 'call of distress,' the 'cry out of the depths,' that is, the lament, is an inevitable part of what happens between God and man."[85] To lose lament results in "the loss of genuine covenant interaction."[86] To allow for and give space for lament "makes an assertion about God: that this dangerous, available God matters in *every* dimension of life."[87] And thus, "The passionate prayers of lament and protest assume that God can be affected, that God is vulnerable to the cries and questions of the afflicted."[88] Therefore, in the light of the "context"

---

84. Brueggemann, "Psalms as Prayer," 34.
85. Westermann, *Praise and Lament*, 261.
86. Brueggemann, "Loss of Lament," 102.
87. Ibid., 106.
88. Billman and Migliore, *Rachel's Cry*, 113.

section above, expression of lament is always directed towards God because he is the covenant partner and therefore has responsibility to uphold his side of the covenantal relationship. If the situation of the sufferer is such that the suffering being experienced may be thought to result from wrong action on the part of God, who else should protest be directed at?

At this point a specific definition of lament is called for. In his work on the Psalms Brueggemann defines lament as "a painful, anguished articulation of a move into disarray and dislocation. The lament is a candid, even if unwilling, embrace of a new situation of chaos, now devoid of the coherence that marks God's good creation."[89] As medical doctor Barry Bubb suggests, "Simply stated, a lament is an expression of suffering, a crying out of pain—physical, emotional, and spiritual."[90] In addition to this, we may agree with Billman and Migliore when they state, "Intense pain . . . borders on the inexpressible, and our resources to speak of it are sparse."[91] Their response to such an experience is that, "The prayer of lament is the language of the painful incongruity between lived experience and the promises of God. Without it we would be left speechless and hopeless in the midst of affliction."[92] What we may say from these definitions is that lament is voiced expression of pain experienced in relationship with, and directed at, God, and it pushes language as description and expression to its absolute limits. We can also say, with Balentine, that, "lament expresses what one actually feels in the throes of suffering, not what tradition or the canons of orthodoxy propose that one ought to say."[93]

To explore the concept of expression further it is worth employing a framework used by a variety of scholars to great success when looking at lament in the Old Testament. The structure of this framework, generally, is as follows:

i. Address

ii. Complaint

iii. Confession of Trust

iv. Petition

v. Vow of Praise.[94]

---

89. Brueggemann, *Message of the Psalms*, 20.
90. Bubb, *Communication Skills*, 102.
91. Billman and Migliore, *Rachel's Cry*, 105.
92. Ibid., 107.
93. Balentine, *Prayer in Hebrew Bible*, 150.
94. Billman and Migliore, *Rachel's Cry*, 27. See also Westermann, *Praise and Lament*, 52 and 170. Brueggemann, who, building on Westermann's work, makes some adjustments in form, still retains a similar structure. See Brueggemann, *Message of the*

A Dramatic Pentecostal/Charismatic Anti-Theodicy

This framework holds as a general rule but the order varies and the presence of various sections of it alters depending on the individual context. As Brueggemann notes, "It will be understood that no single psalm follows exactly the ideal form, but the form provides a way of noticing how the psalm proceeds."[95] However, in what follows we shall use it as a framework for examining how lament is expressed.

Address

As stated above, lament is directed at God and, as Westermann highlights, involves expression about any combination of three specific parties—self, God, and enemies—and how they are or are not interacting with one another.[96] In specific reference to Ps 109 Brueggemann states, "the speech is an opportunity for realism that gives freedom of expression to those raw edges in our life that do not easily submit to the religious conviction we profess on good days."[97] To restate a re-occurring theme, the address occurs within the context of the covenantal relationship and in the light of the experience and history of that relationship. As Brueggemann notes, "The complaint is not spoken by one who is a stranger to Yahweh, but one who has a long history of trustful interaction."[98] God is seen as transcendent and therefore understood, as Rigby states, as "a God who is distinct from human beings and in some sense has the power to influence human circumstances."[99] However, this God is also understood as immanent, present and deeply interested in the life of his people to the point where they appear to be able to affect him. As R. W. L Moberly suggests, "How people respond to God *matters* to God, and *affects* how God responds to people."[100] This is the seemingly irresolvable paradox of a God who is both "above the fray" and "in the fray."[101] When a prayer of lament is uttered it is done with the assumption "that

---

Psalms, 54–56; and Brueggemann, "From Hurt to Joy," 70.

95. Brueggemann, *Message of the Psalms*, 54.
96. Westermann, *Praise and Lament*, 169–94.
97. Brueggemann, *Message of the Psalms*, 85.
98. Ibid., 54.
99. Rigby, "Someone to Blame," 80.
100. Moberly, "'God is Not a Human,'" 115.
101. These are expressions coined by Brueggemann in the light of work by Brevard Childs and Norman Gottwald. See Brueggemann, "Shape for Old Testament Theology I," particularly 28–32, and "Shape for Old Testament Theology II."

God can be affected, that God is vulnerable to the cries and questions of the afflicted."[102]

A God who is totally transcendent is a disinterested one that has little room for interactive relationship. To this God there seems little point in lamenting. On the other hand, a God who is fully immanent may be a God who is deeply interested in the lives of his people but is at the same time unable to offer any real help beyond human capacity.[103] Neither of these is the God addressed in Scripture but instead, the God addressed there can be addressed *because* he is believed to have the capacity to change things, but, at the same time, *because* he is in faithful, loving relationship with his people and is both deeply interested and deeply affected by their state. This is the God addressed with the cry of lament. It is a voiced desperation to the loving life partner of this people.

Complaint

As would be expected by the title of this section, lament commonly involves a specific articulation of the problem that has led to the suffering being experienced. As was stated above, the content of this articulation usually involves self, God, or an enemy, or any combination of the three, but is always addressed to God.

When talking of self, this is often via descriptive language of the physical, emotional, psychological and spiritual state of the lamenter. It is worth noting that these are often intertwined or shown to have influences on each other. This shows the sufferer's belief that to be human is to be an integrated whole, and that when one area of life is affected, the whole of life is affected. It also shows that all areas of life are equally important and are therefore equally important to God.

When the sufferer addresses God as the source of the problem, no stone is left unturned in the descriptions of how they are feeling. These feelings range from abandonment and rejection right through to deception and rage, and description of them often contains some strong accusations against God. Complaint also involves a significant amount of questioning. Patrick Miller notes,

> When one is in distress and trouble, the questions that always come roaring to the forefront of the mind and heart—and here

---

102. Billman and Migliore, *Rachel's Cry*, 113.

103. This restates a point made in chapter 2 above regarding problems that emerged with the theology of some anti-theodicy proponents. See the "Critical Reflection" "On the Nature and Role of God" in the "Anti-Theodicy" section of chapter 2.

A Dramatic Pentecostal/Charismatic Anti-Theodicy

articulated in prayer—are "*Why* is this happening?" or, to God, "*Why* are you doing this (letting this happen, etc.)?" and the complaining query, "*When* is this going to end?" or "*How long* do I have to endure this suffering?" The complaint to God in these prayers thus gives voice to the most fundamental of human questions when life is threatened and falls apart.[104]

These kinds of questions suggest that many experiences described in the Biblical narrative are ones that lasted for prolonged periods of time. It is worth noting again the importance of the context of relationship in which the complaint is made to God. As Westermann highlights, "never do they condemn God, for the utterances are never objective statements. They always remain personal address."[105] Lament is never the production of a theodicy. Instead, it is always about face to face confrontation in the context of relationship, where honesty rules and the soul of the lamenter is laid bare before God.

When lament is addressed to God about enemies, the vigor with which it is done is no less powerful. Again, with this the lamenter holds nothing back in description or feeling, but instead is quick to point out all details. These details often include who the enemy is and what they are doing, as well as how this is affecting the one lamenting. The complaint is always addressed to God because, as stated above, it is believed that God has the capacity to affect the situation, and more than that, *should* affect the situation. Because of this, when lament is done towards God about a third party, there is often a complaint about the problems and emotions caused by God's lack of intervention, or even, in some cases, the kind of intervention carried out.[106] The case of complaint to God about an enemy is given extra

---

104. Miller, *They Cried*, 72. The question, "How long?" is found in Pss 6:3; 13:1–2; 35:17; 62:3; 74:10; 79:5; 80:4; 89:49; 94:3. The question, "Why?" is found in Pss 10:1; 22:1; 43:2; 44:23–24; 74:1, 11; 88:14.

105. Westermann, *Praise and Lament*, 177.

106. In cases such as this the lamenter may feel somehow short changed if retribution or revenge is not carried out in the way or to the degree expected. For a detailed overview of complaint in the psalms in particular, but also in the rest of the Old Testament, see Miller, *They Cried*, 68–86. Bauer suggests that "lament is a mode of dealing with suffering that may suspend an arbitrary desire to 'annihilate enemies,' handling the hatred towards them and easing the conflict by opening up an eschatological horizon" ("Enquiring into Absence," 26). Although this may well be true, and I would argue that it is, it would seem to be stretching the evidence to suggest that this was the reason why the various biblical lamenters engaged in this particular type of lament. My argument would be that they whole heartedly desired retribution and revenge (hence their possible feelings of disappointment if this desired divine action was not undertaken), but, in vocalizing this, they unknowingly opened up the way for the possibilities that Bauer suggests. Pembroke argues, "Psychological research indicates that simply venting anger

force because the lamenter commonly believes the enemy to not only be their enemy, but, due to the covenantal relationship with Yahweh, to also be the enemy of Yahweh.

In sum,

> The complaining person is one who treats his or her troubles as serious and legitimate and not to be accepted as normal. The complaining person refuses silence and resignation, but rather issues a vigorous and shrill protest grounded in the covenantal right to be granted well-being and to be taken seriously.[107]

In following on from the vocalization of the problem via complaint, petition of God is commonly not far behind. However, before we discuss petition, a brief word must be said about the next section of the expression of lament—the vow of trust.

Vow of Trust

The vow of trust, sometimes found amidst the complaint and petition in lament, particularly in the Psalms, is further evidence of the depth of relationship that exists between the two parties. Middleton argues, "The genre of lament is predicated on the expectation that God can and will rescue the supplicant."[108] Such a belief is built on the trust that stems from the covenantal relationship and is maintained by the memory of Yahweh's past actions—as noted in the "memory" section above.

In the book of Job, although not structured in the same systematic way as is being examined here, Job's lament contains an underlying vow of trust that manifests itself on a number of occasions. The most poignant yet surprising way in which this is seen is in Job's want for a hearing to appeal against God's judgment. As the drama unfolds Job asserts that he wants a hearing with God in the context of a law court so that he may plead his case (Job 23:1–7). However, the paradoxical twist comes in the role, or rather

---

does not usually lead to a significant reduction in the angry feelings. In order to bring at least partial resolution, the emotional ventilation needs to be accompanied by a cognitive reinterpretation of the relevant event or events and of the attitudes and behavior of those involved" (*Pastoral Care*, 46). To refer back to Bauer's point, it seems that in the expression of emotion before God, a horizon is opened up that otherwise would not have been, in which divine action can lead to a fresh perspective. As we will see below, the lament is not the end, rather, it is the means of moving through difficult times in the relationship towards a place of re-orientation.

107. Brueggemann, *Theology of the Old Testament*, 470.
108. Middleton, "Why the 'Greater Good,'" 100.

roles, that Job sees God taking. As would be expected he sees God as the judge, but, he also appeals to God to be his defender and avenger (Job 14:13; 19:25–27). This is a succinct picture of the paradox at the heart of lament. God is complained to and petitioned due to his actions or lack thereof, but he is also appealed to as the covenantal partner who must do right and defend his people.[109] Gutiérrez states that, "This painful, dialectical approach to God is one of the most profound messages of the Book of Job."[110] I would add to this that it is probably one of the most profound truths of the performance of lament in general in the Old Testament, and it hangs on the existence of an on-going vow of trust that is juxtaposed with the complaint and petition of the lamenter. Brueggemann affirms this by suggesting, "the complaints insist upon Yahweh's faithfulness and protest against Yahweh's refusal to be visibly and effectively faithful."[111]

Petition

The petition continues the holding together of the two poles that we saw demonstrated by Job's dialectical view of God. In the petition—what Miller describes as "the specific or general plea for God to help"[112]—is found a variety of suggestions regarding *what* God should do in the situation, combined with suggested reasons or "motivations" as to *why* he should act.[113] As Brueggemann notes, "in petition the needy person addresses Yahweh in an imperative."[114] Again, the petition and motivation is only possible because of the covenantal relationship and the promises and expectations that come with that.

Often, when petitioning God, the motivation for doing so is the apparent innocence of the sufferer.[115] Although one may respond to this with the Pauline theme of all having sinned and fallen short of the glory of God (Rom 3:23), such use of that theme misses the point of this particular petition. The plea of innocence is not, as we see explicitly in Job, that of com-

---

109. I am aware that there is debate regarding who it is that Job is appealing to. I here side with those that believe Job's defender to be of a divine nature, however, full explanation and defense of this approach must wait until chapter 6.

110. Gutiérrez, *On Job*, 65.

111. Brueggemann, "Psalms as Prayer," 54.

112. Miller, *They Cried*, 86.

113. Brueggemann separates "motivations" off into its own category in his breakdown of the form of the lament Psalms. See Brueggemann, *Message of the Psalms*, 54–55.

114. Brueggemann, *Theology of the Old Testament*, 471–72.

115. Ps 17 is a particularly good example of this.

Humans, Evil, and Suffering—A Theo-Dramatic Perspective

plete innocence in one's life or one's community's life, but more the plea that the punishment does not match the crime (or lack thereof!). Again this view is founded on the cause and effect worldview and thus, to some degree, this worldview is retained. However, at the same time the sufferer is stating that the system is failing and it is Yahweh's fault, and, he should do something about it as the blame cannot possibly rest on the innocent sufferer.[116] In this sense there is also an appeal to God's justice, righteousness and faithfulness. Miller notes,

> All those complaints that seek to establish the injustice and unrighteousness of the enemies and the innocence and faithfulness of the petitioner are giving a reason, implicitly or explicitly, for a just and righteous God to help, hoping thereby to move God to intervene in behalf of the just and innocent petitioner.[117]

A further motivation for the petition of the sufferer is their memory regarding previous personal experience of the acts of Yahweh, or knowledge of stories about the previous acts of Yahweh that have been passed down through the generations, as was noted in the "memory" section above. In the light of such memories, petition can involve recounting these previous acts of Yahweh in an attempt to motivate him to act in a similar fashion, or, motivate him to fulfill a previous promise (Ps 89:49). In a brief examination of Ps 22 Miller notes of vv. 3–5, "The recital is . . . a reminder of the way God has been in order to evoke a similar response in the present situation."[118]

In connection to the actions of God, the sufferer, on some occasions, is seen to petition God based on the possible consequences if God were to remain inactive. The consequences vary but include the potential result that if the sufferer is destroyed by the circumstances, there would be no one left to tell of Yahweh and proclaim his name and his works (Pss 6:5; 88:10–12). A further consequence may be that Yahweh's reputation would be marred if he remained inactive (Ps 79:9). When Yahweh has told his people that he is the only authentic God and his people have proclaimed this to their neighbors, Yahweh's inactivity and his apparent lack of holding to his part of the covenant places his reputation at great risk.

In addition to this kind of petition, if we consider the cases in which the lamenter turns to Yahweh in complaint about the effects of an enemy's

---

116. We also find in petition and motivation sections of some lament texts the realization that the punishment has indeed matched the crime. However, the current work's focus is on situations in which the sufferer appears to be innocent.

117. Miller, *They Cried*, 118.

118. Ibid., 115.

A Dramatic Pentecostal/Charismatic Anti-Theodicy

actions, petition may move as far as calling for vengeance.[119] Motivations are mixed here. In some cases we see that the lamenter wants vengeance as justice for what they have experienced—again pointing towards the system.[120] In other cases we see that a response of aggressive retribution by Yahweh on the lamenter's enemies is asked for on the grounds that these enemies are also enemies of Yahweh, and once again, inactivity places his reputation at risk.[121]

The petition section of the general lament structure shows much variety in its content, but what is apparent is that the covenant partner is always faced with raw honesty within the expected bounds of the covenantal relationship. Although it is frequently difficult to determine how long the sufferer waits in each example of lament, on most occasions there is sufficient evidence to suggest that Yahweh does respond to his partner.[122] In Psalm scholarship it is often argued that a "salvation oracle" is experienced by the sufferer that leads to a change in attitude towards Yahweh, and a change of emotion and action. However, there is also disagreement regarding whether such an oracle was actually experienced.[123] It is notoriously difficult to determine, on textual grounds, either way, but, as Brueggemann notes, "What is clear in the text is that there is a covenantal-theological move from one part of the text to the next. Beyond that, we are engaged in speculation."[124]

When the move in the text does take place it is a move to what has been labeled the "vow of praise."

Vow of Praise

Brueggemann states, "In the full relationship, *the season of plea* must be taken as seriously as the *season of praise*."[125] As will be discussed in the "Re-

---

119. A famous example is found in Ps 109.

120. One example of this is found in Ps 35. Here the psalmist, from a position of innocence, appeals to the system and the covenant. He has acted rightly (vv. 13–14), but in response, they have not (vv. 7; 11–12; 15–16), and so justice is called for.

121. Ps 74 suggests this, particularly in v. 22 where it is made clear that the enemies "scoff" at Yahweh as well as his people.

122. This is not exclusively the case, Ps 88 being an exception. The place of such examples in the canon will be discussed below.

123. Much belief in the presence of a salvation oracle is due to the hypothesis put forward by Begrich in his article, "Das Priesterliche Heilsorakel." However, Moo, Ellington, and most notably Conrad, all contest the presence of such an oracle: see Moo, *Old Testament*, 227; Ellington, *Risking Truth*, 144; and Conrad, "Second Isaiah." Brueggemann is undecided but would perhaps seem to side with Begrich—see *Message of the Psalms*, 57–58.

124. Brueggemann *Message of the Psalms*, 58.

125. Ibid., 57.

orientation" section of this chapter, praise is the natural progression out of lament. However, whereas current western Christianity—in particular Pentecostal/Charismatic Christianity—has placed great emphasis on the triumphalistic nature of the praise of God and his mighty works at the cost of lament, Old Testament theology does not.[126] Brueggemann's point is that the relationship between Yahweh and Israel is one that gives equal space to lament *and* praise.

As would perhaps be expected, the vow of praise often corresponds to the type of suffering being experienced. When this is the case it is commonly assumed that God has moved in a way that has physically altered the situation for the good of the lamenter.[127] In other cases, praise comes in a form that suggests the lamenter has *heard* from God rather than having experienced a physical change.[128] In both cases, the seeming absence of God has been superseded by evidence of his presence, which brings with it fresh assurance and hope for the sufferer.[129] Miller notes that, "In some instances, it is difficult to tell whether the declaration of praise at the end of the prayer is a vow in anticipation or the words of praise uttered upon receipt of a divine word of assurance or God's intervention to help."[130] It is thus worth noting that the vow of praise sometimes comes due to anticipation and expectation of the forthcoming actions of God rather than because God has already evidently moved.

At this point an important exception to the structure being explored here needs to be highlighted. In his extensive work on the Psalms Westermann states that, "There is not a single Psalm of lament that stops with lamentation."[131] However, on closer inspection, this is not true. In Ps 88 there are significant aspects of the characteristic form of lament with the notable exception of any evidence of a response from God. There is also no sign of resolution and therefore no vow of praise. Brueggemann states, "It simply reports on how it is to be a partner of Yahweh in Yahweh's inexplicable absence."[132] Whatever the details are of a situation that causes

---

126. For an insightful examination of this issue, see Ellington, "Loss of Testimony."

127. In Ps 13 we may find an example of this. Verse 6 in particular seems to suggest that God has acted to alter the situation with the psalmist's enemies. See also Isa 38:17–19.

128. In Ps 6 we see a turn at v. 8 that we are told is due to the psalmist being "heard" by Yahweh.

129. Ps 22 is possibly one of the most powerful examples of a turn that leads to joyous praise.

130. Miller, *They Cried*, 132–33.

131. Westermann, *Praise and Lament*, 266.

132. Brueggemann, *Message of the Psalms*, 79.

such lament, what we can say is that it is clearly a desperate one. In such a situation the only options open to the sufferer are to repeat this psalm until a resolution arises or, simply wait in silence. As Brueggemann notes regarding the reality of the relationship between Israel and Yahweh, "To be Israel means to address God, even in God's unresponsive absence."[133]

A second psalm that does not fit the typical structure of lament is Ps 109. In a similar way to Ps 88 there is no resolution here, however, the content is starkly different. This psalm is a vindictive response to a neighbor. The sufferer in question desires vengeance for something done to them and vengeance in this instance touches on every part of the enemy's life. As stated, there is no resolution and no reasons given as to why such an extreme response has been aroused.

A third example that exists outside the psalms is of the weeping and mourning of Rachel, who refuses to be comforted (Jer 31:15). Having seen her children either slain or carried off into exile, Rachel is understandably inconsolable. But, "In refusing to accept easy consolation, Rachel does what is right. Her resistance is both a protest to and a waiting on God. In her own way, Rachel holds open the possibility of again praising the God of justice and new life."[134] Billman and Migliore continue by stating, "Rachel's lament is not contrary to praise but the pre-condition of authentic, honest praise."[135] In all these examples we see the mixture of the honest protest to God about the situation, combined with the presence of the covenantal, relational trust that fuels such lament.

When praise does come, this is a sign of the second move, the move that leads to re-orientation.

"Re-orientation"

The second move is one from lament to praise and the state in which the once sufferer finds themselves has been labeled by Brueggemann as "new orientation." Although I have opted to re-label it "re-orientation" for reasons discussed above, it is still important to draw out the "new" aspects of this on-going relationship. This new state of affairs has come about because God has broken into what appeared like a hopeless situation of despair and death and has miraculously brought life and hope. In specific reference to the Psalms, we find this movement reflected in such ways as the "song of

---

133. Ibid., 81.
134. Billman and Migliore, *Rachel's Cry*, 2.
135. Ibid., 3.

celebration,"¹³⁶ which Brueggemann states "is a new song sung at the appearance of a new reality, new creation, new harmony, new reliability."¹³⁷ He continues, "It is the experience that the world has new coherence, that the devastating hopelessness of the lament is not finally appropriate for the way life is."¹³⁸ It may be said of this movement from lament to praise that, "Just as we come to know the true meaning of hope only through the experience of suffering, so we can praise God with a full and joyful heart only if we are free to grieve and lament the real pain and injustice of our world."¹³⁹ One example where the movement from lament to praise is explicit in the Scriptures is in the book of Job.

We see towards the end of the book of Job that Yahweh appears to Job in the form of a whirlwind and engages in dialogue with him (Job 38:1—42:6). It has been suggested that this dialogue shows that Yahweh comes to Job to put him in his place and show him how little he knows and how little power he has in relation to Yahweh. We may say that, based on this understanding, the movement from lament to praise comes about by force that shuts lament down thus causing a forced praise.¹⁴⁰ This interpretation is further supported by use of Job's comment in response to the speeches of Yahweh: "I despise myself and repent in dust and ashes" (Job 42:6). However, this interpretation does not correlate with the positive place given to lament in the rest of the Old Testament texts explored and as Carol Newsome notes, this verse "is not only as terse and enigmatic as the preceding verses but also grammatically ambiguous. Almost every word in v. 6 is susceptible of more than one interpretation."¹⁴¹ Newsome proceeds to offer five different possibilities regarding how this verse may be rendered and states, "Asking which possibility is correct misses the interpretive significance of the ambiguity of Job's reply, which corresponds to the ambiguity that is also part of the divine speeches."¹⁴² Thus the rendering of this verse and the dialogue between God and Job generally, will be based partially on the theological framework of

---

136. Brueggemann, "Psalms and Faith," 9–10 and 14.

137. Ibid., 14.

138. Ibid. Brueggemann expands on the various sub-categories of psalms that make up psalms of new orientation in chapter 4 of *Message of the Psalms*.

139. Billman and Migliore, *Rachel's Cry*, 124.

140. See Westermann, *Structure of Job*, 107–8. Pope states, "No extreme of suffering gives mere man license to question God's wisdom or justice as Job had done. It is apparently on this very point that Job repents and recants" (Pope, *Job*, lxxx). See also Hartley, *Book of Job*, 45–47.

141. Newsome, "Book of Job," 628. See also Clines, *Job 38–42*, 1218–23; Gutiérrez, *On Job*, 86–87; and Middleton, "Does God Come to Praise?," 14–16.

142. Newsome, "Book of Job," 629.

A Dramatic Pentecostal/Charismatic Anti-Theodicy

the interpreter. In this case, although wary of forcing an interpretation onto a text to fit a system, I am employing a canonical approach that, as will be drawn out further in the following chapter, has a Christological key. For the sake of this chapter, as already noted, it is important to attempt to understand this text in the light of less ambiguous texts regarding communication with and about God in times of seemingly innocent, meaningless suffering.

In an unpublished paper, J. Richard Middleton suggests a re-interpretation of the whirlwind speeches and responses of Job that would appear to make more sense in the light of the movement through suffering whilst in relationship with God explored so far in this chapter. Middleton's interpretation also acts as a good example of how the movement from disorientation to re-orientation takes place. In his interpretation, Middleton focuses on the use of the chaos monsters—Behemoth and Leviathan—by the author of Job, and how God sees them and compares them to Job. Interpretation of the comparison of these monsters to Job has sometimes drawn on the concept of them as chaos monsters in the myths that have emerged from the Near East, and has thus understood these monsters as being overcome by God in his bringing of order at creation.[143] In the same way, in the whirlwind speeches God is understood to suggest that he will also overcome Job.[144] However, Middleton points out that in the Job texts the monsters are not portrayed as aggressive or violent if they are left to their own devices. He also points out that God created Behemoth and is proud of the creatures rather than in conflict with them. He does believe however, that "Job is . . . being compared to these beasts."[145] And in agreement with this we see in Job 7:12 that Job compares himself to a chaos monster that needs restraining.

Middleton continues this comparison stating,

> Through a complex web of associations Job's fearless and courageous strength, by which he stood up to the verbal and emotional assaults of his friends, is evoked in the description of Behemoth and Leviathan. Like them, Job has been impervious to the assaults of his adversaries, and this is a good thing.[146]

In how God deals with the sea, Middleton points out that this is not like chaos myths and instead God is inclined to give boundaries to his creation. "The picture is of energetic nurture, rather than anything adversarial."[147]

---

143. See Newsome, "Book of Job," 617–27, for a survey of interpretations of the identity of Behemoth and Leviathan and their interaction with Yahweh.
144. See Habel, *Book of Job*, 557–61.
145. Middleton, "Does God Come to Praise?," 8.
146. Ibid., 9.
147. Ibid.

Humans, Evil, and Suffering—A Theo-Dramatic Perspective

This suggests an interpretation in which Job is comparable to the chaos monsters in how he deals with his friends, but also suggests that God is interested in giving him boundaries and nurturing him rather than "burying" him. Middleton further argues this point by exploring the royal status given to humans as the *imago dei*.[148]

In looking at the necessity of the two speeches as opposed to one, Middleton argues that this is because of Job's passivity after the first speech. God was not interested in shutting Job down but instead, "desired a worthy dialogue partner."[149] After the second speech Job does respond and shows a new level of understanding. This leads up to the difficult statement by Job mentioned earlier (42:6). Middleton argues that this could be interpreted in one of two ways, both of which move away from the passive interpretation of the common English rendering, and both of which are retractions of the passive response post first whirlwind speech. He suggests that in the first of these, Job is repenting *of* dust and ashes, thus following on from Job's general repentance of passivity. In the second, Middleton suggests that Job may be saying that he accepts he is dust and ashes whilst at the same time royal.[150] Either way, this is a far cry from the usual rendering.

Based on this interpretation of the whirlwind speeches we may say that God sees Job as a royal follower who is right to lament over his situation and right to aim it at Yahweh. We may also say that God is interested in nurturing Job and that this is therefore the driving force for Yahweh's encouragement of Job's honest expression of his feelings. What adds further weight to this approach is the way in which Yahweh condemns Job's "friends" for their theology and their worship of the structure. Job is a prime example of the movement from lament to praise, which is brought about by his dialogue and his actions. We may therefore agree with Brueggemann when he states, "the laments show clearly that *biblical faith, as it faces life fully, is uncompromisingly and unembarrassedly dialogic.*"[151] As dialogue is never one-way, most importantly in this transition is the presence of a sal-

---

148. Ibid., 10–13.

149. Ibid., 14.

150. Ibid., 14–16. Although he disagrees with Middleton's rendering and interpretation of 42:6, Clines does aid Middleton's argument by suggesting that "I despise myself" is a poor rendering of the Hebrew. Clines replaces this with "So I submit," which, depending on how this is interpreted in the wider dialogue, may be more affirming of Middleton's argument. See Clines, *Job 38–42*, 1218–20. In a similar way, Janzen replaces it with "Therefore I recant." Unlike Clines, Janzen's rendering and interpretation of 42:6 seems to provide some support for Middleton's, particularly regarding the rendering and interpretation in which Job is understood to see himself as both dust and ashes, and royal. See Janzen, *Job*, 251–59.

151. Brueggemann, "From Hurt to Joy," 68.

vation oracle in the form of a theophany. In this confrontation we thus find an example of Vanhoozer's "dialogical consummation." In first his silence and then in dialogue, Yahweh consummates the character of Job. The necessity of the second whirlwind speech, as argued for by Middleton, as well as Job's response, provide support for this as it is only through *both* speeches (in Middleton's interpretation) that this consummation takes place. It is through *both* speeches that Job is able to make the second move to re-orientation. This re-orientation involves the salvaging of Job's situation, thus causing him to experience the structure as functioning correctly again. We surely must say therefore that the Old Testament suggests that lament done right, in the end, leads to praise, and that God not only encourages it but also can consummate his heroes' characters through it. The new phase of re-orientation thus brings about a new stage in the relationship between God and the sufferer in which a new level of maturity is reached. I concur with Billman and Migliore when they assert, "only relationships that permit us to assert ourselves without fear of shame or punishment, that give us room to take initiative as well as being recipients of the initiative of others, provide the contexts for moral and spiritual growth."[152] In the example of Job explored above is found this principle in a most explicit form.

Conclusion

As this chapter draws to a close there are a number of points to raise to the surface in anticipation of the following chapter.

Firstly, we have seen that as evil and suffering emerge on the stage of creation, nothing on the stage is left untouched and the figure of Satan is always lurking somewhere in the shadows. However, secondly, God, as the divine playwright, scripts a drama in which he draws humans into covenantal relationship with him in order to purge creation of all evil and suffering, with the promise that one day God will bring this purging to completion with the final consummation. Thirdly, the covenantal relationship between God and his people involves certain commitments regarding how each party agrees to act towards the other one. These commitments are freighted with expectation regarding the activity of each party in certain circumstances. Fourthly, in the unfolding of the drama, the experience of Israel is that there are a significant number of occasions when the reality of their experience seems to be incongruent with the expectations they have regarding how the divine partner is to act on these occasions. At this point,

---

152. Billman and Migliore, *Rachel's Cry*, 117.

to use Brueggemann's terminology, "core testimony" is met by "countertestimony" as Israel and individuals grapple with this incongruence.

When this occurs the question that lies at the center of this study emerges in the life of Israel. How do they perform when they are experiencing seemingly innocent, meaningless suffering and the God of covenant appears to be absent? What does it mean to perform fittingly in these situations? What we can gather from the Script is that to perform fittingly in response to experiences that cause this question to emerge is to lament. A significant part of the eschatological consummation of the drama is the expulsion of evil and suffering. In order to carry on their through-line, the actors are called to maintain covenantal relationship with the playwright as they seek to perform fittingly and thus enable the movement of the drama towards eschatological consummation. The direction that appears to emerge from Act 2 of the Script is that the way of doing this, given the experience of the kind of suffering in question, is to perform lament towards God as the only fitting way to maintain covenantal relations *and* honest expression of the experience. In doing so, the actors enable the movement of the drama towards eschatological consummation in a way that would not otherwise have been possible.

As we prepare to enter the next chapter, and thus the climax of the study, we can recall that a point of contention, regarding how much direction we are to take from the performance of Israel, is that we live in a different act of the drama to that which their performance took place in. Their performance took place in Act 2 and we live in Act 4 and in between lies the act in which the most significant performance of all took place—the divine command performance of God incarnate seen in Act 3. We may also recall from chapter 4 that in seeking to give a fitting performance in the current act, we are to improvise on this command performance. In this chapter we have fulfilled the first and second of the four steps laid out in the introduction to this chapter, as we are clear on where we are in the drama and how God, and his people, responded to evil and suffering in Act 2. We are also clear on how Israel performed in the face of seemingly innocent, meaningless suffering when God appeared to be absent. And so, in the light of that, we can move on in the next chapter to complete step three by examining how Jesus improvised on this performance.

With the completion of step three the way is clear to proceed to step four where we reach the climax of the study and answer the central research question. In doing so, what I suggest we will find is that dismissal of Israel's performance of lament in the face of experiences of the type of suffering in question, is done at the actor's peril. What I will also be suggesting is that, rather than being dismissed by the divine actor, it is instead legitimized and added to by his fitting, improvised performance.

6

Improvising on a Divine Performance of Lament

Introduction

WE CAN RECALL THAT the question at the heart of this study is: What does it mean to produce a fitting Pentecostal/Charismatic performance in the face of seemingly innocent, meaningless suffering when God appears to be absent? We can also recall that in the pursuit of finding an answer to this question we began by examining Christian responses to evil and suffering in general (chapter 2), followed by examining Pentecostal/Charismatic responses to evil and suffering (chapter 3). In the light of these two examinations it was highlighted that the Biblically rooted, systematic guidance for the production of a fitting performance that would constitute a suitable answer to the question would require a high view of Scripture in the construction of that answer. With this in mind, a suitable hermeneutical method was developed (chapter 4) that could provide the necessary tools for the construction of such an answer.

In the previous chapter, a four step approach was outlined as the way in which the climax of this study would be reached and the central research question answered, and steps one and two were completed. We thus find ourselves at this point with a clear understanding of where we are in the drama as well as a growing understanding of how God sees and responds to evil and suffering. In conjunction with this latter point, we are also aware that humans are invited to be part of the divine response and further, we have examined what a fitting performance looks like in Act 2 when the actors experience times of seemingly innocent, meaningless suffering and the divine covenantal partner appears to be absent.

Improvising on a Divine Performance of Lament

The challenge in this chapter is to examine the performance of Jesus in the face of evil and suffering in order to provide guidance for a fitting Pentecostal/Charismatic performance in the current act. By examining the performance of Jesus we will firstly, be able to Christologically qualify the response to evil and suffering taken by the divine playwright in Act 2. Included within this, since Jesus is the divine-human actor, we will therefore also be able to Christologically qualify the role set for humans within the divine playwright's response to evil and suffering. The pinnacle of this examination will be in Jesus' response through his Passion, particularly in the Garden of Gethsemane and during his crucifixion. This examination of Jesus' performance will enable the completion of step three of the four step journey, as it will provide the Christocentric lens through which we can complete our examination of the divine response to evil and suffering.

In the light of this examination, we will also be able to complete step four. This is so because we may recall from chapter 4 that in seeking to produce guidance for a fitting performance in the current act, we are to improvise on the performance of Jesus in similar situations with the aim of non-identical repetition. Having provided a context for the performance of Jesus in chapter 5, we are, in this chapter, able to see how he improvises on the performance of Israel. This in turn will enable the provision of guidance regarding a fitting performance and use of the Script in the current act. A twist in the plot comes in the form of the role of the Spirit in our performances, but more will be said about this below.

We begin then by examining Jesus' view of and response to evil and suffering.

Jesus and Evil: A Divine, Command Performance

At the end of Act 2, rather than making progress, the cycle of evil being confronted, judged and stopped, followed by its re-emergence (as noted in chapter 5), was becoming repetitive to the point of stagnation, with no sign of a plot resolution that could break the repetition. Such a situation was due to the fact that evil and corruption was both within and outside of those cast to aid expel it from the cosmic stage. However, the divine playwright could not allow this cycle to continue *ad infinitum* and so there was only one option left to move the drama on. Enter Jesus.

As the curtain rises on Act 3, the entrance of Jesus onto the stage as the divine playwright incarnate offers a number of fresh possibilities. The first of these relates to the divine perspective of evil and suffering as, in Jesus' words and actions, we are allowed to see once more, in the most tangible

A Dramatic Pentecostal/Charismatic Anti-Theodicy

way, what this perspective is. The second is a front row seat to view what a performance in which evil is defeated looks like. The third is access to the prime example of a performance on which we can improvise as we seek to establish what a fitting performance looks like, in the current act, in response to the type of suffering in question. We will examine each of these in turn.

Evil and Suffering Through a Christocentric Lens

The temptation texts in particular offer us a fresh view of the divine perspective on the personal nature of evil (Matt 4:1–11//Mark 1:12–13//Luke 4:1–13). Like Adam and Eve, and then Israel, Jesus experiences the pressure exerted by the presence of evil to think and act in a corrupt manner. He is tempted to give a performance that deviates from the part for which he has been cast. However, unlike Adam, Eve, and Israel, he does not give in to the temptation but wards it off as, in order for Jesus to give a performance of perfection, he must be without sin.[1] A problem with the drama since the moment Adam and Eve gave in to deceit was that no part of the cast from then on would be free from sin. This made it impossible for them to overcome evil and bring the Kingdom of God to bear on the cosmic stage, meaning a completely fitting performance was always out of reach. Jesus is thus improvising firstly, on the part of Adam, and secondly, on the part of Israel, as he carries on his through-line that will move the drama towards eschatological consummation. This scene within Act 3 of the drama emphasizes the importance of remaining free from personal evil in order to carry out a fitting performance of *imago dei*. It also, in connection with the third level of evil, supports the divine understanding of Satan as the ultimate liar and deceiver whose aim it appears to be to tend the drama towards destruction.

We are, through Jesus' performance, given, secondly, a better perspective on the issue of systemic evil. As soon as personal evil infiltrated the cast, corporate and systemic evil, and the infection of the whole of the cosmic stage, followed close behind. Free from personal sin however, Jesus begins opposing evil at the systemic level, thus confirming its presence and the reading of the Script advocated thus far in this study. The exiled Israel had been told by the prophets of a Messiah that would defeat her enemies and restore her to her land where God would reign forever. Wright points out that the "Kingdom of God" "was simply a Jewish way of talking about

---

1. The writer of Hebrews further supports this point in two places, thus confirming the reality of the temptation as well as the reality and importance of Jesus' impeccability (Heb 2:18; 4:15).

Israel's god becoming king."[2] He further states that the key to understanding the return from exile and the reign of the Kingdom of God from Israel's perspective, was "the Jewish expectation of the saving sovereignty of the covenant god, exercised in the vindication of Israel and the overthrow of her enemies."[3] "The time when the blind would see, the deaf hear, the lame walk, and the poor hear good news was the time when Israel would return at last from Babylon."[4] Again, improvising on much of what the prophets had spoken of in the previous act, with his healings and exorcisms, his love and compassion towards outcasts, Jesus begins to implement this return from exile on Israel's behalf. His confirmation of the presence of systemic evil and suffering in creation is achieved by way of his opposition to it. This involved healing those who suffered from evil in biological and ecological systems, challenging corrupt political and religious systems, and breaking down the corruption in sociological systems. All of this had been the task of Israel, who had become so defaced by the evil within that she could not overthrow that, or the evil outside.

The third aspect of evil that Jesus confronts, we have already touched on in his confrontation of the first. Throughout Jesus' ministry he refers to the figure of Satan, which continues to stand behind all other evil and authors lies in order to create opportunities for this evil to continue.

From this brief examination of the divine actor's perspective we can affirm that God, both in his Script and in human form, sees evil, and thus the resulting suffering, with the three tier perspective outlined in chapter 5. What also becomes apparent is that if the drama is to reach its intended conclusion, evil—at all levels—must be defeated, and this defeat can only be brought about through Jesus' performance. By examining the Easter event we can examine how this defeat is obtained.

Easter: The Defeat of Evil and the Climax of the Drama

We begin by returning to the question of personal sin. Jesus had indeed remained free from personal sin in his overcoming of the temptations in the wilderness, but, as we examine his performance in the Easter event we can see afresh the consistency of this aspect of it. We see first, in the Garden of Gethsemane, the temptation to disobey the call to the part he was to play (Matt 26:36–46//Mark 14:32–42//Luke 22:39–46). We can also recall the cries of those standing watching at the cross who taunted him to come

2. Wight, *Jesus and Victory*, 202–3.
3. Ibid., 223.
4. Ibid., 243.

A Dramatic Pentecostal/Charismatic Anti-Theodicy

down and save himself (Matt 27:38–44//Mark 15:25–32//Luke 23:35–39). Throughout these scenes however, Jesus remains impeccable and obedient to the Father.

Secondly, there was the systemic level of evil. To defeat this level required a performance by Jesus that involved embodying Israel, taking her punishment on her behalf, "letting evil do its worse to him" and yet overcome it.[5] Wright states of Jesus, "He would be the means of the kingdom's coming both in that he would embody in himself the renewed Israel and in that he would defeat evil once and for all."[6]

As the opposition from Israel herself, and the political systems around, escalated in response to Jesus' dramatic performance, the climax of the drama neared. Wright suggests that the gospels, "tell the story of how the evil in the world—political, social, personal, moral, emotional—reached its height; and they tell how God's long term plan for Israel (and for himself!) finally came to its climax."[7] At the cross, systemic evil was at its absolute worse as it attempted to annihilate the purest form of goodness and love in creation. The only fitting performance Jesus could give was one that overcame evil *with* that love and goodness.

This brings us to the third tier of evil. Again, behind the temptations and the systemic evil is the figure of Satan, who continues to tempt the rest of creation towards nothingness and destruction and thus attempts to drag the divine actor into his own version of the drama. Wright argues, "Behind his conflict with rival agendas, Jesus discerned, and spoke about, a great battle, in which he faced the real enemy. Victory over this enemy, Jesus claimed, would constitute the coming of the kingdom."[8] This battle "was with the satan; the satan had made its home in Israel, and in her cherished national institutions and aspirations."[9] The only way victory could come for Jesus, Israel, and the rest of creation, and the only way eschatological consummation could be achieved, was if the love and goodness embodied in the divine actor could overcome the ultimate nihilistic tendency of Satan, which was death itself. In his obedience to death and the ensuing resurrection, Jesus experiences the effects of the Satanic performance at all tiers of its manifestations, but, defeats it by overcoming it and shattering its power. In his performance, Jesus remains impeccable, allows Satan to do his worse

---

5. Ibid., 565.
6. Ibid.
7. Wright, *Evil*, 47–48.
8. Wright, *Jesus and Victory*, 200.
9. Ibid., 461.

through the systemic evil, and overcomes the death that such evil brings and which Israel and all of creation deserved.

The performance of *imago dei* that Jesus gave was a fitting performance *par excellence*. He improvised in order to perform the role of priest—in his mediating of the presence of God and as offering sacrifice and prayer for Israel; as prophet—in his calling Israel to repentance, telling of the coming judgment and taking that punishment for her; as king—in being the son of God; and finally as sacrificial lamb. There is no more fitting improvised performance in the drama of salvation than this. This performance carries on the correct through-line and moves the drama towards eschatological consummation in a way no other performance could or would.

In the aftermath of the resurrection and ascension, and therefore the earthly mission of Jesus, there is a fresh commission given to the apostles that, in particular in John's gospel, is reminiscent of the original mission with which Adam and Eve were entrusted.[10] A new act dawns in the drama, a new day in a new week of creation in which the cast are tasked, in the power of the Spirit of the risen Christ, to implement the victory of the Cross over evil, sin and suffering. This is to be a refreshed performance of *imago dei* in which the actors are being renewed and directed by the power of the Spirit to improvise on the Script so far, in the light of the performance of Jesus. The actors in this act are to carry on the through-line of Jesus until he returns to complete the good work that he began and hand it over to the Father for him to be all in all (Phil 1:6; 1 Cor 15:27–28). As we pick up the Script, this is the task of the current group of actors. Script in hand, in community, under the guidance of the Spirit, we are, as we saw in chapter 4, to improvise upon the performance of Jesus, as revealed in the Script, in order to produce a fitting performance of Christ-likeness on the cosmic stage.

There is, however, a problem and a significant one at that. Wright states of the aftermath of the resurrection "on the first Easter Monday evil still stalked the earth from Jerusalem to Gibraltar and beyond, and stalks it still."[11] Regarding the first Christians, and indeed the present ones, he continues, "There was still a mopping-up battle to be fought, but the real victory had been accomplished."[12] So, here is the problem: although Jesus has won the victory over evil, the implementation of that victory is far from complete and will not be completed until Jesus' return at the Eschaton of Act 5. Although we are not to shy away from the task, the reality is that this

---

10. In John 20:19–22 we are told that Jesus appears to the disciples on the first day of the week, suggesting a new week in creation and thus alluding to the first week at the beginning of Genesis.

11. Wright, *Jesus and Victory*, 659.

12. Ibid.

A Dramatic Pentecostal/Charismatic Anti-Theodicy

mission is carried out in what has classically been termed the "now/not yet" period. This means suffering, including seemingly innocent, meaningless suffering, is still experienced, and often, prayer for healing does not work and Satan and his minions do not appear to be primarily behind it. So how are we to perform fittingly in the face of this suffering whilst we await Act 5? My suggestion, as the climax of this study and based on what was examined in the previous chapter, is that we are to perform lament as a method of carrying on our through-line towards eschatological consummation. However, is such a performance legitimized by the performance of Jesus?

There has been and still is, amongst scholars and lay people alike, the suggestion that what we should be experiencing now is the "now" of the Kingdom, thus making lament an outdated performance. This hangs on a particular concept of what Jesus did at the cross and the resultant effect of that act. My contention with this is that firstly, it seems to ignore the testimony of the New Testament that only Jesus, upon his return, can consummate the work that he has begun. But secondly, and most importantly for this study, I further suggest that if we examine the event of the cross closely, what we will find is that Jesus himself improvises on the lament tradition and performs it as part of his carrying on of his through-line. If we are to improvise on Jesus' performance in developing a fitting one of our own, when we look at how to perform in the face of the type of suffering in question, we must begin with Jesus. In doing so, I suggest that we can develop guidance for a fitting performance of lament that is loyal to a Christocentric, Spirit-filled reading and fitting performance of the Script. To do this we must begin by examining the event of the cross.

A Divine Performance of Lament

An obvious point that requires making is that although there are points of similarity between the performance of Jesus and the rest of the cast that follow Him—as there must be if we are to be able to improvise on his performance—there are also some clear dissimilarities. Before proceeding further it is important that we are clear on what the relevant similarities and dissimilarities are.

Dissimilarities between the Human and Divine Actors

The dissimilarities between Jesus' performance and ours are linked and have their roots in his divinity. We have already seen that from divinity flows impeccability (and therefore obedience) but, there is an additional difference that needs highlighting which Vanhoozer has labeled "covenantal concern-based theodramatic construals."

In *Remythologizing Theology* one of the subjects Vanhoozer sought to address was that of how and what God feels. Of particular interest to the current work is the appropriation by Vanhoozer of the concept of "concern-based construals" developed by Robert Roberts.[13] Vanhoozer begins by filtering the term "emotions" into the categories of "affections" and "passions." Of passions he states, "To be subject to passions . . . is to be acted upon by outside forces."[14] To be moved by emotion in this sense is to be involuntarily subjected to non-cognitive desires or forces. Affections, on the other hand, refer to "thoughts of the heart" and are feelings that are felt rightly, based on the situation, and are in line with the will.[15] This is the kind of emotion Vanhoozer argues the divine experiences. At this point Vanhoozer draws in Roberts' concept in order to suggest how divine affections might operate. The process of development of a concern-based construal is that, firstly, there is a mental awareness of a situation towards which, and from which, emotions emerge. Secondly, the type of emotion experienced hinges on the construal of the situation where "To construe something is to characterize it in a certain way, to perceive, believe, or imagine it *as* such-and-such."[16] This construal is done within a particular narrative and is concern-based because it "is one . . . loaded with value."[17] Drawing this together Vanhoozer states, "We can think of the affections . . . as godly emotions: construals—or more importantly, *dispositions to act*—based on divine concerns."[18] If we then add in the fact that God is a covenantal God, which thus governs his perceptions etc., we can say with Vanhoozer that "God's emotions are covenantal concern-based theodramatic construals."[19]

As God incarnate, Jesus' emotional response to any situation is also based on covenantal concern-based theodramatic construals. Because of this, he can choose a fitting response, both physically and emotionally, to any situation based on his obedience, impeccability and construals. Thus, as Vanhoozer notes, Jesus is not at the mercy of creation but *chooses* the experience of suffering that he endures with a clear understanding of what is

---

13. Vanhoozer, *Remythologizing Theology*, 408. See also Roberts, *Emotions*, in particular chapter 2, where Roberts outlines and defends the concept.
14. Vanhoozer, *Remythologizing Theology*, 400.
15. Ibid., 401–3.
16. Ibid., 409.
17. Ibid., 410.
18. Ibid., 411.
19. Ibid., 414.

going on and how it will end.[20] Although we have a good idea of the end in that all will be raised to life—like Jesus—and God will be all in all, in the individual episodes of suffering we experience, more often than not, we do not know how they will end. We also rarely have a full comprehension of what is happening or why. If we combine this with a lack of full knowledge of self or perfect relationship with God, it becomes obvious that we can neither fully control our emotional responses nor respond fittingly to the situations we face. However, this latter point should give us cause to follow the actions of Jesus even closer for, if we do not know fully what is a fitting performance in a particular situation, is it not best to look to the author and perfecter of the faith for direction? We come then to examine the similarities between our performance and the performance of lament of the divine actor.

Similarities between the Human and Divine Actors

We saw in chapter 5 that the presence of covenant is of great significance in the practice of lament, and this is no less the case here. We will recall that lament often occurs when the human covenant partner believes themself to have kept their side of the covenant whilst experiencing suffering seemingly due to the divine partner not keeping his side of the covenant. As we look at the performance of Jesus on the cross, and in his earthly life generally, we can see that covenant, and obedience to that covenant, was central to his actions. As Vanhoozer notes, "The cross is the climax of the courtroom drama where God judges the covenant unfaithfulness of humankind and displays his own covenant faithfulness, his love and his justice. Jesus is the principal actor who takes up the part of both God and man, victor and vanquished."[21] The drama goes, we will recall, that God was covenanting from the start with the express aim of perfect union and communion with his creation. Humans were unable to keep their side of the covenant and so entered evil and sin onto the stage. Rather than abandon his creation, God both defeats evil and takes the punishment for sin at the cross. The new covenant may now be experienced "in Christ" by all those who wish to participate. Covenant then is central to the life of Jesus as he succeeds in performing *imago dei* where all others had failed. However, obedience to the covenant for him entailed innocent suffering as it was undeserved by Him. Even though he freely chose to experience the evil and punishment for sin at the cross, the

---

20. Vanhoozer states that "the Son is not merely active but sovereign in his suffering" (*Remythologizing Theology*, 430).

21. Vanhoozer, *Drama of Doctrine*, 52.

key point remains: this is innocent suffering experienced during covenantal obedience.

If we recall Brueggemann's paradigm for moving through the process of suffering examined in chapter 5, whilst simultaneously examining the drama of the innocent suffering of the Passion, the move within the Father-Son relationship during the Passion can be characterized as a transition from orientation to disorientation. By obediently keeping the covenant with the Father, the Son appears to experience an absence of the Father in the deepest moments of the most innocent suffering ever to be seen on the stage. The form that Jesus carries through by performing *imago dei* in a fitting manner requires an improvisation on the lament tradition in order to carry on his through-line and move the drama towards eschatological consummation. A perfect covenantal concern-based theodramatic construal for Jesus entails a performance that leads to disorientation and the suffering of the cross. In the midst of that suffering, and the dislocation in relationship between Father and Son that ensues, the practice Jesus performs is one of lament, a cry of dereliction, pain, and abandonment. Before we can suggest how the performance of Jesus can give direction to the actors in the current act though, we must look closer at the details of his performance.

Divine Lament in the Passion

In *The Psalms of Lament in Mark's Passion: Jesus' Davidic Suffering*, Stephen P. Ahearne-Kroll investigates, from the perspective of the writer of Mark, what it may mean for "Jesus the Messiah to die 'as it is written of him.'"[22] His aim is to argue that Mark's use of Davidic lament psalms in his writing of the Passion is meant to show Jesus following in the line of David in his suffering, over and above the Suffering Servant of Isaiah. Underlying Ahearne-Kroll's method is that of "Ziva Ben-Porat's four-step poetics of allusion."[23] This method begins by firstly, identifying an evocation in a text, followed by, secondly, identifying the evoked text. In this case the evocation is identified in Mark's Passion narrative and the evoked texts are that of some of the Davidic psalms of lament. The third stage is to read the evoked text (the Davidic psalm) in its context, followed by the fourth stage of reading the allusion (the place of evocation) in its context in the light of the evoked text/s. This method appears at first glance to fall in line with the Vanhoozian method that has been adopted in this study. However, whereas with the Vanhoozian

---

22. Ahearne-Kroll, *Psalms of Lament*, 1.

23. Ibid., 25. Ahearne-Kroll references Ben-Porat's "Poetics of Allusion" as his source for the method.

A Dramatic Pentecostal/Charismatic Anti-Theodicy

method the aim is to see how Jesus improvises on the text to perform fittingly in the drama, Ahearne-Kroll's adaptation of Ben-Porat's method does not consider Mark canonically, and only considers what Mark was trying to show to his reader. This, firstly, ignores any sense of the bigger picture of the canon as brought together by the divine author through his Holy Spirit, and secondly, it appears to render unimportant the belief that Jesus actually existed and actually said and did the things Mark reports. It would be naïve to suggest Mark simply transcribed what happened, as all authors have an agenda. However, it also seems naïve to suggest, as Ahearne-Kroll does, that the use of the psalms by Jesus is simply a Markan construct.[24] Rather than following this view, I shall work with the premise that Jesus knew exactly what he was doing with the words and actions he used, and in so doing, gives us direction for performance. With this correction of Ahearne-Kroll's method in place, it is still useful to proceed with the four stage evocation/allusion method as a way of exploring how Jesus improvises. Of particular focus will be the Gethsemane scene and the crucifixion.

In the Gethsemane scene found in Mark 14:32–42, Jesus appears to be, firstly, deeply distressed and disturbed by where obedience to the covenant is leading him, and secondly, struggling with temptation in the face of that obedience. We have noted above the impeccability of Jesus in tandem with his ability to experience temptation, but, what we see here is how he responds when in a situation of deep stress and temptation that appears to be further heightened by the silence of his Father. Jesus is aware of the suffering that is approaching, and in a sense is already here, and has in fact chosen this path, but still he experiences how it feels to take on this role. We must assume from this that such a response is therefore a fitting one. The suggested texts that are evoked by this scene are those found in Pss 42 and 43, which some scholars argue were originally one psalm.[25] The markers in the Gospel narrative are found in the description of Jesus' emotion in Mark 14:34, as well as the threefold repetition of prayer that Jesus offers to his Father. These two points linked together evoke in particular Ps 42:6, 12 and Ps 43:5. Embedded in a psalm that grows in disillusionment and angst at the absence of God in the face of suffering caused by enemies around the lamenter, there is a repetitive cycle displayed in these three verses that seeks to motivate God and conjure hope. Ahearne-Kroll suggests, "If we take the imagery of Pss 41–42 seriously, Jesus' great distress . . . has clear overtones

---

24. Ahearne-Kroll suggests that "he [Mark] puts the language of most of these psalms on the lips of Jesus" (ibid., 80).

25. Ibid., section 2.4 of chapter 4.

Improvising on a Divine Performance of Lament

of abandonment and rejection by God."[26] He continues, "It is clear that Jesus knows God's will, but in a sense the prayer also expresses Jesus' search for an understanding of God's will—the necessity of suffering for Jesus mission."[27] Ahearne-Kroll concludes by stating, "in the end, Jesus chooses to deny his will and choose God's will that he suffer and die, but this choice does not resolve the tension in the story. Jesus carries that tension with him to the cross."[28] If we are to maintain the argument that the path Jesus takes is chosen and understood by Him, then we can rebut elements of Ahearne-Kroll's argument in order to produce a more fitting one.

Firstly, Ahearne-Kroll seems to premise his reading of the allusion on the idea that Jesus does not fully understand what he is doing, a suggestion that seems flawed if we are to take Jesus' words as his own and contextualize this scene within the wider Gospel accounts. Secondly, if we rightly premise our understanding of the evocations in this allusion with the view that Jesus knows exactly what he is doing, then we can understand Jesus' words of struggle and despair as a fitting performance when faced with the temptation and impending suffering that this path brings about. There will indeed initially be the experience of abandonment and rejection as part of the covenantal agreement that exists in the Godhead, and when this occurs, how is Jesus to carry on his through-line towards eschatological consummation in order to perform fittingly? The answer is that he laments by improvising on the Script. He uses a previous psalm of lament and gives an improvised performance of it. Disorientation has rightly come in the relationship and a covenantal concern-based theodramatic construal demands a performance of lament to carry on Jesus' through-line. By evoking and improvising on a psalm that fits his situation, Jesus gives the perfect performance as well as shedding light on how we are to perform, a point we shall come to below. Those who betray and abuse are driven by the amassing of all the sin and evil in the drama, which will be allowed to do its worse to him as he confronts it and Satan. As we recall Ps 43:5, we can also suggest that Jesus, in the midst of his lament, is spurred on by the knowledge of what the Father has done and will do, and the response that will elicit. But, in the meantime, as the disorientation worsens, the lines of communication are kept open by way of lament as Jesus allows us a glimpse of what a fitting performance in the face of suffering looks like.

---

26. Ibid., 185. Note that Ahearne-Kroll uses a different rendering of psalm numbering hence the change from 42–43 to 41–42 between his work and mine.

27. Ibid., 186.

28. Ibid., 191.

A Dramatic Pentecostal/Charismatic Anti-Theodicy

A more explicit use of a lament psalm is found in Jesus' words on the cross in Mark 15:34 (//Matt 27:46). It is no secret that this marker evokes Ps 22 in its allusion. In its form and structure this psalm follows the classic pattern of lament that was outlined in chapter 5, and again, as with the scene in the Garden of Gethsemane, I suggest that in his use of this section from this psalm, Jesus is evoking the whole of the psalm. The parallels between the psalmist and Jesus are numerous particularly in the sense of the role of the enemies that surround Him, the apparent absence of the Father, and the pain and suffering that Jesus is experiencing. At this point we must repeat that Jesus has knowingly chosen this path and is impeccable in walking it, however, that does not mean that he does not feel, and most importantly, endure, all that this path brings. And again, we can point to the fact that in his performance of this role, the hero carries on his through-line by expressing lament towards the Father, and in doing so is being dialogically consummated.

What is disputed about Jesus' use of this psalm is firstly, whether he intended an evocation and re-appropriation of the psalm only up to and including v. 21. And secondly, if he intended a re-appropriation of the whole of the psalm, how are we to understand v. 22 onwards? We shall tackle these queries in reverse order.

The dispute surrounding v. 22 onwards revolves around whether the closing section of the psalm is the praise that follows some sort of change for the lamenter, or, whether it is a promise of what the lamenter will do *if* God acts. Ahearne-Kroll suggests the latter of these arguing that the intention of the lamenter is to use a description of what he will do *if* God acts as further persuasion for God *to* act.[29] However, if this is a correct translation it seems odd that most commentators do not entertain the idea. More importantly, it also seems to be reading too much into the text to suggest that there is an underlying motive of persuasion in a section of the psalm that gives no direction that it should be read in such a manner. What is more feasible in close relation to this idea is that, as Dahood suggests, "Convinced of the forthcoming help, the psalmist makes a vow to praise God in the great assembly."[30] In a similar way Rogerson and McKay argue that the psalmist "is neither praising God for past deliverance, nor promising praise for future deliverance, but is asking for help now and simultaneously praising God for giving it."[31] Both of these views support

---

29. Ibid., 88–109. Most notable is footnote 23 on p. 88 and section 2.2.2.c on pp. 101–7.

30. Dahood, *Psalms I: 1–50*, 138.

31. Rogerson and McKay, *Psalms 1–50*, 96.

Improvising on a Divine Performance of Lament

the idea that although not apparent yet the psalmist believes a change in circumstances *will* come and is either promising praise when it comes or is praising because he believes it will come. Central to these views is the idea that somehow the psalmist knows that God has heard him.[32] At this point we risk stepping into the on-going debate about the presence or absence of salvation or priestly oracles in the psalms. Scholars such as Peter Craigie argue that an oracle must be presupposed in the psalm, whereas, as noted in chapter 5, there are those who contest a belief in salvation oracles *per se*.[33] My suggestion is that the presence or absence of such an oracle does not concern us here. What is important is not *how* the psalmist knows but *that* he knows that God has heard him. Ahearne-Kroll aside, the central feature of most interpretations of this text is that the psalmist believes that God has heard him and that either God has answered or will answer. This is an important point to be carried forward as we look to Jesus' intentions in quoting the opening verse of the psalm.

In our exploration of those intentions we should perhaps begin with a note of caution by bearing in mind Donald Hagner's belief that what is occurring in this moment "is one of the most impenetrable mysteries of the entire Gospel narrative."[34] Absolute conclusions will be hard to come by, however, this does not mean no conclusions are possible.

As with the questions about the end of Ps 22, there is mixed opinion regarding how we are to read Mark and Matthew's accounts of Jesus' appropriation of this psalm. There are those, like Ahearne-Kroll, who argue that the author of the Gospel constructed the account in a certain way to make a certain point, and that Jesus probably did not quote this psalm at all, an approach I have rejected above.[35] There are also commentators who make the point that quoting the opening lines of a psalm implies that the whole psalm should be recounted by the hearers/readers.[36] Moo dismisses such an approach arguing that traditionally this only applied to a liturgical context.[37] In contrast, there are those who are reticent to look towards the positive conclusion of the psalm because "the reality of his [Jesus] sense of

---

32. Schaefer suggests that "God answers the desperate cry. The transition from tears to joy is sudden and without apparent cause (v. 22)" (Schaefer, *Psalms*, 55).

33. Regarding v. 22 Craigie suggests, "The words come in such striking contrast to the preceding lament and prayer, that one must presuppose the declaration of an oracle . . . announcing healing and health, after the prayer (vv. 20–22b), which give rise to this sudden declaration of confidence" (Craigie, *Psalms 1–50*, 198).

34. Hagner, *Matthew 14–28*, 845.

35. See Collins, *Mark*, 753–55.

36. See Nineham, *Gospel of St. Mark*, 428; and Hill, *Gospel of Matthew*, 355.

37. See Moo, *Old Testament*, 271–72.

A Dramatic Pentecostal/Charismatic Anti-Theodicy

abandonment must not be minimised" and looking towards the conclusion of the psalm risks doing just that.[38]

With this mixture of approaches to interpreting the text, a way forward is not easy to come by. However, if we recall that what we are aiming at is as thick a description as possible as to the situation and the speech-act that is being elicited, and that is to be gained with a Christocentric, canonical, typological method, a substantial way forward can be developed.

With that in mind my argument is that a fitting understanding of Jesus' performance of this lament psalm is one in which the cry calls to mind the first twenty-one verses, but points to v. 22 onwards. In this sense it is the most perfect performance of lament because Jesus performs it at the climax of the drama and the climax of the assault of evil and corruption on that which is most pure. In doing so he also points ahead, as he and the drama have done all along. As Douglas Moo suggests, "if Jesus quotes Ps. 22:1 contextually, it is reasonable to expect that the first verse has direct reference to his present experience, and that the triumphant conclusion alludes to the circumstances of the Resurrection and its consequences."[39] In his evocation of this psalm Jesus does indeed point ahead to God hearing and acting. The lament in the face of the most fierce of circumstances possible in the drama will be matched by the most awe-inspiring response by the Father that not only brings salvation to the lamenter but to the whole of creation. This in turn must elicit the most profound and heartfelt praise. However, as a counterbalance I suggest we must also follow Hagner when he states, "In no way however does this lessen the reality of the present abandonment . . . and it is going too far to take Jesus' cry as a cry of victory."[40] My suggestion is that Jesus' use of this lament psalm is the epicenter of his performance that, as we shall see, provides us with a performance on which to improvise. Before we move to our performance however, there are two last points to be made.

Firstly, as Jesus nears death he still has the strength to give out a loud cry. Although I am in agreement with Hagner about this not being a cry of victory, I suggest that this does point to the fact that he is still very much in control of the situation that he himself has chosen until "it is finished." As France points out, "The loud cry which precedes Jesus' death, and his equally loud shout in v. 46, indicate that, unlike most crucified men, Jesus

---

38. Evans, *Mark 8:27—16:20*, 507. See also France, *Gospel of Mark*, 652–53; Filson, *Commentary on Matthew*, 297; Anderson, *Gospel of Mark*, 345–46; Öhler, "To Mourn," 152.

39. Moo, *Old Testament*, 272. See also Cole, *Gospel According to Mark*, 243–44; Albright and Mann, *Matthew*, 353.

40. Hagner, *Matthew 14–28*, 844.

died in full control of his faculties, perhaps even that he died when he himself chose."[41]

Secondly, in affirmation of this first point, Jesus willingly and actively hands his Spirit over to the Father when the task at hand is done. There are very clear points of activity in Jesus actions that rebut the idea that he was unwillingly at the mercy of outside agents. The importance of this will become clear as we move through the next section regarding our performance in the light of Jesus's.

A Dramatic Pentecostal/Charismatic Anti-Theodicy: Improvising on a Divine Performance of Lament

We must reiterate the fact that as the curtain rises on the current act, evil and its effects in creation are still very much apparent. The divine actor has won the victory at the cross but this victory is to be implemented by his followers as they seek to give a fitting improvised performance in the aftermath of Jesus's. In addition, we shall recall that to aid in this we have been left with a Script that offers direction and the Spirit of the resurrected Christ as prompt for our performances. We must ask afresh then, in the light of what has gone before: What does it mean to produce a fitting Pentecostal/Charismatic performance in the face of seemingly innocent, meaningless suffering when God appears to be absent in Act 4 of the drama?

A Provision of Christological Inspiration and Hope

To answer this we begin by recalling the end of the drama as we have been told it so far. In the end it is God that consummates and completes the victory. We therefore begin with a realization that the implementation of victory will always be part of the performance until the day of consummation. That said, it logically follows that suffering will also therefore be with us until that day. The gap between the Kingdom breaking in and the consummation—the "now/not yet" tension—characterizes the current act in the drama. We are to implement the victory in our own lives and also in the world around us but, we will inevitably come up against suffering in the midst of that. As we look to Jesus to help us perform our parts fittingly, we can begin to notice that he moves from a place of orientation, through the suffering and disorientation, to a place of resurrection or new orientation. What I wish to suggest is that this linear motion Christologically qualifies the spiral

---

41. France, *Gospel of Matthew*, 1074.

A Dramatic Pentecostal/Charismatic Anti-Theodicy

paradigm in the Old Testament and signifies the spiral-like nature of our parts prior to the consummation. Whereas Jesus moves from orientation to disorientation to perfect re-orientation, until the final resurrection—of which Jesus is the first fruits—we are caught in an upward spiral in which the re-orientation we experience will turn into orientation and disorientation that will then move to re-orientation once more as we spiral upwards. Where Jesus' motion through this was linear, ours is spiraling, and with each turn we add fresh experience that provides fresh memories and hope for the next cycle—as was outlined in chapter 5. By qualifying the response of Israel in Act 2 of the drama in this way, Jesus' performance brings to the fore at least two points regarding how we, as current actors in the drama, are to view and take direction from Act 2 of the Script.

Firstly, rather than simply seeing it as an outdated performance superseded by the performance of Jesus, the examination above provides substantial support for the argument that the performance of Israel in situations of suffering similar to that being considered here, is to be examined with a high degree of attention. This is so because Act 2 contains important parts of the Script that not only provide background information but also direction for current performances. Although the argument being made in this study is that Jesus' performance qualifies them and in some senses modifies them (as will be discussed shortly), understanding the qualifications and giving a fitting performance in the light of them is only possible if the scenes in the act being qualified are understood and taken seriously. To refer back to the dramatic hermeneutical method outlined in chapter 4 that is being used here, we are aiming at non-identical repetition that improvises on a previous performance in order to produce a fitting one in the current act. And, we may further recall that to produce non-identical repetition and to improvise on a previous performance means that the previous performance must be well understood and taken seriously. This is so because, although it is "non-identical," the current performance is repetitive, meaning that an improvised performance will have significant overlap with the performance it is improvising on. In this case, as there is significant overlap between Israel's performance in Act 2 and Jesus' performance, in seeking to improvise on the performance of Jesus, performances by the current actors should also have significant overlap with Israel's performance. Therefore, to dismiss Israel's performance as outdated is to severely hinder one's ability to perform fittingly in the present.

That said, the second point is that in the specific case of lament in the face of seemingly innocent, meaningless suffering when God appears to be absent, the Script offers direction regarding how to perform. As was noted in chapter 5, although there is some variation in form, there is a clear structure and framework present in Act 2 regarding provision of direction for fitting performance in the face of the type of suffering in question. To ignore such clear direction is to risk failure of carrying on our through-line towards eschatological consummation.

As noted though, the term "Christological qualification" is not a vacuous term and so in the occurrence of the qualification there are some modifications that take place regarding how lament is to be performed. There are at least two alterations that take place in between the performances of Act 2 and fitting performances in the current act.

Firstly, in Christologically qualifying the performances of lament prior to his performance, Jesus offers fresh provision of inspiration and hope to the current actors. This is so because, whereas the Old Testament offers only vague ideas as to how the spiral will eventually conclude, Jesus literally places flesh on the bones with his performance. He not only provides a more detailed picture of what that conclusion will look like, he actually embodies it, thus providing a source of inspiration and hope previously unseen. It is this memory, this testimony, as recorded in Scripture, that infuses all other memories of the salvific actions of God—both those that have occurred and those that will—with fresh life and power. In terms of resisting those who try to shut down the voice of the one lamenting, following Metz, this is the most dangerous memory of all. This memory provides fuel for the cry that this is not how life should be and silently continue to be, for salvation has come, is coming and will come. This memory of the performance of Jesus provides voice to those who protest regarding the painful absence of the "now" of the Kingdom in the "not yet" of the present, as those two poles are held in tension. This memory therefore offers greater anchorage than was previously possible, as well as greater fuel for the hope that drives lament along.

The performance of Jesus, secondly, opens up a new dimension to the performance of lament previously unavailable to the actors, a dimension of particular interest to Pentecostal/Charismatic theology—the aid of the Holy Spirit in the performance. This is a crucial point for this study, so we need dedicate an extended examination.

A Pneumatological Aid

Drawing on a point made by Gutiérrez about Job highlighted in chapter 5 of this study, I wish to suggest that a possible role for which the Holy Spirit is sent is to help the sufferer to lament. To draw this point out further we must begin by returning to Job.

A Dramatic Pentecostal/Charismatic Anti-Theodicy

The Joban Roots

In three places in the book of Job (9:33; 16:19; 19:25), amidst his suffering, Job appeals to a mysterious other to aid him in his somewhat tumultuous relationship with God. In the first of these instances the general consensus amongst commentators is that Job wishes there was some sort of arbiter between him and God. Balentine points out that "Elsewhere in the Hebrew Bible, the môkîah is described as a third party, who listens to disputes between two persons and offers a judgement that both accept as appropriate (cf. Gen 31:37)."[42] Taking this verse alone it is hard to make any headway regarding who this could be and if they even exist, but, if we examine the second of the verses, further clues emerge. However, this is also where opinion begins to differ as to the identity of this character.

In 16:19, Job appeals to some sort of heavenly witness who will vouch for him. Opinion is divided as to whether this character is God or not and where it is not thought to be God, various theories have been suggested.[43] As the drama moves on, in 19:25 we find further mention of who it is that Job is appealing to, but this time we are allowed a clearer picture of who this character is. The Hebrew term gō'ēl is understood by most commentators to refer to a "kinsman-redeemer," which in the Old Testament was the person who looked after and redeemed his fellow kinsman by avenging them, buying them back from slavery and defending them, amongst other things. As Pope puts it "the gō'ēl is the defender of the widow and orphan, the champion of the oppressed."[44] Balentine also points out that "In religious usage, God is described as the gō'ēl of those who have fallen into distress or bondage (e.g., in Egypt: Exod 6:6; 15:13; Ps 74:2; in Babylon: Isa 43:1, 14; 49:7–9)."[45] He continues stating, "It is noteworthy that God's responsibilities as gō'ēl includes pleading the case (ryb), that is, providing 'legal aid,' for those too helpless or too vulnerable to obtain justice for themselves (Ps 119:154; Prov 23:11; Jer 50:34; Lam 3:58)."[46] However, the split over the identity of the character remains intact amongst commentators in the light of this verse as well.

---

42. Balentine, *Job*, 172. See also Anderson, *Job*, 151; Clines, *Job 1–20*, 243; Gutiérrez, *On Job*, 56–59; Habel, *Book of Job*, 196; Hartley, *Book of Job*, 181; Pope, *Job*, 76.

43. Andersen, Gutiérrez, and Hartley all suggest that the heavenly witness is God. See Hartley, *Book of Job*, 264; Andersen, *Job*, 182; and Gutiérrez, *On Job*, 56. Balentine, Clines, Habel, and Pope, however, suggest that it is something or someone else.

44. Pope, *Job*, 146. See also Gutiérrez, *On Job*, 64–65; Habel, *Book of Job*, 305; Balentine, *Job*, 297; Clines, *Job 1–20*, 459; Hartley, *Book of Job*, 292–93.

45. Balentine, *Job*, 297.

46. Ibid.

What then are we to make of this issue? It is clearly difficult to ascertain who exactly Job is appealing to, but this raises the further issue as to whether Job knows fully who it is he is appealing to. Commentators on both sides of the fence seem to assume that Job is clear on who the mysterious character is, whether God or not. Those who dismiss the idea of it being God generally do so on the grounds of it being illogical, since Job also sees God as enemy at these points.[47] My contention is that this argument is based on the concept that logic remains pure and intact in times of intense pain and crisis, a point anyone who has experienced such times, directly or indirectly, knows to be absurd. However, perhaps we also must tread carefully in strongly affirming that Job is clearly and without question referring to God at these points.

Gerald Janzen states regarding 16:19, "The point is precisely that, in the face of a universe whose earthly and heavenly figures—friends and God—are all against him, Job imaginatively reaches out into the dark and desperately affirms the reality of a witness whose identity is completely unknown to him."[48] Perhaps it is closer to the truth to suggest that Job believes both in his own innocence and cause and in a divine being who will vouch for him, but, at the same time, is struggling with the God who appears to be afflicting him. A paradox this may be to cold hard logic but, in the blind cries of the suffering believer reaching in the dark for some relief and help, such an interpretation seems to be the most sensible. However, we are in a more privileged position than Job, as we can read this text afresh in the light of Jesus and the whole canon. My suggestion in doing this is that not only will it shed light on how we can understand this paradox afresh, it will also show how Job's approach can be re-appropriated by Pentecostal/Charismatic Christians in their practice of lament. To do this we must turn first to the Paraclete sayings in John's Gospel, as these sayings are authorized by Jesus as the speaker of them and directly relate the work of the Holy Spirit to that of an advocate, thus linking in with the type of divine aid Job appears to be requesting.

The Paraclete Sayings

In chapters 14, 15 and 16 of John's gospel we find that on five occasions John tells us that Jesus explained to the disciples that he would send the Spirit to teach them, remind them, testify about Jesus and glorify Jesus, and that the Spirit would be a helper, or advocate and would "prove the world wrong

---

47. See Habel, *Book of Job*, 305; and Pope, *Job*, 125.
48. Janzen, *Job*, 125.

about sin and righteousness and judgement," (John 14:16, 26; 15:26; 16:7–11, 12–15). Raymond Brown sums these roles up stating, "the basic functions of the Paraclete are twofold: he comes to the disciples and dwells within them, guiding and teaching them about Jesus; but he is hostile to the world and puts the world on trial."[49] Regarding the term "Paraclete" Beasley-Murray points out that, "In secular Greek it was used especially of one called to help another *in court*."[50] Regarding John 16:7–11 in particular, Barrett writes, "The Paraclete will convict (ἐλέγξει) the world. ἐλέγχειν means 'to expose,' 'to bring to the light of day,' 'to show a thing in its true colours'. It is the activity of a judge and prosecuting counsel in one."[51] Although Barrett pushes the point that, "he [Paraclete] is a prosecuting rather than defending counsel" I suggest that the Paraclete does not need to be limited to this role but can be called on in defense as well, as shown by Jesus' words to his disciples in Mark 13:11.[52] This fits Beasley-Murray's understanding of a helper in court as help can be in the form of prosecution or defense.

Several scholars make a link between the Paraclete sayings and the texts in Job discussed above.[53] Such links are partially based on the idea of spiritual beings who make intercession in the heavenly court on behalf of humans that emerged in Jewish Scriptures and Second Temple Judaism.[54] However Herman Ridderbos contests such an idea as well contesting the idea of the Paraclete in John's Gospel being a legal advocate.[55] Whether the term originates from Jewish thought matters little here though. The point that needs to be drawn out for the sake of this study is not whether the source of the concept is in Job or some other Jewish texts but rather, when read canonically with a Christocentric key, whether the Johannine and Joban texts enable a clear model of lament to emerge—of which I suggest they do. However before we can fully tie these texts together we must turn to a final text in the canon in order to add further clarity—Romans 8. This text is selected because it is arguably the only example in the early church in which the practice of lament and the work of the Holy Spirit within that is explicitly discussed. It is also a text

---

49. Brown, *John (xiii–xxi)*, 1136.

50. Beasley-Murray, *John*, 256. See also Lincoln, *Gospel According to St John*, 393; and Morris, *Gospel According to John*, 649.

51. Barrett, *Gospel According to St. John*, 90.

52. Ibid., 462. See also Brown, *John (xiii–xxi)*, 1136.

53. See Brown, *John (xiii–xxi)*, 1138, Lindars, ed., *Gospel of John*, 478; Schnackenburg, *John*, 3:146.

54. See Brown, *John (xiii–xxi)*, 1138; and Lincoln, *Gospel According to St. John*, 393.

55. Ridderbos, *Gospel of John*, 502–3.

that Pentecostal/Charismatic scholars and non-scholars alike have drawn on in discussing the practice of Pentecostal lament.

Romans 8

In Paul's letter to the Romans we find that in chapter 8 Paul sheds further light on the role of the Spirit. In vv. 15–17 he points out that our cries to God as Father are only possible because of the Spirit at work within us. Joseph Fitzmyer suggests that "Christians cry 'Abba, Father' because the Spirit so enables them and cries with them."[56] Gordon Fee notes, "The Spirit is God's abiding presence, but he does not eliminate our humanity; he has redeemed it and now works through it."[57] As adopted children of God, we still have responsibility for our actions, but we are now aided by the Spirit. As Fee further states, "the coming of the Spirit does not overtake or overwhelm. Rather the Spirit has come to do what Torah could not—inscribe obedience on the heart in such a way that God's people will follow in God's ways by his direct help."[58]

In the verses that follow, Paul explains the broken situation of creation and the vision that gives hope and he states specifically of humans, "not only the creation, but we ourselves, who have the first fruits of the Spirit, groan inwardly while we wait for adoption, the redemption of our bodies," (v. 23). The picture Paul seems to be painting here is one not unlike the form of lament seen in the Old Testament tradition. There is the reality of the situation which Moo describes as "frustration at the remaining moral and physical infirmities that are inevitably a part of this period between justification and glorification."[59] But, there is also the hope of resurrection and eternal life—which in this case, believers have been given a taste of by the presence of the Spirit as first fruits. We have here then the two key elements that are characteristic of lament—the painful reality of the current suffering and the hope of resolution that both anchors the sufferer in a particular understanding of the drama as well driving the lament forward in anticipation of resolution.

The difference in this act of the drama, as pointed to in Act 2 by Job, is brought to light as Paul continues: "Likewise the Spirit helps us in our weakness; for we do not know how to pray as we ought, but that very Spirit intercedes with sighs too deep for words. And God, who searches the heart,

56. Fitzmyer, *Romans*, 501.
57. Fee, *God's Empowering Presence*, 567.
58. Ibid., 569.
59. Moo, *Romans*, 519. See also Dunn, *Romans 1–8*, 490.

knows what is the mind of the Spirit, because the Spirit intercedes for the saints according to the will of God," (vv. 26–27). John Murray states, "The hope and expectation of the glory to be revealed sustains the people of God in the sufferings and groanings of this present time."[60] Although Murray is partially right, he also, I suggest, has not grasped the full force of what Paul is saying. It is not just hope that Paul suggests sustains the people but, in the light of the lament tradition, it is the very groanings themselves and more than that, the Spirit aiding them in their groanings. Fee notes, "What we learn is that the Spirit's presence not only guarantees our future hope (v. 23), but he also takes an active and encouraging role as we await its realization by assisting us in prayer and interceding with God on our behalf."[61] Lament here is not discouraged but instead is met with the promise that when words fail and the lamenter does not know what to pray, the Spirit is given as aid—"the 'like-wise' in verse 26 indicates that the Spirit's 'coming to help' is comparable to the Spirit's 'bearing witness with our spirit [v. 16] that we are children of God.'"[62] Keck continues, "the weakness itself is met by the power of the Spirit."[63] Charles Talbert sums up how the Spirit assists in the practice of lament in this act of the drama when he states, "This comes in two ways: the presence of the Spirit in the present, functioning as a guarantee that the future is certainly coming (v. 23), and the intercession of the Spirit to enlist God's aid in their present journey (vv. 26–27)."[64] As further encouragement, Fee highlights that "The God who searches our hearts also knows the mind of the Spirit; thus the Spirit's 'appeal' is simultaneously in keeping with God (i.e., according to God's will) and on our behalf."[65]

With regards to its relevance to this study, it may appear that the particular Romans passage in question here has been satisfactorily covered. However, contrary to most scholars who have examined this passage, Fee thinks that there is something, particularly significant for Pentecostals and Charismatics, still left to be said regarding the work of the Spirit in the act of "groaning."

In approaching this we must first note that where Paul states "we do not know how to pray as we ought," (v. 26), Fee argues that this "does not refer to our not knowing *how* to pray, as though method or method and

60. Murray, *Romans*, 310.
61. Fee, *God's Empowering Presence*, 576.
62. Keck, *Romans*, 214.
63. Ibid.
64. Talbert, *Romans*, 220–22 (p. 221 contains a side article that is not part of the main text of the commentary, hence such a short quote appears to run across a number of pages).
65. Fee, *God's Empowering Presence*, 577.

Improvising on a Divine Performance of Lament

content together were at issue."[66] Instead he argues that "these words imply that . . . our lack of knowledge has to do with the larger picture, as it were, thus '*what* to pray.'"[67] Building on this Fee highlights the fact that often the "inwardly" of v. 23 in conjunction with the Spirit using "sighs too deep for words," (v. 26) results in an understanding of prayer that is "not really 'groaning' at all, but is simply silent praying" and that this praying is "of a kind that is so deep and profound there simply are not words available for the Spirit to use."[68] This, Fee notes, "seems supported further by the explanation that God 'searches the heart,' implying that what he sees in the heart need never be spoken to us."[69] However, at this point Fee begins to draw in Paul's first epistle to the church in Corinth to make the case that what may actually be being suggested here is the use of tongues as "groaning" and that far from being silent, this use of tongues in most definitely vocal.[70]

In order to do this, Fee begins by arguing for the fact that prayer, whether in private or public, alone or with others, in the culture and context in which Paul was writing was generally done aloud.[71] He then draws on 1 Cor 14:14–15 in which Paul makes the distinction between praying "with the spirit" and praying "with the mind." In both cases, Fee suggests that these prayers are *spoken*, with the difference being that Paul *understands* that which is generated in his mind. That which is not generated in the mind, "praying with the spirit," Fee argues, "in that context can refer only to the praying in tongues about which he [Paul] speaks in vv. 2, 19, and 28—private, articulated but 'inarticulate' with regard to his mind (that is, the Spirit prays and the mind itself is unfruitful in this case), and 'to himself and to God.'"[72] In such cases these utterances are understood to not require interpretation, unlike when tongues are used in public gatherings (vv. 27–28). Fee also links the mixed language of "my spirit" and "the spirit"

---

66. Ibid., 578.
67. Ibid., 579.
68. Ibid., 580.
69. Ibid.
70. In "Pauline Theology," Fee summarizes the "three realities" that changed his mind regarding his belief that "inarticulate groanings" in Rom 8:26 refers to glossolalia. Key to this change of mind was his engagement with 1 Cor 14:14–19 in particular. See "Pauline Theology," 29–31.
71. Fee, *God's Empowering Presence*, 581.
72. Ibid. In his commentary on 1 Corinthians Fee argues that a key difference between Paul praying with his spirit (and therefore in tongues) and praying with his mind was that the former, as it was not understood by his fellow believers, was "for his own sake," whereas the latter, which was in the vernacular, was "for the sake of others." See Fee, *First Corinthians*, 670.

A Dramatic Pentecostal/Charismatic Anti-Theodicy

in the context of prayer in vv. 14–15 by interpreting it as "the Spirit prays in tongues through me."[73]

In correspondence to the Romans passage Fee notes that in both cases, "the Spirit prays within the believer, and . . . does so with 'words' that are not understood by the person praying."[74] In addition Fee also notes that in the same way that Paul switches between "my spirit" and "the spirit" in 1 Cor 14:14–15, he also seems to switch between the Spirit crying "Abba! Father!" in Gal 4:6 and the believer offering that cry in Rom 8:15, and the believer groaning inwardly in Rom 8:23 and the Spirit groaning or sighing in v. 26. In the light of his examination of 1 Cor 14:14–15 Fee concludes that in the latter two cases as with the first, it shows Paul's belief in the Spirit working from within the believer—thus the fluidity between mention of believer and Holy Spirit.

Far from the inward prayer being silent and wordless then, in the light of 1 Cor 14, Fee's argument is that it is instead private prayer in/with the Spirit that takes the form of tongues. Verse 27, rather than affirming silent prayer, in Fee's thinking therefore affirms his belief that although the believer does not know what the Spirit is praying in the tongues being spoken, God does.

It is here important to note that Fee's interpretation is not without objectors and that he is tentative about his conclusions.[75] However, that said, what Fee is proposing, far from being detrimental to what is being proposed in this study, adds the potential for further solidifying a specifically *Pentecostal/Charismatic* response to the type of suffering in question. If Fee's conclusions are correct, not only are there grounds for arguing for a pneumatological aid in the performance of lament, but specifically, one can propose that it is possible, particularly when one does not know what to pray, that the Spirit aids a fitting performance by enabling lament in the form of glossolalia.[76] Time and space do not allow for a full exploration

---

73. Fee, *God's Empowering Presence*, 582. Again in his commentary on 1 Corinthians Fee suggests, "The most viable solution to this ambiguity is that by the language 'my spirit prays' Paul means his own spirit is praying as the Holy Spirit gives utterance. Hence, 'my S/spirit prays'" (Fee, *First Corinthians*, 670).

74. Fee, *God's Empowering Presence*, 582.

75. Ibid., 584–86.

76. Fee notes that "At the same time glossolalia serves as a constant reminder that we, along with the whole of creation, continue to anticipate our final redemption," ("Pauline Theology," 35). Therefore, there are grounds for arguing that as well as the Spirit enabling lament in the form of glossolalia, the very manifestation of glossolalia, as a reminder of the anticipated redemption that is not yet here in full, provides further fuel for lament by reminding the one lamenting of what it is they are ultimate waiting and longing for. By enabling this practice of glossolalia, the Spirit therefore aids lament,

of this possibility in this study, as deeper exploration is necessary in order to do justice to the construction of a solid theological basis for belief and practice of such a performance. However, what we can say in the light of Fee's work is that he adds further support to the idea of a pneumatological aid generally in the performance of lament, and provides a significant route in to looking at the work of the Spirit as glossolalia specifically, in the performance of lament.

A Canonical Drawing Together

If we bring the various texts under consideration together and once again recall the task of improvising on Jesus' performance, we can see with greater clarity the role of the Spirit in our performances of lament. Arguably, the Spirit who brings unity between Father and Son at the cross is the same Spirit who enabled Jesus' performance of lament in Gethsemane and at the cross. This is so because in the same way that Paul in Rom 8 makes the point that we can call God "Abba, Father" because the Spirit dwells within us, so the same was true of the incarnate Son.[77] In reference to the Gospel of Mark, D. Lyle Dabney suggests, "Jesus is led throughout his mission and ultimately to his death by the eschatological power of God's Spirit."[78] He further notes that at the cross, "the Spirit of the Cross is *the presence of God with the Son in the eschatological absence of the Father.*"[79] A correction that requires making here is that it is a *seeming* absence rather than an actual one, and unity is maintained within this seeming absence by the presence of the Spirit with the Son. It is the presence of the Spirit that moves the Son from the cry of dereliction, through the vow of trust ("Father, into your hands I commend my Spirit," Luke 23:46), to the ultimate salvific act of God (the Resurrection).

That being the case, it is this Spirit who is also sent as helper to aid us to improvise on Jesus' performance in order to produce a fitting one of our own. If we then read again the Job passages, the John passages and the Romans passage in the light of this and in the light of Jesus' performance, we can say that it is the Spirit who helps us to lament in the face of suffering, it is the Spirit who we can call on as advocate, defender and helper as we protest

whilst at the same time providing hope that can fuel that lament. Such a practice potentially provides a unique and powerful illustrative window into the already/not yet tension that characterizes this act of the drama.

77. See Dabney, "*Pneumatologia Crucis*," 523.
78. Ibid.
79. Ibid., 524.

A Dramatic Pentecostal/Charismatic Anti-Theodicy

to God and it is the Spirit who arguably enables glossolalia as lament when we do not know what to pray.[80] It is therefore this Spirit of the resurrected Christ who aids us to maintain unity with God even in his seeming absence. Job read in isolation gives us a glimpse but, as argued above, there is a strong case for suggesting that what Job was grasping after in his wrestling with God is given in the form of the Spirit of God for the actors, in the current act, to aid them in lamenting and groaning as they cling on to the hope of final consummation and restoration. Larry McQueen notes, "the Spirit who has been poured out now flows into the lament, taking it up within the Spirit itself, for the Spirit groans on behalf of the individual."[81] As McQueen highlights, not only does the Spirit therefore aid us in our own lament, he also laments on our behalf.

We can say then that as well as Jesus providing a performance to improvise on in facing suffering, he also sends his Spirit to help, particularly with the performance of lament. In the same way that the Spirit unifies the Son and Father, in the performance of lament by the human actors it is this Spirit, enabling us to perform Christ, who unites us to Son and Father as perfect eschatological unity and communion is brought closer. In the light of Jesus' performance then, we can re-frame our understanding of these texts and specifically the work of the Spirit in the current act.

We are now in a position to fulfill the aim of the study and offer an answer to the question at the heart of it: What does it mean to produce a fitting Pentecostal/Charismatic performance in the face of seemingly innocent, meaningless suffering when God appears to be absent? The answer that we can now offer is: *To produce a fitting Pentecostal/Charismatic performance in the face of seemingly innocent, meaningless suffering when God appears to be absent means, to improvise on the performance of Jesus and lament to the Father with the aid of the Spirit as we seek to carry on our through-line towards eschatological consummation.* We can recall that eschatological consummation will involve the completion of the expulsion of sin, evil and

---

80. Some scholars argue that, based on texts such as Heb 4:14–16, Rom 8:34, and 1 John 2:1, it is Jesus that is our advocate. Miller suggests, "It is *our* loud cries and tears that Jesus now offers up to God" (Miller, *They Cried*, 317). Although there is truth in this, there is also the potential for a category mistake. In these texts, Jesus is the one who, having defeated sin, intercedes on behalf of *sinners*. The central focus here is with regard to the necessity of an advocate—the one who has taken the punishment for the sins of the world—to plead the case of the *guilty*. Although the Spirit is given by Jesus in the light of the Easter event, what I am suggesting here is that the Spirit is understood as the one who aids the seemingly *innocent sufferer* in their lament. The difference then is that the former case of advocate is with regard to the guilty sinner, whereas the latter is with regard to the seemingly innocent sufferer. The roles are thus subtly different.

81. McQueen, *Joel and the Spirit*, 71.

suffering, and that at that time God will dwell fully with his people. We can also recall that actors are to have this objective in view as they seek to find how best to help inaugurate the completion of this objective and move the drama towards its final completion. It is with this objective in view that one is able to carry on one's through-line and perform in a fitting manner to enable the correct movement of the drama. It is also important to recall that carrying on the through-line involves maintaining covenantal relationship with God as a central part of that. Steven Land suggests that Pentecostals believe "the power of the Spirit strengthens, sustains and directs all the affections through all the trials and temptations of life toward the goal of the kingdom of God."[82] What is being proposed here thoroughly affirms such a belief. As we reach the climax of this study, what we have established is that in times of seemingly innocent, meaningless suffering when God appears to be absent, a fitting way of performing, that enables the carrying on of ones through-line by seeking to maintain a healthy covenantal relationship with God, means to improvise on the performance of Jesus and lament to the Father with the aid of the Spirit.

Lament as "Dialogical Consummation"

There is a further point to consider here too as we re-engage with Vanhoozer's work. The concept of dialogical consummation was mentioned above, as was the apparent flaw when this idea was combined with the "effectual call." However, I suggest there may be potential in Vanhoozer's concept of prayer as a part of this dialogical consummation that we can use in our examination of the performance of lament.

Vanhoozer states, "*prayer is an asymmetrical dialogical interaction whereby God effects in us, through word and Spirit, a freedom of consent.*"[83] In bringing light to the eyes of our hearts and minds through word and Spirit, we can do nothing but respond, and in responding—via prayer—we are made into the likeness of Christ and our wills come in line with God's. Vanhoozer's prime example of this is in a passage already examined here: the Gethsemane scene in the Synoptic Gospels where Jesus' petition in prayer enables the move to obedience. The petition allows opportunity for the two wills to become one. In an earlier discussion on the book of Job, Vanhoozer concludes, "the theme of Job is arguably not the question of unjust suffering but that of right Author-hero dialogical relatedness."[84] In a similar fashion,

---

82. Land, *Pentecostal Spirituality*, 138.
83. Vanhoozer, *Remythologizing Theology*, 383.
84. Ibid., 346.

A Dramatic Pentecostal/Charismatic Anti-Theodicy

Scott Ellington, in a discussion of the end dialogues in Job, states, "This raises the intriguing possibility that *right speech* may, in certain contexts, include *wrong content* from a theological perspective."[85] Although I raise issue with Vanhoozer's concept of the "effectual call," if we apply firstly, the importance of dialogue, particularly over content, in the continuance of the divine-human relationship, and then secondly, add the concepts of dialogical consummation and determination, we can begin to see a fresh perspective on the performance of lament.[86] Dialogue via lament in a time of crisis in relationship keeps communication open and honest and therefore keeps the outcome of the dialogue (from a human perspective) open. This in itself would dialogically consummate the lamenter as it discloses where and how they turn in times of suffering. However, as followers of Christ and with the aid of the Spirit as helper and advocate in this process, dialogical *determination* can take place as the Spirit aids us with what to say, and in so doing brings unity between us and the Godhead. If we refer back to Jesus at the cross, we can say that it is the Spirit that enables his dialogical consummation and determination as he moves from dereliction to resurrection.

I am, however, reticent to take Vanhoozer's approach as far as he does on this matter as the conclusion would seem to be that in performing lament in suffering I will eventually come to see the hand of God in it and submit to his will. Such a view quickly gathers speed as it moves towards the conclusion of God ordaining all suffering for a particular reason and that we simply need to come round to his way of thinking. This, to me, severely oversimplifies a very complex problem, as does suggesting that the silence of God makes space for our consummation—a further point Vanhoozer argues for.[87] Although much of what Vanhoozer says is helpful for the discussion here, there appears to be a contradiction in his understanding of the revelation of God that is not as helpful. On the one hand he goes to great lengths to maintain the distinction between the economic trinity and the immanent trinity and the belief that what we know of the immanent is only glimpsed via the economic. However, on the other hand, some of the conclusions that he reaches regarding the immanent based on the revelation of the economic seem at best stretching the evidence and at worst presumptuous. The case in point here is an example of a dangerous presumption. The concepts of dialogical consummation and determination when applied in the fashion suggested here, in the light of the work of the Holy Spirit do

---

85. Ellington, *Risking Truth*, 118.

86. For Vanhoozer's discussion of "dialogical determination," see *Remythologizing Theology*, 381–86.

87. See Vanhoozer, *Remythologizing Theology*, 448–55.

further present the case that the Holy Spirit can be seen as being a very real aid in the performance of lament. He is an important part of us performing fittingly, as it is he that gives us direction, in conjunction with the Script, as to how to improvise on the performance of Christ in a situation of suffering. However, there remains a large element of mystery, as we see in a mirror dimly, regarding the silence of God, the timing of God and the actions of God that cannot, at least currently, be penetrated. I therefore suspect Vanhoozer overplays his hand on just how much we can see into the workings of the immanent trinity, which, in the case of the subject being discussed here means that he is suggesting more than he can prove. That said, we must hold on to the positives to be drawn from seeing the Spirit as aiding dialogical consummation and determination in lament.

Review and Categorization

We have, to this point, established a solid basis for firstly, holding to the belief that lament is an approach amidst innocent, meaningless suffering that was performed, and is therefore sanctioned, by Jesus. We have also, secondly, argued, following on from this, that the lament to be performed in the current act is enabled and aided by the Holy Spirit. If we return to the categorization of responses to evil and suffering outlined in chapter 2, we are now in a position to place this approach within them. It will come as little surprise that what is proposed here may be described as a Pentecostal/Charismatic Anti-Theodicy. In proposing guidance for performance that is Biblically rooted and, in particular, Christologically qualified and justified, as well as being pneumatologically aided, this approach uses positive aspects of the various Anti-Theodicy approaches discussed and overcomes the problems. Rather than offering a theoretical answer to a post-Enlightenment problem, it offers guidance for a practical response that is anchored in the Script. It thus qualifies as an Anti-Theodicy. It also acknowledges the importance of the work of the Spirit in that response whilst not dismissing belief in divine healing, exorcism and the educational nature of some suffering. In this sense it remains conducive to Pentecostal/Charismatic belief and practice whilst overcoming the issues raised with some of those beliefs and practices in chapter 3.

Having dealt with the role of the Script and the Spirit in the performance of lament, one area still remains to be discussed though—the performance of the acting community.

A Dramatic Pentecostal/Charismatic Anti-Theodicy

Practical Suggestions: Testimony

We must once more recall that the aim of this study has been: to answer the central research question by developing Biblically rooted, systematic guidance for the production of a fitting Pentecostal/Charismatic performance in the face of seemingly innocent, meaningless suffering when God appears to be absent. Engagement in a detailed conversation with a concrete community regarding the application of such guidance in their particular community rests well outside the bounds of this study. However, having brought the definition and justification of that guidance to completion I will close this chapter by suggesting how it may challenge and modify the theology and practice of testimony in Pentecostal/Charismatic communities. My justification for focusing on this particular practice is that, as will become clear, the use of testimony is central to the life of a Pentecostal/Charismatic community and so modification of its use in the light of the importance of lament will be paramount to any wider incorporation of the practice of lament in those communities.[88] Testimony, as may be noted from the work so far in this study, is also an important part of the practice of lament. Therefore, if the guidance offered in this study is to be seriously engaged with by Pentecostal/Charismatic communities, examination of the theology and practice of testimony as understood by those communities is unavoidable.

The following section will therefore begin by briefly outlining the function and role of testimony generally before moving to a more detailed examination of the function and role of Pentecostal/Charismatic testimony. This will be done by primarily following Tony Richie's work on Pentecostal testimony in his published Ph.D thesis, *Speaking by the Spirit*.[89] Having done this, a critique will be offered in the light of the

---

88. Three further practices that may also be re-appropriated in the light of this study are "glossolalia," "tarrying," and "praying through." One reason why I have not discussed re-appropriation of tarrying and praying through is because, important though these ideas may be to some, they are not necessarily universally used and understood in the types of communities to which this work is aimed, whereas testimony, it is suspected, is. I have not opted to discuss glossolalia at length because of time and space constraints. Given the nature of the content of this work, offering direction for the modification of the theology and practice of testimony also seemed a more natural direction in which to go than attempting the same with glossolalia.

89. Richie, *Speaking by Spirit*. In engaging with Richie the term "Pentecostal" will become dominant, as opposed to "Pentecostal/Charismatic." This is so because, although the conclusions drawn from this section are intended to be applicable within *Pentecostal/Charismatic* communities where testimony of the kind examined here is practiced, Richie is, in his work, focusing mainly on classical Pentecostal communities and their theology and practice. Therefore, the language used in the following discussion will reflect this. However, the use of "Pentecostal/Charismatic" will re-emerge due to this author's intent

latter examination in particular, and the argument made in the study thus far. This will then be followed by suggestions for modifications in theology and practice of Pentecostal/Charismatic testimony, in continued engagement with Richie's work, in order to develop Pentecostal/Charismatic testimony as Anti-Theodicy. This section will then close with some "Practical Directives" for how the modifications could be introduced into Pentecostal/Charismatic communities. We shall begin by briefly examining the function and role of testimony generally.

The Function and Role of Testimony

Richie highlights the point that "Apparently testimony is universally prevalent among humans but present in varied ways, occurring in juridical, religious, or social contexts."[90] Following J. L. Austin, testimony can be understood as a particular speech-act which Austin bracketed in the category of "expositives" alongside "reporting," amongst others.[91] To refer back to speech-act theory, although "testimony" can, in terms of illocution, be universally categorized in this way, the perlocution—the intended result— of any particular testimony will vary depending on the intentions of the speaker and the context of the testimony. In short, the one giving testimony is bearing witness to something in order to produce a certain response in the hearer/s, but the reason for bearing witness and the response sought after will vary depending on context. Testimony is therefore, also, a source of knowledge and thus a source that aids construction of worldview as well as initiating and aiding change of worldview. C. A. J. Coady, in his defense of the legitimacy of testimony as a source of knowledge, places it alongside perception, memory and inference with "perception at the centre."[92] Mark Cartledge, in a similar exploration of the place of testimony as a source of knowledge, draws on Robert Audi's "five sources of knowledge" in which testimony is placed alongside perception, memory, consciousness and reason and draws on all four of them as sources for its own generation.[93] As social creatures, and particularly in the context of a worshipping community, testimony is therefore of the utmost importance for the continuation

---

to make the conclusions of the discussion as widely applicable as possible.

    90. Ibid., 130.

    91. Austin, *Things with Words*, 160–63.

    92. Coady, *Testimony*, 147.

    93. Cartledge, *Testimony*, 4–5. See also Audi, *Epistemology*, particularly the Introduction and chapter 5.

A Dramatic Pentecostal/Charismatic Anti-Theodicy

and modification of a worshipping community's story and worldview as it is a source of edification, modification and challenge.

The Function and Role of Pentecostal/Charismatic Testimony

Testimony has traditionally been a particularly important feature of Pentecostal/Charismatic practice and, as would be expected, there are certain characteristics regarding how it is practiced and why, that mark it out as different from the practice of testimony in other contexts and communities. In suggesting how Pentecostal testimony could provide a unique Pentecostal contribution to interreligious dialogue, Tony Richie sought to define such testimonies as well as contextualize them in order to further clarify their theology and practice. With regard to definitions, Richie confined his discussion to the categories of "Function-Practical," "Transformational," and "Liturgical."[94] With regards to context his categories were, "Autobiographical," "Biblical," "Theological," "Pastoral," "Doxological," "Pneumatological," "Historical," and "Sociological."[95] In what follows I will firstly outline the content of Richie's definitions, followed by an outline of the various contexts. In doing this a clear understanding of Pentecostal testimony will be generated in order to engage with and modify by way of developing Pentecostal/Charismatic testimony as Anti-Theodicy. We begin with Richie's definitions.

DEFINITIONS

"Functional-Practical"

Richie notes generally, "Pentecostal testimony is primarily a grateful public sharing of God's gracious work in one's own life to the glory of God. Testimony is a telling of the story of God's words and acts in one's own life."[96] In this sense it "is a distinctive act of ritual worship. As such, it is addressed primarily to God and is expressed primarily for God."[97] What Pentecostal testimony generally is *not* is "creedal or dogmatic confession" or "evangelistic proclamation," and it may not necessarily be didactic.[98] Instead "Pen-

---

94. Richie, *Speaking by Spirit*, 132–35.
95. Ibid., 138–47.
96. Ibid., 3–4.
97. Ibid., 166.
98. Ibid., 3.

tecostals tend to understand testimony more functionally"[99] and therefore "more in terms of what it does or helps to do than through cognitive terminological nuances."[100] In terms of Richie's "Functional-Practical" definition of testimony, as well as offering praise and worship to God, testimony functions as a practical reminder to the community that the Holy Spirit is still working through signs and wonders in the present, as he was in the New Testament, and it challenges the hearers to seek participation in the work of the Holy Spirit. As Richie notes,

> Whenever a Pentecostal testifies to their being saved, sanctified, and filled with the Holy Spirit, or to their being healed and delivered, or to an amazing or possibly miraculous answer to prayer or divine intervention of some kind, the always implicit, and sometimes quite explicit, message is God still does these things today.[101]

"Transformational"

Richie states, "Life experiences, curses as well as blessings, are addressed publicly to the glory of God in the context of the Christian story. Testimonies and the personal experiences they recount all stand under the final authority of inspired Scripture."[102] Pentecostal testimony is not simply accepted without question. Here we return again to corporate involvement in the practice of interpretation. Richie notes, "testimony requires interpretation, evaluation, and judgement, as well as weighing against the character of the one who testifies."[103] In the context of Pentecostal testimony, it is understood that the community interprets and judges, with the aid of the Holy Spirit, "under the final authority of inspired Scripture." This in turn leads to the almost certain occurrence of transformation on the part of some, if not all those involved (including the one testifying), as correct interpretation is discerned and reception of that interpretation and the influence of the Holy Spirit take effect. It is, therefore, not a given that the testimony will be legitimate, but instead it is weighed in the light of Scripture and in the power of the Holy Spirit in order to discern the presence of God in the words and actions of the one testifying.

99. Ibid., 132.
100. Ibid., 133.
101. Ibid.
102. Ibid.
103. Ibid., 130.

A Dramatic Pentecostal/Charismatic Anti-Theodicy

"Liturgical"

Testimony as practiced in worship services has a liturgical nature about it in that it is a ritual practice engaged in as part of that service. As has already been noted, testimony is about what God has done and is offered as praise to God. In worship services in particular, it therefore provides a vehicle for challenge and engagement with God by way of the Holy Spirit for all those present. As Richie notes, "Pentecostal testimonies express the stories of God's people in ways that transform the spiritual reality of worshipers as an important element in encountering God's Spirit and power in and through worship."[104] Therefore, although not liturgical in the sense of some more established denominations, testimony still may be defined as such within Pentecostal communities.

Context

Having briefly outlined Richie's definitions, we can move on to briefly outline the various contexts he uses to further examine Pentecostal testimony. We begin with "Autobiographical."

"Autobiographical"

As has been noted above, Pentecostal testimony is not an intellectual statement of ascent and so is not formal in the way that a creedal statement or a dogmatic confession is. Due to the narrative nature of Pentecostalism, testimony is instead autobiographical in context as it recounts the activity of God in the unfolding story (or perhaps drama!) of the life of the one testifying. As Richie highlights, "They are autobiographical and doxological stories of God's activity as experienced in human lives here and now."[105]

"Biblical"

Given the high view of Scripture maintained by Pentecostals, the Biblical context is an extremely important one for testimony. Richie suggests, "In the Old Testament, testimony has to do mainly with God's self-revelation to Israel, and in the New Testament, with the additional revelation of Jesus

---

104. Ibid., 135.
105. Ibid., 138.

Christ to the world."[106] With the story of Salvation History as the backdrop, particularly the story of the victory of Jesus at the cross, Pentecostal testimony involves "the telling of one's personal narrative or spiritual story as it participates in or illustrates the story of Christ and his gospel."[107] Richie also goes on to note that Biblically, "What has happened and is remembered from the past informs the needs of the present and results in experiences of fresh encounters with God that may result in some reinterpretation of the past."[108] He continues, "In Pentecostal testimony, the deeds of God are told in faith that these deeds will be repeated in different contexts as the need arises."[109] Pentecostal testimony is therefore produced through the lens of the Biblical testimony of Salvation History whilst at the same time enabling interpretation of that story.

"Theological"

In following on from the "Biblical" context the theological context of testimony is entwined with it. In contrast to more cerebral, intellectual modes of doing theology, testimony embraces story-telling in the dynamic relationship between Salvation History as portrayed in Scripture and the reality of the continual unfolding of that history in the life of the one testifying. Embedded within the testimonies of these current characters in the story are theological truths that must not be ignored or missed just because they are not communicated in a more clinical, propositional fashion. As Richie warns, "Missing the theological content of Pentecostal testimony because of its mode of communication would be a categorical mistake."[110]

"Pastoral"

Drawing on the work of Robert McCall, Richie highlights the decline in story-telling in the pastoral context of Pentecostal communities, which is understood as a very negative occurrence. If testimony could be encouraged and thus increase in frequency, McCall suggests that it could "help us deal with our own insecurities, inconsistencies, and uncertainties through shared testimonies and stories in a secure environment where fellow believers are

---

106. Ibid.
107. Ibid., 139.
108. Ibid., 139.
109. Ibid.
110. Ibid., 140.

willing to listen with interest and respond with understanding, care and mutual support."¹¹¹

"Doxological"

As has already been mentioned, the giving of one's testimony generally occurs in the course of a worship service, but there are occasions when there will be "testimony services" that are entirely dedicated to the giving of testimonies. Richie states, "Pentecostal testimonies are soteriologically based doxological narratives of historical occurrences viewed through the lens of faith."¹¹² By this he means that testimonies are accounts of powerful, often miraculous and healing acts of God in the life of the one testifying that are understood in the light of the gospel of Christ and are recounted with the intent of praise and worship to God by both the one testifying and those listening. By aiming at drawing all present into celebration and praise by way of testimonies it is suggested that this becomes an occasion of "liberated and liberating worship," free from the limits of acceptable worship in other contexts.¹¹³

"Pneumatological"

Rather than simply being a purely human authored recounting of the events, instead, testimony is commonly understood within Pentecostal communities to be speech that is aided by the work of the Holy Spirit. I agree with Richie when he states, "For our purposes, it is enough to understand that in certain circumstances, that is, when the Spirit so leads and moves, in Pentecostal worship services testimony can function as Spirit-inspired speech."¹¹⁴

"Historical"

One of the most important access points to the history of Pentecostalism is the testimonies offered within Pentecostal communities. Given the oral-narrative nature of Pentecostalism, this is commonly how history is

---

111. R. D. McCall, "Storytelling and Testimony: Reclaiming a Pentecostal Distinctive." DMin diss., Columbia Theological Seminary, 1998, 52, cited in Richie, *Speaking by Spirit*, 143.

112. Richie, *Speaking by Spirit*, 144.

113. Ibid.

114. Ibid., 145.

conveyed. However, due to this method, although that which is recounted corresponds with reality, the content of testimony is the result of a certain interpretation of that reality as well as selection and rejection of aspects of it when deciding on the content and structure of the testimony. This must be borne in mind when considering the historical context of testimony.

"Sociological"

Richie states, "Testimony may be the moment when irreversible bridge burning occurs."[115] This is so because in testifying in the way common in Pentecostal practice, one is choosing to affirm a certain worldview and therefore reject others. Pentecostal testimony thus constitutes a significant method for affirming a particular social narrative of a specific community as well as showing that one agrees with that narrative. Testimony therefore plays an important part in determining whether one is accepted by a community and how one is viewed within that community.

Having considered Richie's definitions and contexts of Pentecostal testimony we can summarize by saying that Pentecostal/Charismatic testimony continues and reinforces a particular worldview that centers on the drama of Salvation History and the victory of Jesus by way of testifying to how that drama is being played out in the current scenes of the life and community of the one testifying. Of particular importance is the work of the Holy Spirit in the life of the one testifying. In recounting the acts of the Spirit in the scenes of their life, the one testifying aims, at least partially, to edify the community of believers. Their testimony also challenges hearers to seek to engage with the drama by seeking encounters with the Holy Spirit (like those testified about), as well as challenging them regarding how they have interpreted the scenes of their lives thus far. At the center of this practice of testimony is the aim of giving glory to God.

With this as an examination of the function and role of Pentecostal/Charismatic testimony, we are one step closer to being able to offer an argument for how such testimony may be modified in the light of what has been offered so far in this study. However, before this can be done, we need first, in a similar way to what has already been carried out in this study, highlight relevant problems within the understanding and use of Pentecostal/Charismatic testimony thus far explored.

---

115. Ibid., 146.

A Dramatic Pentecostal/Charismatic Anti-Theodicy

A Critique

As stated above, Pentecostal/Charismatic testimony is commonly understood to partially function as a practice that reinforces key beliefs of the worshipping community and challenges and modifies others. However, the central criticism to highlight here, particularly in the light of the argument being made in this study, is that it can also give rise to deciding whether a person is accepted or rejected by a community—or at the very least, whether their worldview is accepted or rejected. This is so due to the issues raised in chapter 4 regarding where authority lies in determining right belief and practice from wrong.[116] Although it is claimed that interpretation and determination of the legitimacy of testimony is ultimately brought under the authority of Scripture, we have already seen that, in reality, Pentecostal/Charismatic communities place a far greater weight of authority on their particular selective reading and interpretation of Scripture than they are often willing to admit. The result of this is that a testimony's legitimacy is commonly decided by how it measures up to a particular community's use of and interpretation of Scripture, and thus its worldview, beliefs and practices. For those that challenge or contradict these, rejection of their worldview, at the very least, will more than likely be immanent.

In his research on narratives used in worship in Pentecostal communities, Jean-Daniel Plüss, under the influence of Ricoeur, writes, "Testimony . . . is understood as a discourse in which event and meaning are fused by means of a symbolic tradition. This symbolic tradition mediates a relation between meaning and event, and thus manifests an interpretation."[117] He later states, "Their [Christian] testimony is a mediator between the secular and the Sacred, between the meaning of life and the events that shape it."[118] The basic point to be drawn out here is that in the actual creating and giving of testimony by the one testifying, the worldview in which they are embedded is used to supply the events experienced with a certain meaning as noted in the "Historical" section above. This is, of course, true of all of us. However, what is particularly important about this fact with regards to Pentecostal/Charismatic communities is that, generally speaking, this worldview is, as stated above, anchored in a *selective* use of and reading of Scripture (thus giving authority largely to the community), and it is a worldview that rejects significant challenges to that use of and reading of Scripture.

---

116. The examination of criteria that determines the *reliability* of a testimony is, of course, also a significant issue, however, time and space do not allow for a discussion of this issue here. For one example of such a discussion see Coady, *Testimony*, chapters 1–3.

117. Plüss, *Narratives in Worship*, 55.

118. Ibid., 77.

Further on in his exploration, Plüss discusses Vladimir Propp's idea that there is a limited amount of "functions" that a character can carry out within a story.[119] Applying this concept to Pentecostal testimonies, Plüss highlights the presence of common functions within these testimonies and in the light of this creates a fictional one in order to test whether it resonates with Pentecostals—which on the whole he finds it does.[120] The relevance of this is that Plüss' research seems to confirm that if one is embedded in a Pentecostal tradition, one is expected to see the world in a particular way and thus perceive, interpret and testify to a certain view of the world and events within it. In doing so, the very structure and content of what is an expected and acceptable testimony becomes rigidly fixed. This is all good and well unless conflict emerges between experience and worldview and there is no better example of when this occurs than when someone experiences some form of suffering. Where suffering, particularly of the seemingly innocent, meaningless variety, occurs, in a community that expects the intervention of the Holy Spirit in miraculous ways, questions must be asked as to how this event is understood in the light of the larger narrative. We saw in chapter 3 that the tendency within Pentecostal/Charismatic theology is either to blame the sufferer for not claiming their healing, or, to passively accept that God knows what he is doing. A result of this is that, "The great majority of public testimonies have a happy end. There is no sense of the tragic, except in the case of prolonged suffering, which then is interpreted as a period of catharsis, of purification and self-examination."[121] However, as Charles Farah was correct to point out, presuming to know the intentions of the divine playwright is a dangerous game to play, but so, it would appear, is lamenting within a community that determines such a response to be invalid. Scott Ellington warns, "If suffering is denied and lament is suppressed, complaint will continue in the community."[122] And, rather than in a healthy way, as suggested in the Script and particularly in the performance of Jesus,

> Feelings of anger and confusion, because they are suppressed and given no legitimate means of articulation, will be expressed in inappropriate and distorted ways that do not serve to build up

---

119. "Function is understood as an act of a character, defined from the point of view of its significance for the course of action" (Vladimir Propp, *Morphology of the Folktale*, 21, cited in Plüss, *Narratives in Worship*, 164).

120. Plüss, *Narratives in Worship*, 164–77. As with Richie, Plüss's research focuses specifically on Pentecostal communities, hence the narrower use of language in labeling.

121. Ibid., 186.

122. Ellington, "Loss of Testimony," 59.

A Dramatic Pentecostal/Charismatic Anti-Theodicy

in the community the expectation that God will act again as he is remembered to have done in the past.[123]

To further highlight the root issue that leads to such a rigid understanding of what constitutes an acceptable testimony, we can note Richie's belief, as stated above, that "In the Old Testament, testimony has to do mainly with God's self-revelation to Israel."[124] Although Richie may be right regarding the majority of testimony, he appears to miss the fact that significant parts of the Old Testament—large sections of the Psalms and Job in particular—are testimony to the very opposite of this—what Brueggemann refers to, as noted in chapter 5, as "countertestimony." This particularly highlights the fact that although testimony is brought under the authority of Scripture to test its legitimacy, it is a reading of Scripture that ignores significant sections of examples of testimony that run contrary to that advocated by Pentecostal communities. It is also interesting that Richie states that, regarding Pentecostal testimony, "Equal appreciation goes to the wisdom of the words of the oppressed and poor with those from other strata of society."[125] To further state the point I am making here, in reality, appreciation is only really likely to be given, regardless of status, if one's testimony follows a certain pattern. If one's experience does not match up to the expectations of that pattern, to testify honestly about those experiences would inevitably lead, not to liberation—as Richie suggests in the "Doxological" context but, more than likely, to becoming the one that is oppressed, and this is simply not what is advocated by Scripture. Richie suggests, "Those that seem different or just unfamiliar become first known and then loved as they tell testimonies revealing who they are and what they are about in the context of their faith life."[126] However, one cannot help but imagine, particularly with regards situations, and therefore testimonies, of seemingly innocent, meaningless suffering when God appears to be absent, that becoming "known" and "loved" in the course of such testimonies may well lead to a Job like situation in which his friends (in this case the community) try and brow beat Job (in this case the one bringing a "different" sort of testimony) into a particular worldview that shuts down the voice of the sufferer as well as the possibility that God may be wanting to do something different in this situation. Richie is indeed right in pointing out that, sociologically, the giving of testimony can burn bridges. However, it seems that depending on the content of the testimony,

---

123. Ibid.
124. Richie, *Speaking by Spirit*, 138.
125. Ibid., 137.
126. Ibid., 260.

those bridges could well be the ones that link the testifier with the very community in which they are testifying.

One may be forgiven for thinking at this point that, due to the above critique, I am heading towards arguing for the rejection of Pentecostal/Charismatic testimony as a vehicle for a fitting response to the situations of suffering in question in this study. However, that is not the case. Instead, the above critique sets the stage for the possibility of suitable modifications that, it will be argued, enable the uniqueness of Pentecostal/Charismatic testimony to come into its own in a fresh way. This is so because the modifications will enable the use of lament by way of testimonies meaning that the development of Pentecostal/Charismatic testimony as Anti-Theodicy will be possible. In providing this possibility a practice will be developed that is, perhaps, more fitting, with regard to taking direction from the Script on the subject of responses to the type of suffering in question in this study, than most denominations can offer. It is to these modifications and the development of Pentecostal/Charismatic testimony as Anti-Theodicy that we now turn.

Pentecostal/Charismatic Testimony as Anti-Theodicy

We saw in chapter 5 that the picture portrayed in the lament genre in Scripture is one of a faith that is defined, at least in part, by the fact that in the face of great difficulties and traumas, honesty is the most fitting policy, and sometimes that means that lament is the most fitting performance. In putting to use the hermeneutical tools proposed in chapter 4, what I have argued for in chapters 5 and 6 is guidance for a fitting Pentecostal/Charismatic performance, in the face of the type of suffering in question, that results in the practice of lament. However, we need here to bring that to bear in the practice of testimony specifically.

If we begin by returning to Plüss' research, we find that in response to Propp's analysis of functions, Plüss draws on the work of Claude Bremond, who suggests that Propp's idea that one function leads to another is false and therefore a plot may not necessarily reach the potential of its various functions, an example being that, "a struggle must not always end in victory."[127] With this in mind Plüss suggests, "the theodicy problem could find a more appropriate formulation in the light of contingency. There would be more room for *peripeteia*, the unexpected turn of events."[128] Rather than compromising a true rendering of reality by forcing experiences that chal-

127. Plüss, *Narratives in Worship*, 176.
128. Ibid., 177.

A Dramatic Pentecostal/Charismatic Anti-Theodicy

lenge a worldview into a mold that misrepresents that experience, and thus closes out challenging voices, Plüss calls for "testimonies of defeat" or "anti-testimonies." He suggests, "The danger of glossing over the problem of theodicy could be countered by the inclusion of 'testimonies of defeat' which in turn would render the 'testimonies of victory' more credible, and diminish a trivial rendition of existence."[129] If we once again recall the practice of lament examined in chapter 5, that has now been Christologically qualified and justified, we can recall Brueggemann's paradigm of "core testimony" and "countertestimony." In the light of this I wish to suggest that Plüss' labeling of "testimonies of defeat" or "anti-testimonies" be replaced by "countertestimonies." This is so because "anti-testimony" suggests one is somehow against testimony *per se*, which I am not, and "testimonies of defeat" suggests that the individual's story has concluded and there is no possibility of any positive outcomes. Countertestimony maintains the importance of testimony, particularly testimony that runs counter to the "core testimony," creates space for verbalizing a story which, as yet has not found any positive outcomes, but also leaves space for the possibility of such outcomes. We also saw in chapter 5 that the space created by countertestimony allowed lament to emerge as a practice that in turn enabled the maintenance of an honest relationship with God in the midst of deep suffering. I am thus supportive of Plüss' ideas but suggest, in the light of this study, that the above modification is required.

Having modified Plüss' idea in this way, we can move to modify Pentecostal/Charismatic testimony accordingly. In the light of the combination of Plüss' research and Brueggemann's categorization of the testimony of Israel in the Old Testament, we can re-categorize Pentecostal/Charismatic testimony as it currently stands—what Plüss' refers to as "testimonies of victory"—as "core testimony." Having argued for a canonical reading of the Script undertaken by way of a Christocentric key in seeking direction for a fitting performance in the current scenes of this act of the drama, it has been comprehensively argued that "core testimony," important though it is, only accounts for part of testimony as displayed in Scripture. Therefore, vocalization of core testimony only accounts for part of a fitting performance of testimony in the current act of the drama. Although it has an important part to play—a point I shall re-visit below—core testimony is only part of a fitting performance in the face of seemingly innocent meaningless suffering when God appears to be absent. The other significant part is taken up by "countertestimony." If Pentecostal/Charismatic testimony is to be truly brought under the authority of Scripture, the first,

---

129. Ibid., 186–87.

and perhaps most important, modification to be made is with regard to what constitutes "legitimate" testimony. Rather than a selective reading of Scripture that automatically leads to testimony only being acceptable if it is "core testimony," a "testimony of victory," based on the argument made in this study, legitimate testimony must be understood instead to be able to include "countertestimony" as well.

Critics may well feel inclined at this point to argue that I am moving towards watering down and devaluing Pentecostal/Charismatic testimony to the point of it losing its unique quality and power. However, this is not so. Instead, to return to Plüss' point above, the use of countertestimony, alongside testimonies of victory—core testimonies—actually makes those testimonies more credible. In addition to this, as I have already hinted at above, I further wish to suggest, again in the light of this study, that the testimonies of victory are actually an important, if not indispensable, part of the performance of lament and need sit alongside countertestimony within that performance. Here the idea of "modification" (rather than dismissal) gains greater clarity as, what has previously been designated as simply "testimony," is re-designated as "core testimony" and placed within a wider understanding of testimony, which now includes "countertestimony." In the same way that lament in the Bible often includes vows of trust that are based on the core testimony, lament in Pentecostal/Charismatic communities, having been Christologically justified and legitimized as a sound practice in the preceding chapters of this study, will include recollection of victories, by way of these testimonies of victory. Such testimonies will then sit alongside countertestimonies. In doing this the sufferer can be reminded of what God is capable of, which therefore provides hope that God can act again, and so act as fuel to drive the lament forward. Such testimonies can also be used, again as has been noted regarding the form and structure of lament in the Psalms, as prayer to God to motivate God to act. In this sense "testimonies of victory" as "core testimony" are vital to the performance of lament and the use of countertestimony within that.

Having established the importance of testimonies of victory and countertestimony as complimentary and jointly necessary parts of the wider Biblical understanding of testimony, the way is paved for this understanding of "testimony" to open up into a performance of lament. In order to show that this is so we need first recall, as detailed in chapter 5, the general form and structure that lament takes: address, complaint, confession of trust, petition, vow of praise. Testimonies of victory naturally enable confessions of trust because they recount positive acts of God and encourage hearers to believe God still acts, by way of the Holy Spirit, in such ways. They also encourage praise of God due to what God has done—as testified to—and by way of

A Dramatic Pentecostal/Charismatic Anti-Theodicy

affirming the character and nature of God as revealed in Scripture—which naturally calls for praise. In this sense, testimonies of victory on certain occasions work as stand alones. However, countertestimony—the recounting of events that run contrary to who God is supposed to be and how God is supposed to act—is not to stand alone if healthy, covenantal relationship is to be maintained. To simply recount such events serves no particular purpose. Recounting such events to God (address and complaint), which is then juxtaposed with confessions of trust (based on testimonies of victory), followed by petition (which may involve requesting God to act in ways similar to those recounted in the testimonies of victory), followed by a vow of praise (either because God has acted, or, some assurance had been gained that God will act, or, in addition to the petition as an attempt at persuasion), does, however. This is so because, as has already been shown in this study, such a performance enables the maintenance of healthy covenantal relations, particularly in periods of seemingly innocent, meaningless suffering when God appears to be absent. Therefore, although there are times when testimonies of victory may stand alone, when a countertestimony is offered, testimonies of victory are necessary for a fitting performance—a performance of lament—to be undertaken.

In order to further highlight the importance of modifying a Pentecostal/Charismatic understanding and practice of testimony and show critics and none alike how such modifications are possible whilst still retaining the unique characteristics of traditional testimony, I return to the work of Tony Richie. In what follows I will show how the wider modified understanding of "testimony" that opens the way to lament (thus testimony as Anti-Theodicy) still suits his definitions and contexts and can therefore still find a home in Pentecostal/Charismatic theology and practice.

Definitions

In terms of the "Functional-Practical," what is being suggested here does not detract from the notion that testimony involves recounting God's acts in the life of the one testifying, nor does it deny that such acts occur and that telling of them should be encouraged as praise to God and motivation and challenge to hearers. The point is that such testimonies should be re-designated as "testimonies of victory" and subsumed under a re-definition of testimony that also contains "countertestimony." If done, testimony still remains functional and practical in the way Richie defines it, but also now includes a vehicle for expressions of suffering that can enable the legitimate and healthy practice of Pentecostal/Charismatic lament. There is perhaps a

Improvising on a Divine Performance of Lament

question mark over whether this is praise and worship but I shall address this issue in the "Contexts" section below.

With regard to the definition of testimony as "Transformational," again, one is not detracting from bringing all of life's "curses as well as blessings" before God, the community and Scripture. Instead what is being suggested here is that that should be affirmed and is not actually currently being allowed to happen. This is so, as noted above, due to how Scripture is used by the community, and therefore what is understood as a legitimate testimony. With the wider understanding of "testimony" argued for here, and Scripture *truly* being authoritative, one would *really* be able to honestly bring all of life's experiences before God. In the case of those experiences that involve suffering, the testifier would legitimately be allowed to use testimony as a way into, and part of, lament. In doing so, space would be opened up for asking afresh where God is and what God is doing in such situations, without feeling the need to reject aspects of the testimony that are unresolved or difficult to listen to. Testimony defined in this way would open up the possibility of transformation for all involved in a way that the current, narrower, more restrictive understanding does not.

A continuing theme emerges upon consideration of testimony as liturgical. In modifying the understanding and use of Pentecostal/Charismatic testimony, I am not suggesting that by introducing countertestimony as part of that practice, it can no longer be defined as liturgy. Countertestimony as part of lament psalms has not detracted from such psalms still being understood as liturgy and they have, historically, been used as such. As noted in chapter 5, countertestimony is practiced alongside testimonies of victory, within these psalms, as part of the practice of lament. Therefore, although testimonies of victory may be used alone as one type of liturgy, the subsuming of such testimonies into the general category of testimony, alongside countertestimonies, allows for a different type of liturgical testimony, but it is testimony as liturgy nonetheless. Therefore, such a modification is possible and justified within Pentecostal/Charismatic testimony.

Having shown how the modifications suggested do not detract from, but, in some cases, enhance Pentecostal/Charismatic testimony, we move on now to briefly see how such modifications impact upon or modify the contexts of Pentecostal/Charismatic testimony.

Context

It is perhaps obvious to make the point that although modifications have been made to what defines a Pentecostal/Charismatic testimony, at no point has it been suggested that it may no longer operate in an autobiographical context. Instead, by way of modification, testimony, as is being suggested here, allows for greater space to include *all* of life's experiences, including those that involve suffering, and is therefore supportive of a much broader understanding of an autobiographical context.

With regard to Biblical and theological contexts, again it is being affirmed that in introducing countertestimony as part of the practice of testimony, an oral-narrative method is still being applied. And further, this method still involves: i.) the recounting of acts of God in the lives of those testifying, ii.) the belief that God continues to act in such ways now, and iii.) that all such accounts are to be understood in the light of the unfolding of Salvation History, and in particular, the performance of Jesus as recorded in the Gospels. However, in the light of the argument made in this study, that therefore also means that one must take into account the whole of the canon, when seeking to perform fittingly, and in particular, the entirety of the performance of Jesus as the source for our own improvised performances. In addition one must also understand that the act of the drama in which we find ourselves involves the now/not yet tension and so suffering, of the seemingly innocent, meaningless variety, continues. Therefore, modifications in these contexts, as already argued in this study, must include the practice of countertestimony as part of a fitting performance of lament, in the midst of relevant experiences. This does not reduce the Biblical or theological contexts of testimony but instead provides a fuller account of them and in doing so provides a Christologically justified, Biblically rooted method for the practice of testimony in *all* of life's situations.

This naturally leads into three of the biggest contextual modifications—the pastoral, the sociological, and the historical contexts. The pre-modified understanding of testimony left no room for honesty regarding difficult experiences of suffering, particularly the type this study focuses on. Therefore, in such situations, either the voice of the sufferer is shut down or they are forced to provide a false testimony in order to be accepted, which would involve a misrepresentation of history. With the use of Scripture advocated in this study, combined with the modified understanding of testimony, safe pastoral space is created for honest testimony to be safely given, and a performance of lament undertaken where appropriate. This is so because testimony now includes making space to seek the presence and will of God rather than presuming to know the mind of God and thus restricting what sufferers can safely testify about. This use of testimony thus creates the possibly of safe sociological space where healthy pastoral care can take place. In doing so a Biblically informed rendering and recounting of history is still undertaken, however, the whole canon is the grounding

Improvising on a Divine Performance of Lament

for this rendering rather than selected texts. Therefore, the oral-narrative nature of testimony is retained, but a rendering of history occurs that is done in the light of the *whole* of Scripture.

A further seemingly tricky modification is with regard to the doxological context. As noted above, the use of countertestimony and lament does not seem to sit well with a doxological context for Pentecostal/Charismatic testimony. The first point to make here is that if one is going to be Biblically rooted, then the simple fact is that not all testimony is explicit praise and worship. That said, it is important to recall from chapter 5 that sitting behind the performance of lament is the belief that God can do what he currently is not doing, as well as a belief that he should do it, all of which is based on the fact that God has acted in such positive ways before. Therefore, although not explicit praise and worship throughout, as has already been noted, testimony in its modified sense when used as part of lament, firstly, does often contain explicit doxology, and secondly, may be said to contain implicit praise and worship. This latter point is so because the very fact that such a performance is being undertaken is founded on certain beliefs about God and the relationship that the one lamenting has with God. Therefore the very act of using testimony as part of lament is an implicit act of worship. When understood in this way the modifications made still, arguably, result in an understanding of testimony that is acceptable to Pentecostal/Charismatic theology in the context of doxology.

Perhaps the most important modification for Pentecostal/Charismatic testimony is with regard to the Pneumatological context. As has already been argued for in this chapter, the reading of Scripture proposed here is one in which the Holy Spirit is understood as one who aids with the performance of lament. Therefore, as well as testimonies of victory being understood as Spirit-inspired, it is legitimate to also believe that countertestimony and the performance of lament generally can also be Spirit-inspired. In addition, as has also already been argued, there are grounds for suggesting that the Spirit laments on our behalf. Therefore the modifications suggested here enhance rather than detract from the Pneumatological context of testimony.

In the light of the suggested modifications and their impact upon the definitions and contexts of Pentecostal/Charismatic testimony, it is possible to propose that Pentecostal/Charismatic testimony as Anti-Theodicy is both legitimate and justifiable as well as a concept that is to be embraced and practiced. Far from Pentecostal/Charismatic theology and practice being diametrically opposed to an Anti-theodical performance of lament, in the light of the argument made in this study regarding producing directions for a fitting performance in the face of the type of experience of suffering in question, the modifications to the theology and practice of Pentecostal/

A Dramatic Pentecostal/Charismatic Anti-Theodicy

Charismatic testimony proposed here, create an extremely fitting vehicle for enabling such a performance. Therefore, it is possible to say that the modified version of Pentecostal/Charismatic testimony proposed can indeed, in the right circumstances act as a vital Anti-theodical performance that naturally enables the fitting performance of lament that direction had been offered for in this study. In this sense, Pentecostal/Charismatic testimony as Anti-Theodicy has been achieved. The last task of this chapter is to suggest how this concept may begin to be integrated into concrete communities.

Practical Directives for a Modified Use of Testimony

A realistic suggestion as a practical starting point may be to begin with the leaders and teachers in churches starting to teach and talk—both in congregational meetings and small groups—about the times when God does not answer or act in ways we would like or expect, and then how we are to respond to these times. In conjunction with this, another practice that may help this integration is leading a congregation in corporate lament over a situation of devastation in the world such as 9/11, the Japanese earthquake and Tsunami, or the Norway massacre etc. This introduces the concepts of countertestimony and lament in a practical way, but the issue/s at hand may be far enough away geographically and emotionally that to lament about them may not place the same amount of strain on the theology of those lamenting as crying out over an issue closer to home perhaps would. If and when such a practice has been integrated, alongside the on-going teaching and example being set by the leaders, then a move can perhaps be made regarding encouraging a practice of lament about subjects closer to home i.e., loss of a close relative, redundancy, terminal or long term illness. Again this must be encased in teaching that supports such a practice—such as has been laid out in this study—in order for theory and practice to go hand in hand. Perhaps the example of giving countertestimonies would need to be set by the leaders in order for other members of the congregation to feel safe to follow suit. With this practice slowly being integrated into the congregation, it would be hoped that it would then become a theory and practice that finds its way into the more private side of individual's lives.[130]

---

130. I am appreciative of Scott Ellington and Ali Walton for their suggestions on this matter. Michael Adams has also made suggestions as to how lament may be incorporated into the musical aspect of worship in Church. See Adams, "Music."

Conclusion

In chapter 5 a four step approach was set out regarding how this study would reach its climax with steps one and two being completed in that chapter. The aim of the current chapter was, therefore, to complete steps three and four. In doing this the divine view of and response to evil as begun in chapter 5 was Christologically qualified by way of an examination of Jesus' response to evil and suffering, with particular emphasis on his performance at the cross. By completing step three in this manner the way was paved for completion of step four—the production of Biblically rooted, systematic guidance for a fitting Pentecostal/Charismatic performance in the face of seemingly innocent, meaningless suffering when God appears to be absent.

In following the hermeneutical method developed in chapter 4 the argument that unfolded at the climax of this study was that, rather than dismiss the lament genre of Act 2 of the drama, in seeking to improvise on the performance of Jesus, this practice must be examined and embraced. However, a further point was that in doing so, it must be examined and embraced through a Christological lens that both retains much of the form and content of Israel's lament tradition, whilst also modifying it in the light of the Easter event.

In carrying out the necessary modifications it was noted that of particular importance for this study is the role of the Holy Spirit in the performance of lament. This in turn led to the fulfillment of the aim of the study by way of production of an answer to the question at the heart of it: *To produce a fitting Pentecostal/Charismatic performance in the face of seemingly innocent, meaningless suffering when God appears to be absent means, to improvise on the performance of Jesus and lament to the Father with the aid of the Spirit as we seek to carry on our through-line towards eschatological consummation.* In addition, it was also noted that the presence of the Holy Spirit as aid was understood to help enable dialogical consummation and determination as our through-lines in the drama are carried on, even amidst times of deep suffering.

In attempting to address the role of the Script, the Spirit *and* the community in how lament is to be performed, direction was suggested as to how the performance of the community could be modified in the light of the argument at the center of this study. In doing so the area of testimony was examined with suggestions as to how modification could take place that would lead to Pentecostal/Charismatic testimony as Anti-Theodicy.

In summary, this chapter has provided a fitting climax to the study by both answering the central research question and providing stage direction as to how that answer might be translated into action. As we reach the conclusion to the study it is important to reflect on where we have been and where we are now, in order that we may look ahead to where we may go next.

7

Conclusion

Introduction

HAVING REACHED THE CLIMAX of this study, a natural question that emerges is "where do we go from here?" There are of course many answers that could be offered as a response to this question, of which some will be discussed below. However, in order to provide a suitable backdrop for such explorations it is important to firstly, summarize where we have been in this study, and secondly, to remember afresh where we are in the light of it. We will then be in a better position to make suggestions regarding future research.

Summary

We can recall from the Introduction that the question this study has been seeking to answer is: What does it mean to produce a fitting Pentecostal/Charismatic performance in the face of seemingly innocent, meaningless suffering when God appears to be absent? In embarking on the quest to provide an answer—and in so doing give guidance for right belief and practice (or rather, a fitting performance)—the journey began with an exercise in ground-clearing and contextualization.

Chapter 2 provided a critical overview of the plethora of responses from Christianity to the problem of evil and suffering. By providing such an overview it was possible to clearly notice that much of what has passed for "Christian responses" is neither overly practically useful to the sufferer/s, nor particularly well rooted in Scripture. Both of these issues cause somewhat

Conclusion

of a problem for Pentecostal/Charismatic theology as generally, a high view of Scripture and practical usefulness are characteristics of such theology. In the light of this it became apparent that any response developed in this study would find more of an affinity with those responses loosely categorized as "Anti-Theodicy." However, it was also noted that, although there was much that was good in Anti-Theodicies, there was no approach that was either problem free or that therefore offered a satisfying answer to the question around which this study centers. Chapter 2 thus enabled the clearing of space for the approach to be developed, the provision of a context in which it would emerge, and the highlighting of points of contact with that context.

In a similar way, chapter 3 provided an examination of specifically Pentecostal/Charismatic responses to evil and suffering—again with the intent of ground-clearing and contextualization. The result of this examination was that, as a general rule, in the face of seemingly innocent, meaningless suffering, one can either blame the sufferer or those praying, or accept the sovereignty of God in silence. Although practical in response, in the sense that they are not purely theoretical, such responses raise the issue of the view and use of Scripture by Pentecostals and Charismatics. What emerged was that although there may be *some* Biblical grounding for *some* of the approaches, all approaches are experientially generated and employ a "proof-texting" use of Scripture as the support for their authority. It was noted that there is, therefore, an inconsistency between what is believed about Scripture, and the practice that goes with it, and that this in turn leads to a lopsided response to suffering and evil. Chapter 3 thus further supported the point that the approach to be developed in this study needed to be built on a high view of Scripture and be practically useful. It also highlighted the necessity of addressing the issue of the hermeneutical method to be employed to make such a construction possible.

Having cleared ground in preparation for construction of an answer to the central research question, the task of chapter 4 was to provide tools for that construction. This came in the form of a hermeneutical method that was conducive to Pentecostal/Charismatic theology, but that also overcame the inconsistencies unearthed in chapter 3. The result of the ensuing three-way conversation between Thomas, Archer and Vanhoozer that was developed in chapter 4 was a Dramatic Pentecostal/Charismatic hermeneutical method. This method sought to make space for the roles of Scripture, community and the Spirit in a way that is acceptable to Pentecostal/Charismatic theology, whilst also maintaining Scripture as the norming norm. With that in place it was possible to return to Scripture as Script in order to obtain a divine perspective of evil and suffering and so begin to construct the foundations on which guidance for right belief and practice could be built.

A Dramatic Pentecostal/Charismatic Anti-Theodicy

In the light of chapter 4, the task for the company of actors in the current scenes is to seek to produce a fitting performance by improvising on the performance of Jesus. In the case of this study specifically, that means examining how Jesus responded in the face of similar types of suffering to that which is in question here, with the aim of being able to generate guidance for a fitting performance for the current Pentecostal/Charismatic actors. In order for that to be possible, an examination of the performances on which Jesus was improvising was necessary. Chapter 5 thus sought to firstly, clarify where we are in the drama, and secondly, examine the divine perspective on evil and suffering as well as how God responded to it in Acts 1 and 2 of the drama. This also involved an examination of how his company of actors responded to it having been drafted in to aid with the divine response. Of specific focus in chapter 5 was how the company of actors responded in times of seemingly innocent, meaningless suffering when God appeared to be absent. The fitting performance they gave at such points was one of lament, which was examined in detail.

Having provided the background for Jesus' performance in chapter 5, chapter 6 Christologically qualified the divine perspective of evil and suffering and the divine/human response to it examined in chapter 5. The most important result of this was that, far from the performance of Jesus causing a performance of lament to become outdated, his improvisation on the lament tradition, it was argued, authorized the performance of lament as a fitting performance in the current act. In addition to this, it was also argued that the Spirit is given as an aid to such performances. Therefore, as the climax to the study, the answer that was offered to the central research question was: To produce a fitting Pentecostal/Charismatic performance in the face of seemingly innocent, meaningless suffering when God appears to be absent means, to improvise on the performance of Jesus and lament to the Father with the aid of the Spirit as we seek to carry on our through-line towards eschatological consummation. In short, it is only by following Jesus' example at the cross and lamenting to the Father with the aid of the Spirit that healthy covenantal relationship can continue prior to eschatological consummation. Having provided this answer, it was then, in the light of chapter 2, possible to categorize it as a Pentecostal/Charismatic Anti-Theodicy. Chapter 6 concluded by offering stage directions as to how changes could be made in belief and practice in Pentecostal/Charismatic communities in the light of the answer provided, focusing particularly on the modification of testimony. This brings us to where we are now.

Conclusion

The Current Scene: Where We Are Now

Having got to this point in the study we need take stock of what has been achieved, and also, what has not. The aim of this study was: to answer the central research question by developing Biblically rooted, systematic guidance for the production of a fitting Pentecostal/Charismatic performance in the face of seemingly innocent, meaningless suffering when God appears to be absent. In pursuing this aim guidance has been offered that is Biblically rooted whilst maintaining a high view of Scripture. It is guidance that is practically useful and qualified and authorized by the divine incarnate. It is guidance that makes space for the tangible activity of the Holy Spirit. And, it is guidance for communities and individuals alike. It is therefore rightly categorized as a "Pentecostal/Charismatic Anti-Theodicy." Everything that was intended to be achieved has been. This study therefore provides a seemingly unprecedented challenge to those in Pentecostal and Charismatic communities who are grappling with questions of what it means to "perform fittingly" in the face of seemingly innocent, meaningless suffering when God appears to be absent. It offers a challenge to them to reflect on their beliefs and practices in the light of this research and to question both what they believe and what they do. In the same vein, this study therefore also offers a resource, previously unavailable, that can open up fresh avenues regarding how those who are suffering in our midst are cared for and enabled to grow in community with others and with God. It is a resource that recovers a rich but overlooked practice in a way that does not require the rejection of the core aspects of what it is to be Pentecostal/Charismatic. There is then much that has been achieved by way of this research. However, there is much still to do.

As was noted in the introduction, there are limitations to this study. The greatest of these is perhaps the distance that exists between what has been suggested here and the reality of an actual community. The trade off in aiming to make a project such as this as broadly applicable as possible within certain parameters is that, at this stage, the practical viability of it remains largely uncharted territory. The term Pentecostal/Charismatic was purposely broad, but, the question remains, how will what has been developed here work in specific "on the ground" communities within the various and unique socio-historical and theological contexts? Although a theological argument has been made and "stage direction" has been offered, how does a Pentecostal/Charismatic individual or community re-appropriate Biblical laments? Or even, in the light of guidance offered by the Script, how do they construct their own laments?

A Dramatic Pentecostal/Charismatic Anti-Theodicy

At the conclusion of this study it is the juxtaposition of the achievement that has occurred in its making and the questions over the application of the findings that mark where we now stand. In the light of this it seems fitting to close the project by returning to the question posed at the start of the conclusion—"where do we go from here?"—and suggest possible avenues for future research.

Future Research

There are four directions in which I wish to point in attempting to offer a preliminary answer to this question, all of which will require the help of scholars and communities alike. The first of these involves Pentecostal/Charismatic communities and practical theologians.

As noted above there is significant potential for there to be a gap between what is being suggested in this study and the reality of the actual situations in any particular Pentecostal/Charismatic community. The problem this causes is one of application. How are the findings of this research to be engaged with and applied in any particular community? An answer I wish to suggest, that acts as the first direction in which we may go, is for practical theologians to examine just this question. By empirically researching how specific communities respond to the type of suffering in question in this study and placing their findings in conversation with what is being presented here, there is the potential for a two way yield. On the one hand the empirical research, in conjunction with this research, may result in the modification of beliefs and practices in the communities in question in a way that enables those communities to be more authentically Christian. On the other hand, as all conversations are at least two-way, the empirical research could offer significant challenge to suggestions in this research. Engagement by practical theologians thus provides one way in which we can, in conversation, move forward together in our desire for right Christian belief and practice.

The second direction that I wish to suggest as a way forward from this point involves Biblical scholars and Pentecostal/Charismatic communities—or more ideally, Pentecostal/Charismatic Biblical scholars and Pentecostal/Charismatic communities. This study proposes guidance for right belief and practice, however, the "doing" of that practice is a further challenge that this study has only touched on. Although I have justified the use of lament as a legitimate response to the situations of suffering in question for Pentecostal/Charismatic communities, there is the significant question of: what would a Pentecostal/Charismatic appropriation of lament texts look like? In one sense this could be a question that potentially proceeds from the empirical research suggested above, but, there is also the possibility that the desire to answer that question may emerge from communities apart from such endeavors.

A small number of scholars have begun suggesting, in the light of the Biblical texts, what modern day laments could look like.[1] However, as yet, unsurprisingly, there have been no such endeavors from within Pentecostal/Charismatic communities. As noted in the section discussing the work of John Christopher Thomas in chapter 4 of this study, there are, however, Pentecostal commentaries emerging. This being the case, in the light of the present work, one wonders if a question it asks is whether a Pentecostal commentary on the Psalms, or perhaps Job, may be possible, and what they might look like?

With regard to the use of the Psalms, the third direction—which again may open up as a result of empirical research or, apart from it—is an examination of the place of lament in the music of Pentecostal/Charismatic communities. In the introduction to this study Michael Adams was highlighted as one Pentecostal scholar who had begun to examine the possibility of incorporating lament into Pentecostal worship. However, also highlighted in the introduction was the unsolved problem of the way the Easter event affects the use of Old Testament lament texts. Having dealt with that problem in this study, there is fresh impetus with which to carry on exploring the possibilities of the use of lament in worship.

In connection to the last point, the fourth and final direction in which further research may go is along the route of exploring how the work undertaken in this study could open up the possibility of theologically supporting the practice of glossolalia as lament. As was noted in examining the work of Gordon Fee regarding Rom 8 in chapter 6 of this study, there has already been significant research undertaken that potentially provides the foundation for such a suggestion.[2] What is perhaps required is further extensive engagement with that research in order to solidify such a position and so provide solid foundations and clear guidance for how such a practice may occur in Pentecostal/Charismatic communities.

The four directions offered here are by no means the only ones that could be taken, but are ones which I suggest are important and worthy of exploration. It is hoped that this study will encourage such explorations as well as provide a resource for the journey.

1. See Brueggemann and Frost, *Psalmist's Cry*. Swinton, *Raging*, 126–28; Weems, *Psalms of Lament*; and Pembroke, *Pastoral Care*, chapters 3 and 4.

2. Examples include Smith, "Tongues"; Hilborn, "Glossolalia"; Macchia, "Sighs Too Deep."

Bibliography

Adams, Marilyn McCord. *Horrendous Evils and the Goodness of God.* Ithaca, NY: Cornell University Press, 1999.
Adams, Michael K. "'Hope in the Midst of Hurt': Towards a Pentecostal Theology of Suffering." Paper presented at the Twenty-Fifth Annual Meeting of the Society for Pentecostal Studies, Toronto, Canada, 1996.
———. "Music That Makes Sense: Inclusiveness of the Lament May Be the Key to Renewal in the Church." Paper presented at the Twenty-Third Annual Meeting of the Society for Pentecostal Studies, Guadalajara, Mexico, 1993.
Ahearne-Kroll, Stephen P. *The Psalms of Lament in Mark's Passion: Jesus' Davidic Suffering.* Cambridge: Cambridge University Press, 2007.
Albright, W. F. and C. S. Mann. *Matthew.* Garden City, NY: Doubleday, 1971.
Alexander, Kimberly Ervin. *Pentecostal Healing: Models in Theology and Practice.* Blandford Forum. Dorset: Deo, 2006.
Allan, Richard. "Contemporary Pentecostal Hermeneutics: Toward a Critical Realist Epistemology." MPhil diss., University of Birmingham, 2008.
Anderson, Allan. *An Introduction to Pentecostalism: Global Charismatic Christianity.* Cambridge: Cambridge University Press, 2004.
———. "Varieties, Taxonomies, and Definitions." In *Studying Global Pentecostalism: Theories and Methods,* edited by Allan Anderson et al., 13–29. London: University of California Press, 2010.
Anderson, Francis I. *Job: An Introduction and Commentary.* Leicester, UK: InterVarsity, 1976.
Anderson, Hugh. *The Gospel of Mark.* London: Marshall, Morgan and Scott, 1976.
Archer, Kenneth J. *The Gospel Revisited: Towards a Pentecostal Theology.* Eugene, OR: Pickwick, 2010.
———. *A Pentecostal Hermeneutic For the Twenty-First Century: Spirit, Scripture and Community.* London: T. & T. Clark, 2004.
———. "Pentecostal Hermeneutics: Retrospect and Prospect." *JPT* 8 (1996) 63–81.
———. "Pentecostal Story: The Hermeneutical Filter for the Making of Meaning." *Pneuma* 26.1 (2004) 36–59.
Arrington, French. "Hermeneutics." In *DPCM* 376–89.
Atkins, Peter. *Memory and Liturgy: The Place of Memory in the Composition and Practice of Liturgy.* Aldershot, UK: Ashgate, 2004.
Audi, Robert. *Epistemology: A Contemporary Introduction to the Theory of Knowledge.* 2nd ed. Abingdon, UK: Routledge, 2007.
St. Augustine. *The City of God.* Translated by Henry Bettenson. London: Penguin, 2003.

Bibliography

———. *On Free Choice of the Will.* Translated by Thomas Williams. Cambridge: Hackett, 1993.

Austin, J. L. *How to do Things with Words.* Oxford: Oxford University Press, 1962.

Bakhtin, M. M. "Author and Hero in Aesthetic Activity." In *Art and Answerability: Early Philosophical Essays by M. M. Bakhtin*, translated by Vadim Liapunov, edited by Michael Holquist and Vadim Liapunov, 4–256. Austin: University of Texas Press, 1990.

Balentine, Samuel E. *The Hidden God: The Hiding of the Face of God in the Old Testament.* Oxford: Oxford University Press, 1983.

———. *Job.* Macon, GA: Smyth and Helwys, 2006.

———. *Prayer in the Hebrew Bible: The Drama of Divine-Human Dialogue.* Minneapolis: Fortress, 1993.

Barrett, C. K. *The Gospel According to St. John.* London: SPCK, 1982.

Basinger, David. "Practical Implications." In *The Openness of God.* By Clark Pinnock et al., 155–76. Carlisle, UK: Paternoster, 1994.

Basinger, David, and Randall Basinger, eds. *Predestination and Freewill: Four Views of Divine Sovereignty and Human Freedom.* Downers Grove, IL: InterVarsity, 1986.

Bauer, Jonas. "Enquiring into the Absence of Lament: A Study of the Entwining of Suffering and Guilt in Lament." In *Evoking Lament.* Edited by Eva Harasta and Brian Brock, 25–43. London: T. & T. Clark, 2009.

Beasley-Murray, George R. *John.* Waco, TX: Word, 1987.

Begrich, Joachim. "Das Priesterliche Heilsorakel." *ZAW* 52 (1934) 81–92.

Beilby, James K., and Paul R. Eddy, eds. *Divine Foreknowledge: Four Views.* Carlisle, UK: Paternoster, 2002.

Ben-Porat, Ziva. "The Poetics of Literary Allusion." *PTL: A Journal for Descriptive Poetics and Theory of Literature* 1 (1976) 105–28.

Billman, Kathleen D., and Daniel L. Migliore. *Rachel's Cry: Prayer of Lament and Rebirth of Hope.* Eugene, OR: Wipf and Stock, 1999.

Blue, Ken. *Authority to Heal.* Downers Grove, IL: InterVarsity, 1987.

Blumenthal, David R. *Facing the Abusing God: A Theology of Protest.* Louisville: Westminster John Knox, 1993.

Bray, Gerald. *Biblical Interpretation: Past and Present.* Downers Grove, IL: InterVarsity, 1996.

Brown, Raymond. *The Gospel According to John (XIII–XXI).* London: Chapman, 1971.

Brueggemann, Walter. "The Costly Loss of Lament." In *The Psalms and the Life of Faith*, edited by Patrick D. Miller, 98–111. Minneapolis: Fortress, 1995.

———. "Covenanting as Human Vocation: The Relation of the Bible and Pastoral Care." In *The Psalms and the Life of Faith*, edited by Patrick D. Miller, 150–66. Minneapolis: Fortress, 1995.

———. "The Formfulness of Grief." *Interpretation* 31 (1977) 263–75.

———. "From Hurt to Joy, From Death to Life." In *The Psalms and the Life of Faith*, edited by Patrick D. Miller, 67–83. Minneapolis: Fortress, 1995.

———. *Hopeful Imagination: Prophetic Voices in Exile.* Philadelphia: Fortress, 1987.

———. *The Message of the Psalms.* Minneapolis: Augsburg, 1984.

———. "Prayer as an Act of Daring Dance: Four Biblical Examples." In *The Psalms and the Life of Faith*, edited by Patrick D. Miller, 135–49. Minneapolis: Fortress, 1995.

———. "Psalms and the Life of Faith: A Suggested Typology of Function." *JSOT* 17 (1980) 3–32.

———. "The Psalms as Prayer." In *The Psalms and the Life of Faith*, edited by Patrick D. Miller, 33–66. Minneapolis: Fortress, 1995.
———. "Response to John Goldingay's 'The Dynamic Cycle of Praise and Prayer.'" *JSOT* 22 (1982) 141–42.
———. "A Shape for Old Testament Theology I: Structure Legitimation." *CBQ* 47 (1985) 28–46.
———. "A Shape for Old Testament Theology II: Embrace of Pain." *CBQ* 47 (1985) 395–415.
———. "Theodicy in a Social Dimension." *JSOT* 33 (1985) 3–25.
———. *Theology of the Old Testament: Testimony, Dispute, Advocacy*. Minneapolis: Fortress, 1997.
Bubb, Barry. *Communication Skills That Heal: A Practical Approach to a New Professionalism in Medicine*. Oxford: Radcliffe, 2006.
Cargal, Timothy B. "Beyond the Fundamentalist—Modernist Controversy: Pentecostal Hermeneutics in a Postmodern Age." *Pneuma* 15.2 (1993) 163–87.
Cartledge, Mark. *Testimony in the Spirit: Rescripting Ordinary Pentecostal Theology*. Farnham, UK: Ashgate, 2010.
———. *Testimony: Its Importance, Place and Potential*. Cambridge: Grove, 2002.
———. "'Text-Community-Spirit': The Challenges Posed by Pentecostal Theological Method to British Evangelical Theology." Paper presented at the British Evangelical Identities Conference, King's College, London, July 2004.
———. "Text-Community-Spirit: The Challenges Posed by Pentecostal Theological Method to Evangelical Theology." In *Spirit and Scripture: Examining a Pneumatic Hermeneutic*, edited by Kevin L. Spawn and Archie T. Wright, 130–42. London: T. & T. Clark, 2012.
Clines, David J. A. *Job 1–20*. Dallas: Word, 1989.
———. *Job 38–42*. Nashville: Nelson, 2011.
Coady, C. A. J. *Testimony: A Philosophical Study*. Oxford: Clarendon, 1992.
Cole, R. A. *The Gospel According to St Mark: An Introduction and Commentary*. London: Tyndale, 1968.
Collins, Adela Yarbro. *Mark*. Minneapolis: Fortress, 2007.
Conrad, Edgar. "Second Isaiah and the Priestly Oracle of Salvation." *ZAW* 93 (1981) 234–46.
Copeland, Kenneth. *The Force of Faith*. Fort Worth, TX: Copeland, 1983.
———. *Our Covenant With God*. Fort Worth, TX: Copeland, 1980.
———. *You Are Healed*. Fort Worth, TX: Copeland, 1979.
Copeland, Kenneth, and Gloria Copeland. *Healing Promises*. Fort Worth, TX: Copeland, 1994.
Cotterell, Peter, and Max Turner. *Linguistics and Biblical Interpretation*. London: SPCK, 1989.
Craigie, Peter C. *Psalms 1–50*. Waco, TX: Word, 1983.
Crenshaw, James L. "Introduction: The Shift From Theodicy to Anthropodicy." In *Theodicy in the Old Testament*, edited by James L. Crenshaw, 1–16. London: SPCK, 1983.
Dabney, D. Lyle. "Pneumatologia Crucis: Reclaiming Theologia Crucis for a Theology of the Spirit Today." *SJT* 53.4 (2000) 511–24.
Dahood, Mitchell. *Psalms I: 1–50*. New York: Doubleday, 1973

Bibliography

Davis, Stephen T. "Free Will and Evil." In *Encountering Evil: Live Options in Theodicy—A New Edition*, edited by Stephen T. Davis, 73–89. Louisville: Westminster John Knox, 2001.

Dostoyevsky, Fyodor. *The Brothers Karamazov*. Translated by David McDuff. London: Penguin, 2003.

Dunn, James D. G. "Judaism and Christianity: One Covenant or Two?" In *Covenant Theology: Contemporary Approaches*, edited by Mark J. Cartledge and David Mills, 33–55. Carlisle, UK: Paternoster, 2001.

———. *Romans 1–8*. Dallas: Word, 1988.

Dykstra, Craig and Dorothy C. Bass. "A Theological Understanding of Christian Practices." In *Practicing Theology: Beliefs and Practices in Christian Life*. Edited by Miroslav Volf and Dorothy C. Bass, 13–32. Cambridge: Eerdmans, 2002.

Eco, Umberto. "Between author and text." In *Interpretation and Overinterpretation*, edited by Stefan Collini, 67–88. Cambridge: Cambridge University Press, 1992.

———. "Interpretation and history." In *Interpretation and Overinterpretation*, edited by Stefan Collini, 23–43. Cambridge: Cambridge University Press, 1992.

———. "Overinterpreting texts." In *Interpretation and Overinterpretation*, edited by Stefan Collini, 45–66. Cambridge: Cambridge University Press, 1992.

Ellington, Scott A. "The Costly Loss of Testimony." *JPT* 16 (2000) 48–59.

———. "Reality, Remembrance and Response: The Presence and Absence of God in the Psalms of Lament." PhD diss., University of Sheffield, 1999.

———. *Risking Truth: Reshaping the World Through Prayers of Lament*. Eugene, OR: Pickwick, 2008.

———. "So Much Still to Do: A Response to Leonard Maré, Hannah Harrington, and Blaine Charette." *JPT* 18 (2009) 186–93.

Evans, Craig A. *Mark 8:27—16:20*. Nashville: Nelson, 2001.

Farah, Charles, Jr. "A Critical Analysis: The 'Roots and Fruits' of Faith-Formula Theology." *Pneuma* 3.1 (1981) 3–21.

———. *From the Pinnacle of the Temple*. Plainfield, NJ: Logos, 1970.

Fee, Gordon D. *The Disease of the Health and Wealth Gospels*. Vancouver, BC: Regent College Publishing, 2006.

———. *The First Epistle to the Corinthians*. Grand Rapids: Eerdmans, 1987.

———. *God's Empowering Presence: The Holy Spirit in the Letters of Paul*. Peabody, MA: Hendrickson, 1994.

Filson, Floyd V. *A Commentary on the Gospel According to St. Matthew*. London: A. & C. Black, 1960.

Fitzmyer, Joseph A. *Romans*. London: Chapman, 1993.

France, R. T. *The Gospel of Mark: A Commentary on the Greek Text*. Carlisle, UK: Paternoster, 2002.

———. *The Gospel of Matthew*. Cambridge: Eerdmans, 2007.

Frei, Hans. *The Eclipse of Biblical Narrative. A Study in Eighteenth and Nineteenth Century Hermeneutics*. New Haven: Yale University Press, 1974.

Fretheim, Terence E. *God and the World in the Old Testament: A Relational Theology of Creation*. Nashville: Abingdon, 2005.

Gee, Donald. *Trophimus I Left Sick: Our Problems With Divine Healing*. London: Elim, 1952. N.p. http://www.angelfire.com/la2/prophet1/problemswithhealing.html.

Bibliography

Gill, Robin. "Health Care and Covenant: Withholding and Withdrawing Treatment." In *Covenant Theology: Contemporary Approaches*, edited by Mark J. Cartledge and David Mills, 101–16. Carlisle, UK: Paternoster, 2001.

Goldingay, John. "The Dynamic Cycle of Praise and Prayer in the Psalms." *JSOT* 20 (1981) 85–90.

Griffin, David Ray. *God, Power, and Evil: A Process Theodicy*. Philadelphia: Westminster, 1976.

Gunton, Colin. "Historical and Systematic Theology." In *The Cambridge Companion to Christian Doctrine*, edited by Colin Gunton, 3–20. Cambridge: Cambridge University Press, 1997.

———. "A Rose by Any Other Name? From 'Christian Doctrine' to 'Systematic Theology.'" *IJST* 1.1 (1999) 4–23.

Gutiérrez, Gustavo. *On Job: God-Talk and the Suffering of the Innocence*. Translated by Matthew J. O'Connell. Maryknoll, NY: Orbis, 1991.

———. *A Theology of Liberation*. Translated by Sister Inda Caridad and John Eagleson. Rev. ed. London: SCM, 1996.

Habel, Norman C. *The Book of Job: A Commentary*. London: SCM, 1985.

Hagin, Kenneth E. *The Believer's Authority*. 2nd edn. Tulsa, Oklahoma: RHEMA Bible Church, 1986.

———. *Exceedingly Growing Faith*. Tulsa, Oklahoma: Kenneth Hagin Ministries, 1978.

———. *I Believe in Visions*. Tulsa, Oklahoma: Faith Library, 2003.

Hagin, Kenneth, Jr. *Executing the Basics of Healing*. Tulsa, Oklahoma: Faith Library, 2006.

———. *Itching Ears*. Tulsa, Oklahoma: RHEMA Bible Church, 1982.

Hagner, Donald A. *Matthew 1–13*. Dallas: Word, 1993.

———. *Matthew 14–28*. Dallas: Word, 1995.

Hanson, Paul D. "Divine Power In Powerlessness: The Servant Of The Lord In Second Isaiah." In *Power, Powerlessness and the Divine: New Inquiries in Bible and Theology*, edited by Cynthia L. Rigby, 179–98. Atlanta: Scholars, 1997.

Hare, Douglas R. A. *Matthew*. Louisville: John Knox, 1993.

Hart, David Bentley. *The Doors of the Sea*. Cambridge: Eerdmans, 2005.

———. "No Shadow of Turning: On Divine Impassibility." *Pro Ecclesia* 11.2 (2002) 184–206.

Hartley, John E. *The Book of Job*. Grand Rapids: Eerdmans, 1988.

Hasker, William. "A Philosophical Perspective." In *The Openness of God*, by Clark Pinnock et al., 126–54. Carlisle, UK: Paternoster, 1994.

Hauerwas, Stanley. *Naming the Silences*. 1990. Reprint, Grand Rapids: Eerdmans, 1991.

Healy, Nicholas M. "What is Systematic Theology." *IJST* 11.11 (2009) 24–39.

Hejzlar, Pavel. *Two Paradigms for Divine Healing: Fred F. Bosworth, Kenneth E. Hagin, Agnes Sandford, and Francis MacNutt in Dialogue*. Leiden: Brill, 2010.

Hick, John. *Evil and the God of Love*. Glasgow: Fount, 1979.

———. "An Irenaean Theodicy." In *Encountering Evil: Live Options in Theodicy—A New Edition*, edited by Stephen T. Davis, 38–52. Louisville: Westminster John Knox, 2001.

Hilborn, David. "Glossolalia as Communication: A Linguistic-Pragmatic Perspective." In *Speaking in Tongues: Multi-Disciplinary Perspectives*, edited by Mark J. Cartledge, 111–46. Milton Keynes, UK: Paternoster, 2006.

Hill, David. *The Gospel of Matthew*. London: Marshall, Morgan and Scott, 1978.

Bibliography

Hume, David. *Dialogues Concerning Natural Religion*. Edited by Nelson Pike. London: Macmillan, 1985.

Iser, Wolfgang. *The Act of Reading: A Theory of Aesthetic Response*. London: Routledge, 1978.

Janzen, J. Gerald. *Job*. Atlanta: John Knox, 1985.

Jewett, Robert. *Romans: A Commentary*. Minniapolis: Fortress, 2007.

Kärkkäinen, Veli-Matti. "Pneumatologies in Systematic Theology." In *Studying Global Pentecostalism: Theories and Methods*, edited by Allan Anderson et. al., 223–44. London: University of California Press, 2010.

Kay, W. K. "Introduction." In *Pentecostal and Charismatic Studies: A Reader*, edited by William K. Kay and Anne E. Dyer, 47–51. London: SCM, 2004.

Keck, Leaneder E. *Romans*. Nashville: Abingdon, 2005.

Kelsey, Morton. *Discernment: A Study in Ecstasy and Evil*. New York: Paulist, 1978.

———. *Psychology, Medicine and Christian Healing*. London: Harper and Row, 1988.

Kilby, Karen. "Evil and the Limits of Theology." *New Blackfriars* 84.983 (2003) 13–29.

Knight, Henry H., III. "God's Faithfulness and God's Freedom: A Comparison of Contemporary Theologies of Healing." *JPT* 1.2 (1993) 65–89.

Kübler-Ross, Elizabeth. *On Death and Dying*. New York: Macmillan, 1969.

Kuhlman, Kathryn. *God Can Do it Again*. London: Oliphants, 1970.

———. *I Believe in Miracles*. Alachua, FL: Bridge-Logos, 2006.

Kuhlman, Kathryn, with J. Buckingham. *A Glimpse Into Glory*. South Plainfield, NJ: Bridge, 1983.

Land, Steven J. *Pentecostal Spirituality: A Passion for the Kingdom*. Sheffield: Sheffield Academic, 1993.

Lane, William L. *The Gospel According to Mark*. London: Marshall, Morgan and Scott, 1974.

Leibniz, G. W. *Theodicy: Essays on the Goodness of God the Freedom of Man and the Origin of Evil*. Translated by E. M. Huggard. London: Routledge, 1952.

Lewis, B. Scott. "Evil, Problem of." In *EPCC* 186–89.

Lewis, C. S. *The Screwtape Letters*. London: Fount, 1998.

Lincoln, Andrew T. *The Gospel According to St John*. London: Contiuum, 2005.

Lindars, Barnabas, ed. *The Gospel of John*. London: Marshall, Morgan and Scott, 1972.

Lindbeck, George. *The Nature of Doctrine: Religion and Theology in a Postliberal Age*. London: SPCK, 1984.

Lindström, Fredrik. *Suffering and Sin: Interpretations of Illness in the Individual Complaint Psalms*. Stockholm: Almqvist and Wiksell, 1994.

Lyotard, Jean-Francois. *The Postmodern Condition: A Report on Knowledge*. Manchester: Manchester University Press, 1984.

Macchia, Frank D. "Sighs Too Deep For Words: Towards a Theology of Glossolalia." *JPT* 1 (1992) 47–73.

———. "Theology, Pentecostal." In *NDPCM* 1120–40.

Mackie, J. L. "Evil and Omnipotence." *Mind* 64 (1955) 200–212.

MacNutt, Francis. *Deliverance from Evil Spirits: A Practical Manual*. London: Hodder and Stoughton, 1996.

———. *Healing*. Notre Dame: Ave Maria, 1976.

———. *The Power to Heal*. Notre Dame: Ave Maria, 1977.

———. *The Prayer That Heals: Praying for Healing in the Family*. London: Hodder and Stoughton, 1982.

Bibliography

Maré, Leonard. "Pentecostalism and Lament in Worship." Paper presented at the Thirtieth Annual Meeting of the Society of Pentecostal Studies, Tulsa, USA, 2001.

McCloskey, H. J. "God and Evil." *PQ* 10.39 (1960) 97–114.

McGrath, Alister E. *The Genesis of Doctrine: A Study in the Foundation of Doctrinal Criticism*. Cambridge: Eerdmans, 1997.

McLean, Mark D. "A Pentecostal Perspective on Theodicy." Paper presented at the Twenty-Seventh Annual Meeting of the Society for Pentecostal Studies, Cleveland, USA, 1998.

———. "Pentecostal Responses to the Problem of Evil: Walking the Razors Edge between Deism and Calvinism." Paper Presented at the Thirtieth Annual Meeting of the Society for Pentecostal Studies, Tulsa, USA, 2001.

McQueen, Larry R. *Joel and the Spirit: The Cry of a Prophetic Hermeneutic*. Sheffield: Sheffield Academic, 1995.

Metz, Johann Baptist. *Faith in History and Society*. Translated by David Smith. London: Burns and Oates, 1980.

Meyer, Ben F. *Critical Realism and the New Testament*. Allison Park, PA: Pickwick, 1989.

Middleton, J. Richard. "Does God Come to Praise Job or to Bury Him? The Function of YHWH's Second Speech From the Whirlwind (Job 40:6—41:34 [Heb 41:26])." Unpublished Draft Paper.

———. "Is Creation Theology Inherently Conservative? A Dialogue with Walter Brueggemann." *HTR* 87.3 (1994) 257–77.

———. "A New Heaven and a New Earth: The Case for a Holistic Reading of the Biblical Story of Redemption." *JCTR* 11 (2006) 73–97.

———. "Why the 'Greater Good' Isn't a Defense: Classical theodicy in Light of the Biblical Genre of Lament." *Koinonia* 9, nos. 1–2 (1997) 81–113.

Migliore, Daniel L. *Faith Seeking Understanding: An Introduction to Christian Theology*. 2nd edn. Grand Rapids: Eerdmans, 2004.

Miller, Patrick D. *They Cried to the Lord: The Form and Theology of Biblical Prayer*. Minneapolis: Fortress, 1994.

Mjaaland, Marius Timmann. "The Fractured Unity of God: Lament as a Challenge to the Very Nature of God." In *Evoking Lament*, edited by Eva Harasta and Brian Brock, 99–115. London: T. & T. Clark, 2009.

Moberly, R. W. L. "'God is Not a Human That He Should Repent': (Numbers 23:19 and 1 Samuel 15:29)." In *God in the Fray: A Tribute to Walter Brueggemann*, edited by Tod Linafet and Timothy K. Beal, 112–23. Minneapolis: Fortress, 1998.

Moltmann, Jürgen. *The Crucified God: The Cross of Christ as the Foundation and Criticism of Christian Theology*. Trans. R. A. Wilson and John Bowden. London: SCM, 1995.

Molzahn, David. "Psalms: Lament and Grief as a Paradigm for Pastoral Care." Paper presented at the Twenty-Fourth Annual Meeting of the Society for Pentecostal Studies, Wheaton, IL, 1994.

Moo, Douglas. *The Epistle to the Romans*. Cambridge: Eerdmans, 1996.

———. *The Old Testament in the Gospel Passion Narratives*. Sheffield: Almond, 1983.

Morris, Leon. *The Gospel According to John*. London: Marshall, Morgan and Scott, 1972.

———. *The Gospel According to Matthew*. Leicester, UK: Apollos, 1992.

Murray, John. *The Epistle to the Romans*. London: Marshall, Morgan and Scott, 1970.

Newsome, Carol. "The Book of Job: Introduction, Commentary and Reflections." In *NIB* 4:317–637.

Bibliography

Nineham, D. E. *The Gospel of St. Mark*. London: A. & C. Black, 1968.

Öhler, Markus. "To Mourn, Weep, Lament and Groan: On the Heterogeneity of the New Testament's Statement on Lament." In *Evoking Lament*, edited by Eva Harasta and Brian Brock, 150–65. London: T. & T. Clark, 2009.

Osborne, Grant R. *The Hermeneutical Spiral*. Downers Grove, IL: InterVarsity, 1991.

Pauw, Amy Plantinga. "Attending to the Gaps between Beliefs and Practices." In *Practicing Theology: Beliefs and Practices in Christian Life*, edited by Miroslav Volf and Dorothy C. Bass, 33–48. Cambridge: Eerdmans, 2002.

Pembroke, Neil. *Pastoral Care in Worship: Liturgy and Psychology in Dialogue*. London: T. & T. Clark, 2010.

Perriman, Andrew, ed. *Faith, Health and Prosperity*. Carlisle, UK: Paternoster, 2003.

Peterson, Michael L. *God and Evil*. Oxford: Westview, 1998.

Pinnock, Clark. "Open Theism: An Answer to My Critics." *Dialog* 44.3 (2005) 237–45.

———. "Systematic Theology." In *The Openness of God*, by Clark Pinnock et al., 101–25. Carlisle, UK: Paternoster, 1994.

Pinnock, Clark, et. al. "Preface." In The *Openness of God*, by Clark Pinnock et al., 7–10. Carlisle, UK: Paternoster, 1994.

Plantinga, Alvin. "The Free Will Defense." In *The Problem of Evil*, edited by Michael L. Peterson, 103–33. Notre Dame: University of Notre Dame Press, 1992.

———. *God, Freedom and Evil*. London: Allen and Unwin, 1975.

Plüss, Jean-Daniel. *Therapeutic and Prophetic Narratives in Worship*. Frankfurt: Lang, 1988.

Pope, Marvin. *Job*. Garden City, NY: Doubleday, 1974.

Powell, Mark Allen. *What is Narrative Criticism?* Minneapolis: Fortress, 1990.

Rice, Richard. "Biblical Support for a New Perspective." In *The Openness of God*, by Clark Pinnock et al., 11–58. Carlisle, UK: Paternoster, 1994.

Richie, Tony. *Speaking by the Spirit: A Pentecostal Model for Interreligious Dialogue*. Lexington, KY: Emeth, 2011.

Ridderbos, Herman. *The Gospel of John: A Theological Commentary*. Cambridge: Eerdmans, 1997.

Rigby, Cynthia L. "Someone to Blame, Someone to Trust: Divine Power and the Self-Recovery of the Oppressed." In *Power, Powerlessness and the Divine: New Inquiries in Bible and Theology*. Edited by Cynthia L. Rigby, 79–102. Atlanta: Scholars, 1997.

Roberts, Robert C. *Emotions: An Essay in Aid of Moral Psychology*. Cambridge: Cambridge University Press, 2003.

Rogerson, J. W., and J. W. McKay. *Psalms 1–50*. Cambridge: Cambridge University Press, 1977.

Roth, John K. "A Theodicy of Protest." In *Encountering Evil: Live Options in Theodicy—A New Edition*, edited by Stephen T. Davis, 1–20. Louisville: Westminster John Knox, 2001.

Sanford, Agnes. *Healing Gifts of the Spirit*. London: James, 1966.

———. *The Healing Light*. London: James, 1988.

Schaefer, Konrad. *Psalms*. Collegeville, MN: Liturgical, 2001.

Schnackenburg, Rudolf. *The Gospel According to St. John*. Vol. 3. Tunbridge Wells: Burns and Oates, 1982.

Searle, John R. *Speech Acts: An Essay in the Philosophy of Language*. London: Cambridge University Press, 1969.

Bibliography

Smith, James K. A. "Tongues as 'Resistance Discourse': A Philosophical Perspective." In *Speaking in Tongues: Multi-Disciplinary Perspectives*, edited by Mark J. Cartledge, 81–110. Milton Keynes, UK: Paternoster, 2006.

Soelle, Dorothee. *Suffering*. Translated by Everett R. Kalin. London: Darton, Longman and Todd, 1975.

Stanislavki, Constantin. *An Actor Prepares*. New York: Routledge, 1964.

Surin, Kenneth. *Theology and the Problem of Evil*. Oxford: Blackwell, 1986.

Swinburne, Richard. *Providence and the Problem of Evil*. Oxford: Clarendon, 1998.

Swinton, John. *Raging With Compassion: Pastoral Responses to the Problem of Evil*. Grand Rapids: Eerdmans, 2007.

Talbert, Charles H. *Romans*. Macon, GA: Smyth and Helwys, 2002.

Theron, Jacques, P. J. "Towards a Practical Theological Theory for the Healing Ministry in Pentecostal Churches." *JPT* 14 (1999) 49–64.

Thiselton, Anthony C. *New Horizons in Hermeneutics*. London: HarperCollins, 1992.

Thomas, John Christopher. *The Devil, Disease and Deliverance*. Sheffield: Sheffield Academic, 1998.

———. "Max Turner's The Holy Spirit and Spiritual Gifts: Then and Now (Carlisle: Paternoster Press, 1996): An Appreciation and Critique." *JPT* 12 (1998) 3–21.

———. *The Pentecostal Commentary on 1 John, 2 John, 3 John*. London: T. & T. Clark, 2004.

———. "Pentecostal Theology in the Twenty First Century." *Pneuma* 20.1 (1998) 3–19.

———. "Reading the Bible from within Our Traditions: A Pentecostal Hermeneutic as Test Case." In *Between Two Horizons: Spanning New Testament Studies and Systematic Theology*, edited by Joel B. Green and Max Turner, 108–22. Cambridge: Eerdmans, 2000.

———. "Women, Pentecostals and the Bible: An Experiment in Pentecostal Hermeneutics." *JPT* 5 (1994) 41–56.

Tilley, Terrence. *The Evils of Theodicy*. Washington, DC: Georgetown University Press, 1991.

Tillich, Paul. *Systematic Theology*. Vol. 1. Chicago: University of Chicago Press, 1951.

Tracy, David. *Blessed Rage for Order: The New Pluralism in Theology*. New York: Seabury, 1975.

Turner, Max. "Historical Criticism and Theological Hermeneutics of the New Testament." In *Between Two Horizons: Spanning New Testament Studies and Systematic Theology*, edited by Joel B. Green and Max Turner, 44–70. Cambridge: Eerdmans, 2000.

———. "Readings and Paradigms: A Response to John Christopher Thomas." *JPT* 12 (1998) 23–38.

Vanhoozer, Kevin J. *The Drama of Doctrine: A Canonical Linguistic Approach to Christian Theology*. Louisville, Kentucky: Westminster John Knox, 2005.

———. "Exegesis and hermeneutics." In *NDBT*, 52–64.

———. *First Theology: God, Scripture and Hermeneutics*. Downers Grove, IL: InterVarsity, 2002.

———. "Human Being, Individual and Social." In *The Cambridge Companion to Christian Doctrine*, edited by Colin E. Gunton, 158–88. Cambridge: Cambridge University Press, 1997.

———. *Is There a Meaning in this Text? The Bible, The Reader and the Morality of Literary Knowledge*. Leicester, UK: Apollos, 1998.

Bibliography

———. *Remythologizing Theology: Divine Action, Passion, and Authorship*. Cambridge: Cambridge University Press, 2010.

———. "The Voice and the Actor: A Dramatic Proposal about the Ministry and Minstrelsy of Theology." In *Evangelical Futures: A Conversation on Theological Method*, edited by John G. Stackhouse Jr., 61–106. Grand Rapids: Baker, 2000.

Volf, Miroslav. "Theology for a Way of Life." In *Practicing Theology: Beliefs and Practices in Christian Life*, edited by Miroslav Volf and Dorothy C. Bass, 245–63. Cambridge: Eerdmans, 2002.

Vondey, Wolfgang. Review of *The Drama of Doctrine: A Canonical Linguistic Approach to Christian Theology*, by Kevin J. Vanhoozer. Pneuma 30 (2008) 365–66.

Walsh, Brian J., and J. Richard Middleton. *The Transforming Vision: Shaping a Christian Worldview*. Downers Grove, IL: InterVarsity, 1984.

Warrington, Keith. "The Teaching and Praxis Concerning Supernatural Healing of British Pentecostals, of John Wimber and Kenneth Hagin in the Light of an Analysis of the Healing Ministry of Jesus as Recorded in the Gospels." PhD diss., King's College London, 1999.

Webster, John. "Introduction: Systematic Theology." In *The Oxford Handbook of Systematic Theology*, edited by John Webster et. al., 1–15. Oxford: Oxford University Press, 2007.

Weems, Ann. *Psalms of Lament*. Louisville: Westminster John Knox, 1995.

Weinandy, Thomas G. "Doing Christian Systematic Theology: Faith, Problems, and Mysteries." *Logos* 5.1 (2002) 118–36.

Westermann, Claus. *Praise and Lament in the Psalms*. Translated by Keith R. Crim and Richard N. Soulen. Edinburgh: T. & T. Clark, 1981.

———. *The Structure of the Book of Job*. Translated by Charles A. Muenchow. Philadelphia: Fortress, 1987.

Whitehead, Alfred North. *Adventure of Ideas*. New York: Free, 1967.

———. *Process and Reality: An Essay in Cosmology, Corrected Edition*. Edited by David Ray Griffin and Donald W. Sherburne. New York: Free, 1978.

Wiesel, Elie. *Night*. Translated by Marion Wiesel. London: Penguin, 2006.

Wimber, John, and Kevin Springer. *Power Evangelism*. London: Hodder and Stoughton, 2001.

———. *Power Healing*. London: Hodder and Stoughton, 1990.

Wink, Walter. *The Powers*. 3 vols. Philadelphia: Fortress, 1984–1992.

Wright, N. T. *Evil and the Justice of God*. London: SPCK, 2006.

———. "How Can the Bible be Authoritative?" *Vox Evangelica* 21 (1991) 7–32.

———. *Jesus and the Victory of God*. Vol. 2 of *Christian Origins and the Question of God*. Minneapolis: Fortress, 1996.

———. *The New Testament and the People of God*. Vol. 1 of *Christian Origins and the Question of God*. London: SPCK, 1992.

———. *The Resurrection of the Son of God*. Vol. 3 of *Christian Origins and the Question of God*. London: SPCK, 2003.

Wright, Nigel G. *A Theology of the Dark Side*. Carlisle, UK: Paternoster, 2003.

———. "The Theology of Signs and Wonders." In *The Love of Power or the Power of Love: A Careful Assessment of the Problems Within the Charismatic and Word-of-Faith Movements*, by Tom Smail, Andrew Walker, and Nigel Wright, 37–52. Minneapolis: Bethany House, 1994.

Yong, Amos. "Whither Systematic Theology? A Systematician Chimes in on a Scandalous Conversation." *Pneuma* 20.1 (1998) 85–93.

www.ingramcontent.com/pod-product-compliance
Lightning Source LLC
Chambersburg PA
CBHW051054230426
43667CB00013B/2286